WE ARE EASTER PEOPLE

WE ARE
EASTER PEOPLE

A Commentary for the Time of Resurrection

J. Massingberd Ford
and Ralph A. Keifer

HERDER AND HERDER

1970
HERDER AND HERDER NEW YORK
232 Madison Avenue, New York 10016

Nihil obstat: Leo J. Steady, Censor Librorum
Imprimatur: ✠ Robert F. Joyce, Bishop of Burlington
December 17, 1969

CONTENTS

ABBREVIATIONS

Ab.	Aboth
Ant.	Antiquities (Josephus)
Ber.	Berakoth
B. M.	Baba Mezia
Exod. R.	Exodus Rabbah
Hag.	Hagigah
Hor.	Horayot
J. B.	Jewish War (Josephus)
J. E.	Jewish Encyclopedia
Leg. ad Gaium	Legatio ad Gaium (Josephus)
Mek. Ex.	Mekilta on Exodus
Op. M.	Opus Mundi (Philo)
Sanh.	Sanhedrin
Shab.	Shabbath
T. B.	Babylonian Talmud

WE ARE EASTER PEOPLE

Introduction

As the documents of Vatican II have clearly affirmed, the paschal event, the death and resurrection of Jesus Christ, is the center of the Christian faith. The Easter vigil and mass are the Church's most solemn and exuberant affirmation of that faith. But long before Easter, the Church anticipates the coming vigil. In reality, the paschal vigil is simply an ecstatic summary of all the Church has lingered over through the whole of Lent. The Easter alleluia is the Church's exclamation point after all that has already been said and done.

This book is designed to shed some light on the inseparable connection between Lent and Easter. That connection is already evident in the texts of the Roman liturgy, and will be more evident with coming liturgical reforms. One of the most significant of these reforms is the new lectionary, which is now available. The authors were privileged to see the plans for the new readings, and chose to follow them to prepare this book.

Copious quotations from both scriptural and liturgical texts are provided. This will relieve the reader of the task of juggling Bible, missal, and commentary while he works with the text. For those who cannot attend church services, it should be an aid to prayer and reflection in the spirit of the liturgy.

This book is not a technical study, nor a working model for the preacher or catechist, nor a series of meditations.

Because the commentary is not a matter of technical study, the authors have chosen to omit footnotes, except where they are absolutely essential. For the same reason, points of schol-

3

arly controversy have been omitted by the authors, who have simply followed reputable opinion and probability on certain points, without troubling non-academic readers with the details of academic discussion. For example, for many details the commentary on the history of the Easter celebration relies rather heavily on the *Apostolic Tradition* ascribed to Hippolytus of Rome. The authors are quite aware of the difficulties with regard to Hippolytus' identity and the practices which he describes. But the service in the *Apostolic Tradition* exhibits features which became practically universal. The *Apostolic Tradition* stands as a valuable witness in spite of the controversy which surrounds it. Similarly, we cannot speak with absolute certitude with regard to Jewish practices in the time of Christ, because there are so few sources which date from that time. But the sources we do have allow for a *probable* reconstruction of first-century Jewish practice—a probability which is much more than educated guesswork. If absolute certitude were demanded with regard to every event in history, no history could ever be written.

While the book does not provide a working model for the preacher or catechist, it is meant to speak to those who preach and instruct. But the authors are academicians, and their commentary needs to be translated into homiletic and catechetical terms—the proper work of the preacher and the catechist. The aim of the authors is to indicate something of the sense of the texts and rites of the paschal liturgy. The immediate, here-and-now import of that sense can only be conveyed by those who know their own individual situations. With this in mind, the authors have indicated only the broader issues which must be taken up in liturgical instruction. They leave the rest to those who know the needs of their own people.

Some models for Lenten prayers of the faithful are provided. These are intended not only as an aid to prayer, but also to indicate many of the key themes which the texts suggest.

The aim of this book is to help bridge the gap between scholarly research and worship. It is our hope that the com-

4

mentary that we have provided will be helpful to those who wish to understand more fully the spirit in which the Church worships. Above all, we trust that this book might assist those who are responsible for proclaiming the Word of God in our churches.

Easter and Christian History

The first Christians found their whole lives grounded in the fact of Easter; the message that Jesus had risen from the dead was the heart and center of the new faith. All Christian liturgy was, in a real sense, Easter liturgy; for when the community assembled, the risen Lord was present among them. Whenever Christians met to study the Word of God in the scriptures, whenever they celebrated the eucharist, the risen Lord was there. They gathered to celebrate the resurrection of Jesus, his triumph over sin and death, and to anticipate their own resurrection, when the Lord would come in glory to invite them to the banquet in his kingdom.

Sunday, with the weekly celebration of the eucharist, naturally was celebrated as a weekly festival of the resurrection. But a yearly festival of the resurrection was also celebrated under the influence of the Jewish liturgy. The Jewish Passover was transformed into the Christian Passover, Easter.

The Emergence of the Paschal Vigil

By the second century, Easter began to emerge as a baptismal festival in the West. The Sunday liturgy of the time was simple, even austere, in comparison with our own. Church art had not yet begun to blossom, and the introduction of church music was treated cautiously. While singing was not unknown, there were no musical instruments. There were no vestments, no impressive furnishings, no elaborate ceremonial.

7

But in contrast to the simple Sunday eucharist, the yearly baptismal service had already emerged as a complex, even exuberant rite. One writer has left a detailed description of the practice which in essentials became practically universal.

After a lengthy period of instruction and moral training (sometimes as long as three years), the candidates were carefully examined:

When those who are to be received for baptism have been chosen, their lives are to be examined: have they lived good lives while they were catechumens; have they honored the widows, have they visited the sick, have they done all kinds of good works. If those who have guided them testify that they have done all these things, then let them hear the Gospel. . . . If any one is not good or pure, he should be put aside because he did not hear the word in faith . . .[1]

Then, after a fast on Friday and Saturday, the whole church assembled for an all-night prayer vigil on the Saturday evening before Easter. The candidates were exorcised, presented their offerings of bread and wine for the eucharist, and listened to the readings and instruction which were the heart of the vigil.

Toward dawn, the baptismal water and oil for the anointings were blessed by prayer. Then, one by one, the candidates solemnly renounced Satan. After being anointed with the "oil of exorcism," they were led down into the water for the profession of faith and triple immersion:

When he who is being baptized goes down into the water, the deacon is to put his hand on him and say, "Do you believe in God the Father almighty?" And he who is being baptized shall say, "I believe." Holding his hand on the head of the candidate, the deacon shall immerse him once. And then he shall say, "Do you believe in Christ Jesus, the Son of God, who was born of the Holy Spirit from the Virgin Mary and was crucified under Pontius Pilate and died and was buried and rose living on the third day and ascended into heaven and sat at the right hand of the Father, and is coming

---

1. B. Botte, *Tradition Apostolique de Saint Hippolyte,* Munster, 1963; our translation.

to judge the living and the dead?" And when he says, "I believe," he is again immersed. The deacon then says, "Do you believe in the Holy Spirit in the holy Church and the resurrection of the flesh?" And he who is baptized says, "I believe." And thus he is baptized once in a threefold immersion. (Hippolytus, Chapter 21)

Robed in white, often wearing crowns or garlands, they were then led before the bishop, who laid his hand upon each one, prayed for the grace of the Holy Spirit, and signed them on the forehead with the "oil of thanksgiving."

They then joined in the prayer of the faithful and were welcomed by all with the kiss of peace. The service was concluded with a brief but joyful eucharist.

This primitive celebration was the norm for the Easter celebration for more than a thousand years. Several elements were totally integrated, elements which gradually ceased to have such a direct and obvious connection with one another.

(1) In the West, especially, baptism was a paschal event; that is, it was directly and obviously related to Easter, to the celebration of the death and resurrection of Jesus Christ. This was conveyed, not only by a dramatic use of symbols, but by the fact that the initiation of converts was the heart of the Easter celebration. The way Easter was celebrated was to baptize. Jesus' death and resurrection were commemorated by incorporating new members into his death and life. The Church not only welcomed anew its risen savior; it brought its whole attention to bear on welcoming those who had just entered into his risen life. For these Christians, the festival of the resurrection was not the commemoration of a fact in past history; it was an event which was vividly experienced by the Church in its reception of new members into the life of the risen Saviour. When Christians gathered for the annual commemoration of the resurrection, they could also rejoice in their own rising to new life.

It must have been this experience which made the Passover texts, the Exodus accounts of the deliverance of Israel from Egypt, so real to them. By the end of the second century, the Christian Church was Gentile; it was an urban, Graeco-Roman religion. Culturally, the primitive Church was as far removed from the nomadic and semitic world of the Old Testament as we are. Yet it found no difficulty in using the Exodus accounts to celebrate its own passover. For they, too, had undergone their own exodus. As Israel of old had gone through the Red Sea to escape the hostile Pharaoh and his armies, so the passage through the waters of baptism was a deliverance from Satan and the "powers of this world." As the Israelites followed the pillar of fire on the night of their passage, so the neophytes entered a world illumined by the risen Lord. As the glory of the Lord descended upon the desert tabernacle, so the Church celebrated the glory of its risen Lord present among them. As Israel passed through the sea to be fed on manna in the desert, and crossed the Jordan to a land flowing with milk and honey, so the new Christians emerged from the baptismal water to take their place at the Lord's eucharistic banquet. A hymn from the first part of the third century echoes the readings still found in our own paschal vigil:

> This is the paschal feast, the Lord's passing;
> so cries the Spirit.
> No type or telling, this,
> no shadow;
> Pasch of the Lord it is, and truly,
> The blood that is shed is a sign of the blood to be shed,
> the first indication of what the Spirit will be,
> a glimpse of the great anointing.
> I, seeing the blood, will protect you.
>
> You have indeed protected us, Jesus,
> from endless disaster.
> You spread your hands like a Father
> and fatherlike gave cover with your wings.
> Your blood, a God's blood, you poured over the earth,
> sealing a blood-bargain
> for men because you loved them.
> What anger threatened you turned away from us;
> instead you gave us back God's friendship.

10

The heavens may have your spirit, paradise your soul,
but O may the earth have your blood.

This feast of the Spirit
leads the mystic dance through the year.
The pasch came from God, came from heaven to earth;
from earth it has gone back to heaven.
New is this feast and all-embracing;
all creation assembles at it.

Joy to all creatures, honour, feasting, delight.
Dark death is destroyed
and life is restored everywhere.
The gates of heaven are open.
God has shown himself man,
man has gone up to him a God.
The gates of hell God has shattered,
the bars of Adam's prison broken.
The people of the world below have risen from the dead,
bringing good news:
What was promised is fulfilled.
From the earth has come singing and dancing.

This is God's passing.
Heaven's God, showing no meanness,
has joined us to himself in the Spirit.
The great marriage-hall is full of guests,
all dressed for the wedding, no guest rejected
for want of a wedding-dress.
The paschal light is the bright new lamplight,
light that shines from the virgin's lamps.
The light in the soul will never go out.
The fire of grace burns in us all,
spirit, divine,
in our bodies and in our souls,
fed with the oil of Christ.

We pray you, God, our Sovereign, Christ,
King forever in the world of spirits,
stretch out your strong hands over your holy Church

11

and over the people that will always be yours.
Defend, protect, preserve them,
fight and do battle for them,
subject their enemies to them,
subdue the invisible powers that oppose them,
as you have already subdued those that hate us.
Raise now the sign of victory over us,
and grant that we may sing with Moses the song of triumph.
For yours are victory and power for ever and ever Amen.[1]

(2) Baptism, in this context, was not separated from what we call confirmation and first communion; rather, "baptism" was the total act of initiation—descending and ascending from the baptismal pool, the anointing and laying on of hands, and the eucharist which immediately followed. The first and most obvious purpose of baptism was admission to the eucharist. The rites of anointing and laying on of hands, which would later be known as the sacrament of confirmation, were viewed simply as the completion of initiation, the conclusion of the baptismal rite. These acts were often referred to as the "seal of the Spirit." The image of sealing is instructive. What the early writers have in mind is the image of wine bottle, filled, corked, and then sealed with wax and stamped to certify that its contents are good. In other words, the anointings and laying on of hands were interpreted as the final guarantee of the gift of the Spirit already received in the baptismal immersion, the completion of the process leading up to the first communion. In fact, the very word "confirmation" meant simply the completion of the process of Christian initiation.

The climax of the baptismal celebration was the paschal eucharist. The white-robed neophytes came in triumphal procession to the eucharistic table. A church which saw its worship at the eucharist linked to the eternal praise of the Father in

1. Hippolytus of Rome, "Homily 6 for Easter," in *Early Christian Prayers,* ed. A. Hamman, Chicago, 1961, pp. 31–33.

heaven must have seen the first eucharist of the neophytes as an anticipation of the seer's prophecy in the Book of Revelation:

After this I looked, and behold, a great multitude which no man could number, from every nation, from all tribes and peoples and tongues, standing before the throne and before the Lamb, clothed in white robes, with palm branches in their hands, and crying out with a loud voice, "Salvation belongs to our God who sits upon the throne, and to the Lamb!" And all the angels stood round the throne and round the elders and the four living creatures, and they fell on their faces before the throne and worshiped God, saying, "Amen! Blessing and glory and wisdom and thanksgiving and honor and power and might be to our God for ever and ever! Amen."

Then one of the elders addressed me, saying, "Who are these, clothed in white robes, and whence have they come?" I said to him, "Sir, you know." And he said to me, "These are they who have come out of the great tribulation; they have washed their robes and made them white in the blood of the Lamb.

Therefore are they before the throne of God,
and serve him day and night within his temple;
and he who sits upon the throne will shelter them
with his presence.
They shall hunger no more, neither thirst any more;
the sun shall not strike them, nor any scorching
heat.
For the Lamb in the midst of the throne will be
their shepherd,
and he will guide them to springs of living water;
and God will wipe away every tear from their eyes."

(Rev. 7: 9–17 RSV)

At any rate, the sense of joyful entry into the presence of the Lord led the Roman Church to adopt Psalm 22 (23) as one of its most-used communion psalms:

The Lord is my shepherd, I shall not want;
he makes me lie down in green pastures.
He leads me beside still waters;
He restores my soul.

13

He leads me in paths of righteousness
  for his name's sake.

Even though I walk through the valley of the shadow of death,
  I fear no evil:
for thou art with me;
  thy rod and thy staff,
  they comfort me,
Thou preparest a table before me
  in the presence of my enemies;
thou anointest my head with oil,
my cup overflows.
Surely goodness and mercy shall follow me
  all the days of my life;
and I shall dwell in the house of the Lord
  for ever." (Psalm 23, RSV)

Thus, there was a unified sacramental process: baptism, its completion in confirmation, and the paschal eucharist, as the term, the focus of the process.

(3) Baptism was very much a corporate event in which the whole community actively participated. The whole service constituted a warm welcome into the eucharistic community. The newly baptized were greeted by their sponsors, who had helped to prepare them for baptism, and by fellow Christians, whose appreciation of the event would have been charged with the memory of their own baptism.

This was aided by the vivid, even dramatic use of biblical symbolism. Especially operative in their understanding of baptism was the teaching summarized by Paul in the Epistle to the Romans:

Do you not know that all of us who have been baptized into Christ Jesus were baptized into his death? We were buried therefore with him by baptism into death, so that as Christ was raised from the dead by the glory of the Father, we too might walk in newness of life. For if we have been united with him in a death like

14

this, we shall certainly be united with him in a resurrection like his. (Rom. 6: 3–8, RSV)

The candidates went down into the water as a symbol of burial, and came up from the water as a symbol of resurrection. Even where baptismal pools were constructed in a manner that would prevent total immersion, there were steps down to the pool so that the candidate could descend into the (knee-deep) water, and after the pouring of water over him, rise from it. Baptism by immersion did not entirely die out in the West until the end of the Middle Ages. The 1543 edition of the Sarum Ritual, normative for much of England, contained careful directions for the immersion of infants. The Anglican Book of Common Prayer, heir of much of the medieval tradition, still maintains that infants should be dipped in the font.

Our own liturgy, elaborating the theme, walking in newness of life, mentioned by Paul in the Epistle to the Romans, speaks of the font as a womb from which the newborn Christian emerges as a "heavenly offspring," as an "infant" Christian. The early Christians did not hesitate to dramatize this by baptizing the candidates naked; even jewelry and hairpins had to be removed. The baptismal anointings were also lavish; oil was often poured or smeared over the whole body. The heavy white robes which the newly baptized wore were not only a symbol of innocence and purity; they were also a practical necessity. The robes absorbed the anointing oil; ordinary clothing would have been ruined.

If this sounds all too vivid, it should be noted that there was some discretion about the service. It is not at all certain that the whole congregation always witnessed the actual baptism. Very possibly, only the bishop and his assistants were present, and the candidates were brought in to join the congregation for the celebration of the eucharist only after they had donned their white robes.

An elaborate ceremonial sometimes attended the first communion. The congregation not only received communion under the form of bread and wine, as all communicants did until the High Middle Ages, but two additional chalices were sometimes used for this solemn occasion. Before they received under the form of wine, the neophytes were offered a chalice of water, as a token of inner cleansing, and a chalice of milk and honey:

. . . for the fulfillment of the promise made to the fathers, when he spoke of a land flowing with milk and honey; for which Christ gave his flesh, by which they who believe are nourished like infants. He, by the mildness of his word, makes sweet the bitterness of the heart. (Hippolytus, Chapter 21)

(4) For the candidates, baptism was a vivid personal experience. We do not have to go beyond the New Testament era to see that martyrdom was often the price of baptism. The First Epistle of Peter, leaning heavily on the baptismal liturgy, presents a view of Christian life in which suffering for the faith is expected as part of the normal course of events. The crucified and risen Lord is held up as an example and source of the strength and joy of the newly baptized. The Christian is a pilgrim in exile in an alien and hostile world, who looks forward with eager anticipation to the life of the world to come. The threat of persecution, even to the point of death, was real and imminent up to the beginning of the fourth century. The acceptance of baptism in this world was often, in a very real sense, an acceptance of martyrdom, as the preaching and instruction of the first three centuries was careful to point out.

But persecution, although intense at times, was nonetheless sporadic and intermittent. Christians were able to be grateful for an inefficient bureaucracy which rendered the state's opposition to Christianity ultimately ineffective. There was no "Church of the catacombs," if we mean by that a Church which remained hidden from the public view for the first three centuries of its existence.

But this relative peace was at best an uneasy truce. Apart from the always present if not always realized threat of perse-

16

cution, there was the pagan world which the Christians could not accept. Their opposition to pagan worship which pervaded all public functions virtually cut them off from civic life. Prohibitions against bloodshed led them to oppose military service. Objections to pagan sexual license led them to a negative judgment on much of the art, literature, and entertainment of the time. The Christian protest against the pagan environment, then, made baptism a serious step. The renunciation of "Satan and all his pomps" was not for them quaint rhetoric; it was a solemn renunciation of the paganism which pervaded the society in which they lived. It is no wonder that many Christians were reluctant to baptize their children, and many were content to live their lives as catechumens on the threshhold of the Church. Baptism was an initiation into a new way of life which demanded a solemn rejection of the old. It was an unforgettable personal decision.

The Christian Pasch, then, our Easter, had its center in the celebration of the death and resurrection of Jesus and the entry of the newly baptized into the life of the risen Saviour, a celebration which was at the same time intensely personal and wholly corporate.

A Change in Perspective

The fourth century brought a radical change to the situation of Christianity in the Roman Empire. A wave of bloody persecution was followed by official toleration, and finally by the acceptance of Christianity as a state religion. With the persecutions over, the Church's membership swelled. The rising flood of converts called for a new system of instruction.

The preparation for Easter underwent a gradual development. The weeks preceding Easter had always been marked by a special concern for instruction of converts, and even daily services for this purpose had not been unknown, almost from the very beginning. The cessation of the persecutions and the

17

new Christian influence on the public calendar made it easier for the whole Church to gather for weekday eucharists. Wednesday and Friday had been Christian days of fasting as early as the second century, perhaps even earlier. The new period of peace made it possible for them to become days when the Church gathered to instruct catechumens and celebrate the eucharist. A special solemnity could be given to days which marked stages in the progress of the catechumens, and the days known as the *Scrutinies* received special attention for this purpose. Saturday began to have its own special eucharist as well. Between the fourth and eighth centuries the outline of what we know as the weekday Lenten masses was beginning to appear. The great baptismal vigil, however, remained as the heart and focus of the whole period; everything in the weeks before Easter was directed toward it.

Slowly, however, other factors were beginning to emerge which would radically change the Christian approach to Easter. The time had passed when baptism was an invitation to martyrdom. And the time had passed, too, when the Church required a year's long preparation for baptism. Its standards for membership became less severe. The Church had opened her arms to the weak, the lukewarm, the half-converted. Whether or not this was a "good thing" need not concern us here; however we interpret it, the fact stands that the Church became a "Church of sinners" as she had not been before. With this fact, a new need emerged—a need to develop the Church's penitential system.

As the period before Easter was a period for the instruction of catechumens who were received into the Church and admitted to the eucharist for the first time, so also penance was viewed as a kind of "second baptism," and absolution was given to public penitents on Holy Thursday, as a re-admission to the paschal eucharist. At one point, however, there was a vast difference in the Church's view of baptismal repentance and the repentance of those who were already baptized. She welcomed the newly baptized with rejoicing. But while she was willing to

18

stress God's mercy to the sinner, her attitude toward sin after baptism was one of sorrow and severity. As the number of penitents grew, the joyful anticipation of Easter was more and more muffled by a growing stress on sorrow for sin. With a focus on penitence, a somber note was introduced.

At the same time, another development was taking place; the number of infant baptisms was becoming greater than the number of adult baptisms. Infant baptism had not been unknown in the early Church, but it had not been a universal practice. Some, but certainly not all, Christian parents had their children baptized. Often Christian parents delayed baptism of their children until they had "sown their wild oats." Such a practice may sound slightly cynical, but St. Monica is a witness that this was the attitude even of the most devout. With the emergence of Christianity as a state religion, however, infant baptism became more and more common. As whole towns, and eventually whole nations were baptized, virtually *en masse,* there became practically nobody left to be baptized, except infants.

The ancient vigil held its place for a long time. So carefully was its form retained, that infants still became "catechumens," except that the catechumentate became a series of blessings and exorcisms, without, of course, instruction. Infants were brought to the vigil, immersed, confirmed, and even received communion. But a rite so well suited to adult baptism would gradually fade into the background. The connection between Easter and baptism was gradually blurred as the concern to baptize infants immediately after birth grew, and finally became the rule in the Middle Ages. When the Easter baptisms disappeared, the ancient vigil nearly disappeared. Having lost its central focus, it became a kind of clerical housekeeping ceremony; a time to light new fire for the lamps and bless the water for the font. It was no longer even a vigil; the rites were performed early on Holy Saturday morning, with most of the people absent.

This situation was further complicated by the absence of a vernacular liturgy and a general decline of preaching from the

19

liturgical texts; there was a growing separation between popular piety and the official liturgy.

The piety of the early Church was grounded in a conviction of the presence and power of the risen Lord; he was the triumphant Lord who had conquered sin and death, and by baptism and the weekly celebration of the Eucharist, the believer shared in that victory. Eternal life had already begun for him. The First Epistle of Peter summarizes an attitude which dominated nearly the first thousand years of the Church's life:

But you are a chosen race, a royal priesthood, a holy nation, God's own people, that you may declare the wonderful deeds of him who called you out of darkness into his marvelous light. Once you were no people but now you are God's people; once you had not received mercy but now you have received mercy. (I Pet. 2: 9, 10 RSV)

The early Church was not insensitive to the reminder that "you have been bought with a great price," that the cost of new life had been Jesus' death. But its view of his death was always illumined by the thought of his resurrection. The Good Friday liturgical service, dating from a very early time in our history, faithfully reflects this vision: Jesus is the lowly king who brings victory over sin and death; he is the true Passover lamb who brings deliverance to God's people. The climax of the service is the unveiling of the jeweled cross, symbol of triumph, and the communion, the reception of the *risen* Lord.

But the medieval Church centered its piety more and more in its consciousness of man's sinfulness; and more and more it concentrated its devotion in the crucifix, in the physical sufferings of Christ. Early Christian prayer was dominated by praise and thanksgiving; the first believers spontaneously lifted up their hands to rejoice in God's blessings. Our own *Gloria in excelsis* is a faithful representative of this tradition: "We praise you; we bless you; we worship you; we glorify you." But medieval man turned more spontaneously to prayers of contrition and petition; he knelt and beat his breast. Augustine's

20

joyous cry, "We are Easter men and alleluia is our song," had given way to the doleful declaration, "To thee do we cry, poor banished children of Eve, to thee do we send up our sighs, mourning and weeping in this valley of tears."

Before the end of the Middle Ages, this sin-centered, passion oriented piety had changed the period of preparation for Easter from a period of joyous expectancy to a somber penitential period. To be sure, the Easter communion was the climactic event (all the more so, since communion was, at best, received by the people only on Easter—and sometimes at Pentecost and Christmas); but the faithful now came, not rejoicing in new life, but pleading for forgiveness of their sins. The Anglican Book of Common Prayer incorporated much of the best of medieval piety in its tradition. Its Prayer of Humble Access is a remarkable summary of medieval communion piety:

We do not presume to come to this thy Table, O merciful Lord, trusting in our own righteousness, but in thy manifold and great mercies. We are not worthy so much as to gather up the crumbs under thy Table. But thou art the same Lord, whose property is always to have mercy: Grant us, therefore, gracious Lord, so to eat the flesh of thy dear Son, Jesus Christ, and to drink his blood, that our sinful bodies may be made clean by his body, and our souls washed through his most precious blood, and that we may evermore dwell in him, and he in us. Amen.[1]

Here, in the best of the medieval tradition, we can see a healthy sense of human frailty and a tender piety which produced a genuine sense of the identification of Jesus with suffering mankind. But the darker side of this piety produced a querulous insecurity before a wrathful God and a gloomy pessimism which would later lay Christianity open to the charge of being a sad religion.

The upheaval of the Reformation did not basically change this situation. New Lenten devotions were introduced, but they were essentially adaptations of medieval piety to new condi-

1. From B. Wigan, *The Liturgy in English,* 2nd ed., Oxford, 1964, pp. 7, 8.

tions. It is noteworthy that while new Good Friday devotions appeared, like the Three Hours and the Stations of the Cross, there was no corresponding paschal devotion developed. Some of the more somber aspects of the medieval attitude, however, began to be modified by devotions like the Forty Hours and the promotion of devotion to the Sacred Heart of Jesus. The fruit of the latter was the promotion of more frequent communion, which gradually gained headway after the Council of Trent and came to full growth in our own century.

In our time, we have seen a number of significant changes in the Church's approach to Lent and Easter, beginning with the restoration of the Holy Week Services in 1952. The introduction of a vernacular liturgy and the insistence of Vatican II on the importance of the Word in the liturgy have begun to bring a new attention to the liturgical texts. The reduction of the fasting requirements and the re-introduction of the Good Friday communion have done much to suggest that Lent is not simply a period of mourning for our sinfulness.

The baptismal focus of the Easter vigil has already become clear, especially with the introduction of the renewal of baptismal vows. Many parishes have begun to restore the vigil to its full significance by baptizing adult converts and some infants at the Easter vigil. Outside of the Easter celebration, the paschal character of baptism is being restored by a new baptismal rite, called for by the Council. New funeral rites, indicating the paschal character of Christian death, are already being used experimentally, and can be expected to become practically universal before too many years pass. The new eucharistic prayers and new prefaces are characterized by a renewed focus on the meaning of the paschal event. The liturgical movement is restoring the central fact of the Christian faith, the paschal mystery, to a central place in the lives of Christians.

The First Sunday of Lent

The center of this celebration is the recalling of Jesus' temptation in the desert. It is a capsule summary of the whole Lenten project. Jesus' confident trust in his Father is a model for all who call themselves "the faithful." The liturgy is so insistent upon this theme that is uses parts of Psalm 90 (91) in all the chants for the day. The Tract incorporates practically the whole psalm:

> He who dwells in the shelter of the Most High,
> who abides in the shadow of the Almighty,
> will say to the Lord, "My refuge and my fortress;
> my God, in whom I trust."
> For he will deliver you from the snare of the fowler
> and from the deadly pestilence;
> he will cover you with his pinions,
> and under his wings you will find refuge;
> his faithfulness is a shield and buckler.
> You will not fear the terror of the night,
> nor the arrow that flies by day,
> nor the pestilence that stalks in darkness,
> nor the destruction that wastes at noonday.
> A thousand may fall at your side,
> ten thousand at your right hand;
> but it will not come near you. . . .
> For he will give his angels charge of you
> to guard you in all your ways.
> On their hands they will bear you up,
> lest you dash your foot against a stone.
> You will tread on the lion and the adder,

23

the young lion and the serpent you will trample under foot.
Because he cleaves to me in love, I will deliver him;
I will protect him, because he knows my name.
When he calls to me, I will answer him;
I will be with him in trouble,
I will rescue him and honor him.
With long life I will satisfy him,
and show him my salvation. (Ps. 91)

Already the Church looks toward the paschal vigil, with its affirmation of faith. By taking the attitude of Psalm 90 as its own, the liturgy suggests that faith is a matter of love and trust, and not simply a matter of reciting the creed.

Jesus' sharp rebuke of Satan suggests the ringing baptismal renunciation of Satan. The liturgy evokes a sober assessment of human sinfulness with its portrayal of Jesus' temptation. We see his situation as identical with our own; he has been "tempted in all things like ourselves." But we see, too, the contrast. He has conquered the evil one; he is the Faithful Son of the Father, come to redeem the faithless sons. The Easter vigil will see the Church's sorrow for sin transfigured by joy in the victory of her Saviour: "O happy fault, which merited so great a redeemer!" Into the darkness she will fling her challenge of faith: the light of Christ has come.

Jesus' forty days of prayer suggest that Lent is a time of prayer, of listening to God in his Word, and of responding from the depths of one's own heart. The long prayer vigil on Holy Saturday night is the climax of this season of prayer. Because the Church watches with her Lord, she is sensitive to his coming, to his presence and activity in her midst. Because she has kept vigil, she can cry out, "Alleluia, this is the day the Lord nas made; let us rejoice and be glad in it!"

Christian tradition has always linked this attitude of prayer with fasting. Jesus' own words are instructive. He lays down no rule as to quantity, only as to attitude: "When you fast, do not look dismal, like the hypocrites. . . . But when you fast, anoint your head and wash your face" (Mt. 6: 16, 18 RSV). The reduction of the Church fasts to two days, Ash Wednesday and Good Friday, should be an enormous aid to understanding what Jesus had in mind when he enjoined fasting. Obviously, he expects fasting to be joyful. This does not mesh too well with a notion of fasting as some kind of spiritual push-up or as a self-inflicted punishment. Rather, fasting is an expression of an attitude of prayer, a sign of being at God's disposal. Fasting is simply the physical acknowledgement that obedience to the will of the Father is often difficult; we do not let go of our selfishness easily. But the value of fasting is primarily that of a sign; without a real willingness to die to our selfishness, and a concomitant joy in following the Lord, there can be no genuine Christian life.

The First Sunday of Lent, then, is much more than a pessimistic review of the pitfalls of the human situation, or a call to imitate Jesus' fast. Rather, it is a call to confident faith. Christian repentance is not simply a regret for sin; it is a turning to the one who has overcome all evil.

The First Sunday in Lent

The First Sunday in Lent introduces three themes:
    (1) the creation of Adam and fall of mankind;
    (2) how the new Adam redeemed mankind;
    (3) the temptation of Jesus.

THE FIRST READING, GENESIS 2: 7–9 AND GENESIS 3: 1–7. THE CREATION AND THE FALL OF MAN

. . . then the Lord God formed man of dust from the ground, and breathed into his nostrils the breath of life; and man became a living being. And the Lord God planted a garden in Eden, in

25

the east; and there he put the man whom he had formed. And out of the ground the Lord God made to grow every tree that is pleasant to the sight and good for food, the tree of life also in the midst of the garden, and the tree of the knowledge of good and evil. (Gen. 2: 7-9)

Now the serpent was more subtle than any other wild creature that the Lord God had made. He said to the woman, "Did God say, 'You shall not eat of any tree of the Garden'?" And the woman said to the serpent, "We may eat of the fruit of the trees of the Garden; but God said, 'You shall not eat of the fruit of the tree which is in the midst of the Garden, neither shall you touch it, lest you die.'" But the serpent said to the woman, "You will not die. For God knows that when you eat of it your eyes will be opened, and you will be like God, knowing good and evil." So when the woman saw that the tree was good for food, and that it was a delight to the eyes, and that the tree was to be desired to make one wise, she took of its fruit and ate; and she gave also some to her husband, and he ate. Then the eyes of both were opened, and they knew that they were naked; and they sewed fig leaves together and made themselves aprons. (Gen. 3: 1–7)

The Creation of Man

There are two accounts of the creation of mankind in Genesis—1: 1—2: 3 and 2: 4–24. According to the first account, man was created in the image and likeness of God as the climax of all God's creativity. In the second account, little is said about the creation of the rest of the earth, man is the center of the writer's attention, and the account is far more anthropomorphic than that of the first writer. God formed man from the clods of the earth as a potter moulds a vessel from clay. But then God blew breath into his nostrils and man was transformed into a living being. The word "breathed" means to blow on, blow up, or inflate. The same Greek word is used in I Kings 17: 21 when Elijah restores life to the widow's son and in Ezekiel 37: 9 for breathing life into dry bones lying in a valley. But it is also used

26

in Sirach 43: 4 of the sun which breathes out fiery vapors and in Ezekiel 21: 31 and 22: 20 of God's blowing the fire of his wrath on his enemies. In view of these references it seems that the writer in Genesis wished to convey more than gentle breathing, rather a vigorous, life-giving warmth. It is of special interest to note that John 20: 22 uses the same Greek word for Jesus' breathing on the disciples and giving them the Holy Spirit.

The Jewish writer Philo (almost contemporary with Jesus) identified the breath of God with the Divine Spirit (*Op. M.* 135), and paraphrases of the Bible from about the same date attributed the gift of speech and (spiritual) seeing and hearing to this inspiration; thus God "breathed upon his face the breath of lives, and it became in Adam a Discoursing Spirit" (*Targum of Onkelos,* Etheridge, p. 38), and "breathed into his nostrils the inspiration of life, and there was in the body of Adam the inspiration of a speaking spirit, unto the illumination of the eyes and the hearing of the ears" (*Palestinian Targum, ibid.,* p. 162). Speech distinguished man from the animals.

The Trees

In Genesis, God placed man in a garden in which the focus of attention seemed to be on two trees, the tree of life and the tree of the knowledge of good and evil. These features were obviously a literary device to give a dramatic and concrete form to the story. The tree of life was a common image in the Near East. It symbolized immortality. Its purpose appears to have been to keep from man the fate of death. But the writer of Genesis 2 does not actually say that it gives life. For the Hebrew the true tree of life was wisdom from God (see Proverbs 3: 18; 11: 30; 13: 12; 15: 4). The second tree, the tree of knowledge, symbolized a special knowledge reserved for God and creatures higher than man (see p. 32 below).

27

The Central Points in the Fall Story

When we approach the narrative of the "Fall" we must bear several points in mind. Firstly, the message of the Bible is one which concerns "salvation" rather than "sin"; indeed, the consciousness of sin grew out of Israel's consciousness that she was the channel of salvation for all men and nations. Hence the key to the Genesis story is not the sin of man but the mercy of God. This may be confirmed by the fact that the technical words, which the Hebrews used so frequently throughout the Old Testament to denote various kinds of sins and guilt, do not appear at all in the Paradise story.

Secondly, what we find in Genesis 3 is not the narrative of one specific historical occurrence but a drama which conveys a general truth. It is exquisitely and poignantly told. Everything is expressed in human terms, even the serpent speaks! What the author (or authors) did was to blend skillfully together elements borrowed from non-Israelite cultural traditions and to express through these a spiritual experience common to and often repeated by the whole Israelite nation. These non-Israelite elements were derived mainly from the Mesopotamian and from the Canaanite culture. Material from these sources was used but transformed to be applicable to the Israelite situation —thus, for example, polytheistic elements were excluded.

Thirdly, perhaps the most important points in the drama are the themes of wisdom and covenant.

The Wisdom Theme (Compare "The Trees," P. 27 Above)

Dubarle has suggested that the author was a sage or wise man who meditated on the problem of good and evil. This was a popular theme in the wisdom literature, as in, for example, Sirach 39: 4 where the sage is the man who knows good and evil. There are three motifs in the Genesis story which suggest this wisdom motif:

28

(1) Israel's definition of wisdom and understanding was "living with God and keeping the precepts of the covenant" (Deut. 4: 6–8). Adam and Eve are presented as living in this way before their sin.

(2) In contrast to them, the serpent is represented as shrewd and perverse: he exhibits the antithesis to godly wisdom. This idea of evil shrewdness is shown frequently in the Book of Proverbs.

(3) Ezekiel 28: 12–19 is a variant form of the story of the first man. Here the first man definitely appears to be a sage: even in Genesis this is implied because Adam names or classifies the animals. To give a name to something was to be able to discern the essence of its being and its distinctive characteristics; only a perspicacious man could do this.

The Covenant Theme

A covenant was a bilateral agreement by which both parties accepted certain responsibilities. When God made a covenant with mankind he promised blessings to his people but on their part he required love, worship, and obedience. The covenant theme in this reading is shown in the pattern (1) God's goodness, (2) man's sin, (3) the punishment consequent on this, then (4) the reconciliation made between God and man. This pattern occurs over and over again in the pages of the Old Testament.

This pattern was repeated constantly in the history of Israel. Israel was brought from Egypt, given the commandments, broke them, a penalty was inflicted, but God did not desert his people.

For the writer of Genesis, the pattern of the first sin illustrated the common features of man's failing in his relationship toward God and how God was not indifferent to this but, after facing man with his disloyalty, sought means whereby he might redeem man or bring him back into a right relationship. In Genesis, when God had indicated the punishment which would be inflicted on man, woman, and the serpent, he added a sentence which indicated that this punishment was disciplinary in nature. God was not going to leave man and woman alone but he would try to protect them from the wiles of the serpent. He indicated that from this same man and woman who had sinned would arise someone who would be victorious over the serpent. This promise was indicated, but not clearly defined, in Genesis 3: 15:

I will put enmity between you and the woman, and between your seed and her seed; he shall bruise your head, and you shall bruise his heel.

Catholic theologians have used this verse as a messianic text and have applied it to Mary. The text is difficult to understand and one must be careful how one uses it because the Hebrew here is very uncertain. Further, there is only a little evidence that the Jews applied it to the Messiah. However, one can find at least one example of its use as a messianic text. This is found in the translation of the Hebrew text which Jesus and his contemporaries probably heard in the synagogue:

And it shall be when the sons of the woman consider the law, and perform [its] instructions, they will be prepared to smite thee on thy head to kill thee, and when the sons of the woman forsake the commandment of the law, and perform not [its] instructions, thou wilt be ready to wound them in their heel, and hurt them. Nevertheless there shall be a medicine for the sons of the woman, but for thee, serpent, there shall be no medicine: but it is to be that for these shall be a remedy (or, "Make a bruise with the heel in the days of the king Meshiha").[1]

It would seem, therefore, that almost as soon as God inflicted punishment for sin, he immediately began to think, as it

1. *Jerusalem Targum,* translation by Etheridge, Vol. 1, p. 166. The *Palestinian Targum* or *Aramaic Translation* offers a very similar interpretation.

were, how to redeem man. This idea of the redemption of man is also implied in another text, where it is said that wisdom delivered Adam from his fault; this reads:

The father of the world, the first being to be fashioned, created alone, he had her [wisdom] for his protector and she delivered him from his fault; she gave him the strength to subjugate all things. (Wis. 10: 1–3)

Wisdom here is closely associated with the Spirit of God. It is the Spirit of God who constantly comes to our help after we have committed sin and it is he who helps us to come once again into the right relationship with God.

What Was the Nature of the Sin?

The sin of Adam and Eve does not appear to have been a sexual sin. The Bible and Judaism saw sex as something holy and wholesome. God blessed and commanded procreation. The Jews themselves believed that the begetting of children was the first commandment which God gave to the human race. In addition to this, Wisdom 1: 12–16 stresses the goodness of physical procreation:

Do not invite death by the error of your life,
nor bring on destruction by the works of your hands;
because God did not make death, and he does not
delight in the death of the living.
For he created all things that they might exist,
and the generative forces of the world are wholesome,
and there is no destructive poison in them;
and the dominion of Hades is not on earth.
For righteousness is immortal
but ungodly men by their words and deeds summon death;
considering him a friend, they pined away,
and they made a covenant with him,
because they are fit to belong to his party.

31

Here the notion of "death" deserves attention, it has a wider meaning than merely physical death. Death for the Hebrew did not mean separation of body and soul as it did for the Greek people. Rather it was a loss of vitality in the whole of man's being so that the dead became like shadows or ghosts. This was an existence without joy in which religious activity was either curtailed or completely obliterated; a dead man was a man who could think no more of Yahweh and his wonderful works and deeds for man, he was a man who could no longer praise God in his own works and words. Against this background, we can understand the phrase "you are dead in your sins." By studying the revelation from God and participating fully in his worship, man could imbibe more and more the Spirit of God and therefore become a more vital human being. It is perhaps this idea of "spiritual death" which explains the first sin. Adam and Eve sinned and "died" because they tried to rise above the human condition in which God has placed them: they tried to obtain divine knowledge, not through God, but through their own efforts. The symbolism behind eating the fruit and their eyes being opened conveys the idea that they received a new insight of some kind. They realized, for example, by a sad experience what it meant to resist God and to be alienated from his friendship, to be afraid to be intimate with him. They suddenly appreciated that their blessed condition had been due only to the goodness of God and that left by themselves, they were poor, miserable beings who sought in their embarrassment to hide themselves, not only from God, but from one another. This grasping at divine knowledge may also have included an act of *hubris* or arrogance whereby Adam and Eve may have attempted to obtain the knowledge of secret processes or the inner dynamics of things which fell within the sphere of God rather than man. This may be confirmed by comparison with Ezekiel 28: 1. The Book of Enoch (a non-biblical Jewish work popular among the Christians of the first century) attributed the "Fall" to the acquisition of various magical and technological arts, the abuse, not the use, of the resources of the universe which men were supposed to bring into a special relationship to God.

Perhaps we can conclude this section by saying that we do not know precisely what sin man committed in the Garden of Eden. The narrative's main point was that man's ancient, and also contemporary, folly lies in thinking that he can understand God better from his own point of view and from his own idea of God than he can by subjecting himself to God and learning about him from revelation. The knowledge of good and evil covers more than the moral sphere, rather it comprises everything in man's life. The serpent's temptation was probably to persuade man to extend human existence beyond what God intended for it. This did not mean that man could not increase his intellectual enrichment or his physical well-being, but it did mean that he must respect God's possession of the knowledge of mysteries and of superhuman powers which lie beyond man. If God invited man to partake in some measure in the knowledge of these mysteries and gave him certain supernatural powers, then man could accept willingly, but he is not to grasp these things for himself. We shall see that Jesus himself, even though he was the Son of God, did not grasp at these things. When man does commit this sin, he experiences a disturbance in his whole being because he has tried to become independent of God. To this man reacts with a sense of shame.

The Sense of Shame

When Genesis says that man and woman realized that they were naked and they became ashamed, it does not mean that they were ashamed only in the sexual sense. Nakedness before God and man in the Garden of Eden before the Fall symbolized a complete openness to God and to one's fellow man. It suggested a feeling of relaxation, confidence, and complete lack of artificiality in both the physical and social spheres. It meant that man and woman in their persons without any external trappings, such as clothes, wealth, prestige, and even physical prowess, were acceptable to God and man. When man and woman felt their nakedness, they felt the inadequacy of the human person and they sought, as it were, to make themselves more presentable to God and their fellow men by clothing themselves and by surrounding themselves with signs and symbols of self-esteem. For the Hebrew, clothes, possessions, health, and physical strength and height became signs of distinction. All these things were an extension of the personality of a man or a woman. Thus the Old Testament speaks about Solomon in all his glory, and it enlarges upon this by describing the great economic and social prosperity of Solomon, and, of course, also the glory of the temple which he built for God. On the one hand, when the Hebrews and other ancient people wished to degrade and humiliate enemies they took away all their external trappings and displayed them partly or completely naked before the people who had conquered them. This punishment was inflicted upon prisoners of war (compare Is. 20: 4; 47: 3) and also upon women who were condemned because of adultery (see, for example, Ezek. 16: 37 following). On the other hand, we read that when Saul was overcome by the Spirit of God and began to prophesy, without shame he lay naked all night, and when David danced before the ark of the Lord he also was naked. This suggests that this idea of nakedness in Genesis meant a complete openness to God and man, ease and honesty in their presence, and the realization that it is the whole being of man which is important, not the external possessions with which he surrounds himself. The man or woman who by the grace of God has attained a close mystical union with God does not feel the necessity of possessing a great deal of property or many material things. He or she possesses what we call poverty of spirit and feels completely comfortable with God and with men, even though they may be ill-bred, economically inferior, or even less educated. Such a person has a wisdom, an understanding, and a knowledge of eternal truth which satisfies his whole being and enables him to appreciate

34

the blessings which God has given to mankind. He sees these graces and blessings radiating from himself and also from other people. Therefore, he can look also at the most underprivileged person, underprivileged in other eyes, and yet see in that person the glory of God, his Holy Spirit. When Jesus became incarnate, this was his disposition.

THE SECOND READING, ROMANS 5: 12–19. DEATH THROUGH ADAM AND LIFE THROUGH CHRIST

Therefore as sin came into the world through one man and death through sin, and so death spread to all men because all men sinned—sin indeed was in the world before the law was given, but sin is not counted where there is no law. Yet death reigned from Adam to Moses, even over those whose sins were not like the transgression of Adam, who was a type of the one who was to come.

But the free gift is not like the trespass. For if many died through one man's trespass, much more have the grace of God, and the free gift in the grace of that one man Jesus Christ abounded for many. And the free gift is not like the effect of that one man's sin. For judgment following one trespass brought condemnation, but the free gift following many trespasses brings justification. If, because of one man's trespass, death resigned through one man, much more will those who receive the abundance of grace and the free gift of righteousness reign in life through one man Jesus Christ.

Then as one man's trespass led to condemnation for all men, so one man's act of righteousness led to acquittal and life for all men. For as by one man's disobedience many were made sinners, so by one man's obedience many will be made righteous.

No Systematic Theory of "Original Sin" in Biblical or Jewish Thought

This lesson is patterned on the first reading. St. Paul's consciousness of the superabundant grace of salvation led him to reflect upon the sin of Adam which disturbed the relationship

35

between God and man. But, like the author of Genesis 3, St. Paul was not attempting to explain the historical or prehistorical origin of sin: rather he contemplated the contemporary condition of man and how the life, death, and resurrection of Jesus had altered the sad state of affairs. Romans 5: 12–20 is a meditation on the statement which St. Paul made in Romans 3: 24, when he said that both Jew and Gentile "have sinned and fallen short of the glory of God." One might feel that St. Paul overemphasized the responsibility of the one man Adam. However, this emphasis must be regarded as an individual reflection on the part of the apostle. He did not follow any clearly defined tradition about Adam which he found either in Judaism or in early Christianity. In Judaism there was no uniform doctrine of "original sin" as we call it. Only two books of the Bible, namely, Sirach and Wisdom, give unmistakable references to the sin committed in the Garden of Eden. Other Jewish thought attributed original sin to the "giants," who according to Genesis 6 married the daughters of men. However, the most common theory was that there were two impulses in man, one evil and one good. The evil impulse was sometimes called "the strange god within man" (*Shabbath,* 105b) and "the spoiler who spares none, bringing man to fall even at the advanced stage of seventy or eighty." It was chiefly by the constant study of the Torah (law or revelation) that man could overcome this evil impulse.

Solidarity of the Human Race

The idea which could affect St. Paul was that of the solidarity of the human race. The good or evil perpetrated by an individual was held to affect the whole of his family or clan or even the whole human race but this did not mean that the other individuals, as opposed to the sinner, were responsible for this sin. It was rather a question of a spiritual atmosphere created by men and influencing one's fellow men in their moral and religious attitudes. This influence might jeopardize their response to God's call, to sacred tradition and revelation. One could see, therefore, a kind of legacy, moral, physical, and spiritual, which was handed down within the human race. This legacy comprised a certain loss in man's relationship to God. Just as men could be ministers of grace, one to another, so they could also be ministers of what might be called "gracelessness."

In Romans 5, St. Paul speaks as though the fault of one man brought sin and death to the rest of the world. He was possibly thinking about this legacy of sin and even overemphasizing it. Yet he did understand the responsibility of man for his personal sin. He stressed this in several texts, as for example in II Thessalonians 1: 6–9, II Corinthians 11: 15, and Romans 2: 6–11. Thus:

For he will render to every man according to his works: to those who by patience and well-doing seek for glory and honor and immortality, he will give eternal life; but for those who are factious and do not obey the truth, but obey wickedness, there will be wrath and fury. (Rom. 2: 6–11)

This is consonant with a non-biblical Jewish work called the *Apocalypse of Baruch* (34) which reads:

If Adam was the first to sin and brought untimely death on all those born of him, each has prepared a future punishment for himself . . . Adam is the cause of ruin for himself alone: but each of us is an Adam for himself. (Compare Enoch 98: 4 and IV Esd. 8: 56.)

In Romans 5: 15–17 St. Paul appears to have been carried away by the thought of the excellence of salvation brought through the one man, Christ, and his joy in Christ led him to overstress Adam in contrast.

The tradition of the early Church with reference to the interpretation of this text of Romans was undecided about the consequence of the sin of Adam. The Latin Fathers interpreted Romans 5: 12 to mean that all sinned in Adam, but the Greek Fathers held that the sin of Adam had to be ratified with men's

37

personal sins. Later on, the practice of baptizing infants seems to have influenced the interpretation of this text and to have led to the stress on the sin of Adam, rather than on the individual responsibility for sin. But St. Paul was thinking only of adults.

Also, St. Paul stressed Adam's sin in order to extoll Christ more. In Christ there was redemption offered to all, not only to Jews who were willing to receive it. St. Paul meditated more profoundly than his predecessors and contemporaries and, in reviewing the good news of salvation brought through Jesus Christ, he was able to realize the inferior condition of man before Christ. He rejoiced in the superiority of the present condition. This is clearly expressed in I Corinthians 15: 22–25:

For as in Adam all die, so also in Christ shall all be made alive. But each in his own order: Christ the first fruits, then at his coming those who belong to Christ. Then comes the end, when he delivers the kingdom to God the Father after destroying every rule and every authority and power. For he must reign until he has put all enemies under his feet.

The kingship which could have been Adam's and could have been handed down to his successors was now realized in Christ, and the followers of Christ could receive this dignity once again.

THE THIRD READING, MATTHEW 4: 1–11. THE TEMPTATION OF JESUS IN THE WILDERNESS

Then Jesus was led up by the Spirit into the wilderness to be tempted by the devil. And he fasted forty days and forty nights, and afterward he was hungry. And the tempter came and said to him, "If you are the Son of God, command these stones to become loaves of bread." But he answered, "It is written,
'Man shall not live by bread alone, but by every word that proceeds from the mouth of God.' "

38

Then the devil took him to the holy city, and set him on the pinnacle of the temple, and said to him, "If you are the Son of God, throw yourself down; for it is written,

'He will give his angels charge of you,'

and

'On their hands they will bear you up, lest you strike your foot against a stone.' "

Jesus said to him, "Again it is written, 'You shall not tempt the Lord your God.' " Again, the devil took him to a very high mountain, and showed him all the kingdoms of the world and the glory of them; and he said to him, "All these I will give you, if you will fall down and worship me." Then Jesus said to him, "Begone, Satan! for it is written,

'You shall worship the Lord your God and him only shall you serve.' "

Then the devil left him, and behold, angels came and ministered to him.

Jesus' Baptism and the Temptation

As the Lenten liturgy looks toward our baptism or the renewal of our baptismal vows, one must realize the intimate relationship between Jesus' own baptism and his temptation by Satan. Baptism involves the renunciation of Satan. It is to be expected that it will be followed by temptations which are a challenge for us to put into practice our vows and to develop the potentialities of grace which have been bestowed upon us.

At Jesus' baptism there was a demonstration, not only of Christ's unique relationship with the Father by the voice from heaven, which declared "This is my beloved Son," but also of his brotherhood with mankind. The last point is not quite as obvious as the first, but it is implicit in the scriptural quotations linked with the baptism. The first one is Isaiah 42: 1:

Behold my servant, whom I uphold, my chosen, in whom my soul delights; I have put my Spirit upon him, he will bring forth justice to the nations.

39

This depicts Jesus either as a personification of Israel or as a special servant working and suffering on behalf of God's chosen people, one with them in humanity and in suffering. The second scriptural quotation associated with Jesus' baptism is Psalm 2: 7:

. . . He said to me, "You are my son, today have I begotten you."

This psalm was sung in honor of the King of Israel who was regarded as the adopted son of Yahweh. Jesus, of course, was much more than the adopted son of Yahweh. Yet the quotation draws attention to the fact that there is an intimate and vicarious link between Jesus, God and man, and Israel. Jesus is King, not only on a divine level, but also on a human level. Jesus' temptation, therefore, can be seen as the beginning of his struggle on behalf of mankind, as its brother, indeed, but also as its God. As man, he repudiated Satan as we do at our baptism.

Jesus Could Be Tempted

Our first consideration should be the realization that Jesus could, in reality, be tempted to sin, even though, as the Son of God, he could not sin. When we speak about the person of Jesus, as distinct from one of his natures, either the human or the divine, then we can ascribe properties of both natures to that one person. For example, we can say that Jesus the Person, the only begotten Son of God, suffered; but we cannot say that the divine nature of Jesus suffered. In the same way, we can say that Christ, the man, was tempted; but we cannot say that Christ's divinity was tempted.

The Divine Resources

The temptations show that Christ was determined to experience life exactly as a man, so that as man's brother and his high priest, he could offer to God perfect human obedience;

40

this was the obedience not merely of a privileged person who, as soon as human limitations became inconvenient, was at liberty to fall back on divine reserves. It was the obedience which can be found and practiced by the common man. It was just the use of those divine resources which the devil suggested to Jesus. The devil asked him to turn stones into bread, but Jesus refused miraculous bread for his own needs and in this rejection he perhaps implicitly rejected a means of drawing crowds of people to himself by miracles bringing economic and material advantages. The devil offered him the kingdoms of the world, but Jesus refused political success and preferred the pastorate of souls. The devil tempted Jesus to perform a kind of "conjuring act," as one might say, by throwing himself from the pinnacle of the temple; but, again, Jesus refused to attract people in this sensational way. He did not wish to reveal a miracle-working God, but one who was loving and kind and left people the freedom to come to him of their own will, rather than over-impressing them by his power and might to perform miracles.

Did Jesus Doubt that He Was Son of God?

Yet, beyond these temptations to use divine reserves where these were unnecessary, Christ might also have suffered doubt concerning his own divine sonship. Parallel to the voice which announced his sonship at baptism the diabolical voice insinuates repeatedly, "*If* you are the Son of God. . . ," "If. . . ," "If. . . ," "If. . . ." This emphasis on "if" placed the accent, not so much upon the miracle, but upon the conditional form of the sentence. The devil was saying that if you are the Son of God, show me—in these miraculous ways. In the same way, the second temptation may have been one in which Jesus was tempted to convince himself that he was Lord; similarly, the Israelites wandering in the desert began to wonder whether God was among them (Exod. 17: 1–5). The third temptation

41

was consonant with Psalm 2: 7f. It was on a different level than the rest of the temptations. This Psalm reads:

> Ask of me, and I will give thee the nations for thine inheritance,
> And the uttermost parts of the earth for thy possession.

This was a temptation akin to the temptation of Adam, namely, the belief that man may inherit the promises of God without obedience to the Word of God. Jesus' reply was a quotation from Deuteronomy 6: 13. In the context of this quotation lies the august warning,

> And it shall be, when the Lord thy God shall bring thee into the land which he swear unto thy fathers . . . Then beware lest thou forget the Lord which brought thee forth out of the land of Egypt out of the house of bondage.

Jesus would not forget God and he turned to Satan and bade him go; in his answer he hinted that Satan should be worshipping him, not he Satan. Thus Jesus overcame the temptation to live as an extraordinary man and accepted all the limitations of human existence. He overcame, also, the sin of the first man as depicted in Ezekiel 28. Why was Jesus tempted? Perhaps we can say with a fair amount of confidence that Jesus' temptation is part of his human growth. For St. James says,

> Count it all joy, my brethren, when you meet various trials, for you know that the testing of your faith produces steadfastness. And that steadfastness has its full effect, that you may be perfect and complete, lacking in nothing . . . Blessed is the man who endures trial, for when he has stood the test he will receive the crown of life which God has promised to those who love him . . . (James 1: 2–4, 12)

Jesus' victory over temptation enabled him to become perfect man in the truest sense of the word.

Contrast with Apocryphal Gospels

It is interesting to note that if we turn from the gospels which are contained in the New Testament to the apocryphal gospels, those which the Church rejected, we do not find in these the idea of Jesus being tempted. He is presented as a very precocious little boy and very often performs miracles which do not seem to have any theological meaning. They appear to be much more like magic or spectacular conjuring performances. But our canonical gospels show that Jesus was tempted, just as the Bible and non-biblical Jewish literature shows that the Jewish patriarchs and prophets all endured temptations. Abraham, for example, was supposed to have endured ten temptations.

Temptations in the Rest of Jesus' Life

Jesus' temptations presented to us in this section of the gospel are an epitome of the temptations which he endured throughout his life and which were to culminate at Gethsemane and on the cross. Father Raymond Brown has asked whether St. Matthew's and St. Luke's fuller account of the temptation story, as compared to St. Mark's very brief account (where the evangelist says merely that Jesus was tempted by Satan), are not perhaps a dramatic synopsis of the type of temptations which Jesus actually faced during his whole life. Father Brown makes parallels with John 6–7. Here there is an attempt to make Jesus King (John 6: 15), an implied desire for more bread (John 6: 26), and a request for Jesus to perform a sign or work (6: 30). If so, the temptation narrative was founded on an eyewitness account which had drawn all these temptations together and depicted them under three main headings.

So the crux of the temptations was to seek to win the rule over mankind by a kind of compulsive force, instead of by constraining people by loving example. In being victorious in his temptations, Jesus overcame where Adam had failed and, also, where Israel in the desert had failed. In both cases God seems to have tempted them in order (1) to humble them, (2) to test their devotion to his word or promise of allegiance

43

to him, and (3) to teach that man does not live by bread alone.

As we face the period of Lent, this initial struggle between Christ and the evil one encourages us to place all things and all people in the correct perspective with regard to God; not to force God's hand by asking him to do extraordinary things and to accept with our baptism the necessary temptations and trials which can be overcome in union with Christ. We should bear in mind the text from the Epistle to the Hebrews:

For we have not a high priest who is unable to sympathize with our weaknesses, but one who in every respect has been tempted as we are, yet without sinning. Let us then with confidence draw near to the throne of grace, that we may receive mercy and find grace to help in time of need, . . . (4: 15f.)

Intercession

FIRST SUNDAY IN LENT

The response is
> *Christ, True Image of God, intercede for us.*

(1) That we may reveal to the world the image and likeness of God, let us pray to the Lord . . .

(2) That men and women everywhere may consecrate their talents to their Creator, let us pray . . .

(3) That we may not abuse the resources of the universe to destroy mankind, let us pray . . .

(4) That, during this Lent, we may be raised into a new dimension in our relationship with God, let us pray . . .

(5) That, during this Lent, we may look forward to a special inspiration of the Holy Spirit at Pentecost, let us pray . . .

(6) That we may realize that we do not "live by bread alone," let us pray . . .

44

(7) That we may truly live by "every word which proceeds from the mouth of God," let us pray . . .

(8) That we may not idolatrize the material things of this world, let us pray . . .

(9) That the states and kingdoms of this world may give themselves to the sweet yoke of the Father, let us pray . . .

(10) That God may grant us every good and perfect gift from heaven this Easter, let us pray . . .

The Second Sunday of Lent

The transfiguration obviously looks forward to Easter, with its radiant promise of the risen Lord. Like Peter, we are confused. How are we to respond to this vision? Or more to the point, how are we to respond to the message that Jesus is risen from the dead?

Because popular piety has often concentrated almost exclusively on Jesus' passion, the full impact of the resurrection sometimes escapes us. Viewing the passion and death of Jesus as the acts which brought redemption, we tend to bracket the resurrection as a kind of afterthought. We view it as a wonderful event, no doubt, but somewhat isolated from our situation here and now. It has often been observed that the standard Catholic response to the question, "What is the resurrection?" will be, "It is Jesus' greatest miracle," or "It proves his divinity." We often have failed to grasp the relation of the resurrection to us.

From the perspective of the liturgy, and the biblical sources from which it draws its vision, this relationship is all-important. The glorified Jesus does not stand in splendid isolation. He is the new Adam, head of a new humanity which shares in his glory. By baptism, we too have entered into his risen life.

As the risen Lord does not stand in isolation, neither are we united to him as isolated individuals. Rather, by baptism we are members of his body, united to one another:

For just as the body is one and has many members, and all the members of the body, though many, are one body, so it is with Christ. For by one Spirit we were all baptized into one body—

47

Jews or Greeks, slaves or free—and all were made to drink of one Spirit. (I Cor. 12: 12, 13)

As the Church sees in the transfigured Lord the one who transcends Moses and the prophets, so also she sees herself in her union with the risen Lord as the New Israel, the new People of God. In her, the promise to Hosea is fulfilled:

And I will betroth you to me for ever; I will betroth you to me in righteousness and justice, in steadfast love, and in mercy. I will betroth you to me in faithfulness; and you shall know the Lord . . . And I will have pity on Not Pitied, and I will say to Not my people, "You are my people" . . . (Hos. 2: 19, 20, 23 RSV)

As the Passover was a festival commemorating Israel's deliverance from slavery, so Easter is the Christian Passover. The celebration of the death and resurrection of Jesus commemorates the deliverance of God's new people from sin and death. The vigil sees the passage from Egypt as a type, a promise of the salvation to come in Christ. Jesus is the Lamb who saves God's people. As Israel crossed the Red Sea to safety, so the Christian people, in their passage through the waters of baptism, enter into salvation:

This is the paschal feast in which the true lamb is slain; whose blood hallowed the door-posts of the faithful. This is the night on which you brought our forefathers, the children of Israel, dry-shod through the Red Sea in the flight from Egypt. This is the night on which the light of the pillar of fire destroyed the darkness of sin. This is the night which at this hour everywhere restores to grace and unites in holiness those who believe in Christ, separating them from worldly vice and the darkness of sun.[1]

The light of the risen Lord illumines the Church, like the pillar of fire that went before Israel, and the cloud of glory which from time to time filled the temple. The Church rejoices

---

1. Exultet, Easter Vigil, *The Roman Missal in Latin and English for Holy Week and Easter Week,* Collegeville, Liturgical Press, 1966, pp. 182, 183. Hereafter called *Missal.*

in the everlasting presence of her Lord. She is the new Jerusalem, filled with the light of his glory:

The Lord will create over the whole site of Mount Zion and over her assemblies a cloud by day, and smoke, and the shining of a flaming fire by night; for over all the glory there will be a canopy and a pavilion. It will be for a shade by day from the heat, and for a refuge and a shelter from the storm and rain. (Is. 4: 5, 6 RSV)

In her celebration, the Church rejoices in the very heart and center of her existence. From the font there emerges, not isolated individuals, but the holy people of God. The church can use the language of the Passover, because she too has been delivered from bondage.

The Second Sunday in Lent

The readings for the Second Sunday in Lent present:
  (1) the call of Abraham and the ancestors of the Jewish people from the darkness and foolishness of idolatry to the light and wisdom of the worship of the true God;
  (2) the call of Christians through the revelation of Jesus;
  (3) the glorification of Jesus in his transfiguration.

THE FIRST READING, THE CALL OF ABRAHAM. GENESIS 12: 1–8 (VULGATE 12: 1–7)

Now the Lord said to Abram, "Go from your country and your kindred and your father's house to the land that I will show you. And I will make of you a great nation, and I will bless you, and make your name great, so that you will be a blessing. I will bless those who bless you, and him who curses you I will curse; and by you all the families of the earth shall bless themselves."

So Abram went, as the Lord had told him; and Lot went with

49

him. Abram was seventy-five years old when he departed from Haran. And Abram took Sarai his wife, and Lot his brother's son, and all their possessions which they had gathered, and the persons that they had gotten in Haran; and they set forth to go to the land of Canaan. When they had come to the land of Canaan, Abram passed through the land to the place of Shechem, to the oak of Moreh. At that time the Canaanites were in the land. Then the Lord appeared to Abram, and said, "To your descendants I will give this land." So he built there an altar to the Lord, who had appeared to him.

The Meaning of Idolatry

Abraham and Sarah were the ancestors of the Jewish people and therefore the ancestors also of Jesus. Their parents were pagans and worshipped many graven images. The Jewish people believe that Abraham received from God a special revelation through which he learned to acknowledge the one supreme God who ruled over heaven and earth. He was called by God to leave his homeland, their gods, and possibly many of his friends. He became a semi-nomad in the land of Canaan which God promised to give to him and to his descendants.

One may ask what exactly Abraham and Sarah left when they relinquished idolatry. Idolatry was associated with demons or evil powers and very often also with immoral practices, but it was essentially ignorance of the supreme God, and it was symbolised by the image of darkness. Darkness suggests fear, ignorance, doubt, vexation, frailty, sin and evil, and also impending judgment. For example, in the Book of Job, we read:

Teach us what we shall say to him [God]; we cannot draw up our case because of darkness. (Job 37: 19)

Or, again, the writer of Ecclesiastes writes:

Then I saw that wisdom excells folly as light excells darkness. The wise man has his eyes in his head but the fool walks in darkness . . . (Eccles. 2: 13–14a)

50

One who was trapped in idolatry, therefore, was regarded as someone who lived in darkness and distress. He was like a man who was blind and who might be cut off from so much that is good, lovely, and life-giving in the world. On the other hand, the acknowledgement and worship of the true God was regarded as wisdom and wisdom was symbolized by light. Thus, traditionally, Abraham was regarded as a man of great sagacity and virtue who was said to have kindled a bright light for the Jewish people because he had taught the knowledge of the true God.

Light and Wisdom

How did this association between light and wisdom first originate? Perhaps it was because light was thought to emanate from the "face" of God. In Isaiah 60: 19–20 we read that not the sun nor the moon but the Lord shall be an everlasting light. In Psalm 104: 2 God is described as wrapping himself in light as in a mantle. In the Epistle of James 1: 17 the author says that God is the father of lights. Thus physical, intellectual, and spiritual light were thought to come directly from God. Light was a symbol of life, wisdom, and joy.

In this respect teaching or instruction was likened to light; for example, in one Jewish commentary we read:

The way of the wicked is as [deep] darkness; they know not at what they stumble (Prov. 4, 19). But those who study the Torah give forth light wherever they may be. It is like one standing in the dark with a lamp in his hand; when he sees a stone, he does not stumble, neither does he fall over a gutter because he has a lamp in his hand, as it says, Thy word is a lamp unto my feet, and a light unto my path (Ps. 119, 105), and also, And if thou runnest, thou shalt not stumble (Prov. 4, 12), and also, The spirit of man is the lamp of the Lord (ibid. 20, 27). God said, "Let my lamp be in thy hand and thy lamp in my hand." What is the lamp of God? The Torah, as it says, for the commandment is a lamp, and the teaching is a lamp (ibid. 6, 23). Why is the commandment "a lamp"? Be-

51

cause if one performs a commandment it is as if he kindled a light before God and as if he had revived his own soul, —also called a light, for it says, "*The spirit of man is the lamp of the Lord*" (*ibid.*, 20, 27). Why is the teaching called "*light*"? Because it often happens that when one is eager to fulfill a precept, his Evil Inclination within him dissuades him, saying, "Why do you want to perform this commandment and diminish your wealth? Instead of giving away to others, give it to your own children." But the Good Inclination says to him, "Give rather to a pious cause; for see what it says: '*For the commandment is a lamp*'; just as the light of a lamp is undiminished even if a million wax and tallow candles are kindled from it, so will he who gives toward the fulfillment of any commandment not suffer a diminution of his possessions." Hence, "*For the commandment is a lamp, and the teaching is light.*" (*Exod. R.* 36, 3).[1]

However, one of the most exquisite passages which depicts wisdom as light is found in the Book of Wisdom. Here, throughout the book, the pursuit of wisdom, which is seen as the first creation of God, is contrasted vividly with the practice of making and worshipping graven images. In opposition to the darkness of idolatry, wisdom is said to be "a reflection of eternal light, a spotless mirror of the working of God, and an image of his goodness" (Wisd. 7: 26).

Sons of Light and Sons of Darkness

In Jewish thought this idea of wisdom as light is associated with the idea of the radiance of the Shekinah or, as Christians would say, the Holy Spirit. The radiance of wisdom or the Spirit was supposed to reflect in the angels of light and also to radiate from the faces of scholars and great saints. Therefore it is understandable that good people were called the sons of light (see Luke 16: 8), whereas evil people were called the sons of darkness.

Among some valuable manuscripts found near the Dead Sea about 1947, scholars discovered a Rule written for a Jewish

1. *Midrash Rabbah,* ed. H. Freedman and M. Simon, London, 1961.

religious community which existed around the time of Jesus. In this document the sons of darkness are said to be filled with wickedness and falsehood, with pride, presumption, deception, guile, insolence, shortness of temper, folly, arrogance, greediness, and filthy ways. They are said to possess a blasphemous tongue, blindness of eyes, dullness of ears, stiffness of the neck, and hardness of the heart. It is averred that because of these characteristics they will meet many afflictions at the end of days and be cast into darkness. But the sons of light are characterized by the spirit of humility, patience, abundant compassion, perpetual goodness, insight and perception, and by a sense of the divine power that is founded on a perspicacious comprehension of God's work and plans and by a reliance on his mercy. These people are full of the spirit of knowledge and know how to comport themselves. They are zealous for right government and for overwhelming love for everyone who follows the truth. They have also a self-respecting purity which hates all taint of filthiness. They commune with God and with the saints and angels. They will find that God gives them health and well-being, a long life, and many blessings and joys in the world to come, as well as a crown of glory and a robe of honor. This is a very good illustration of the kind of life from which the Jews believed their forefather, Abraham, and the foremother, Sarah, had rescued their ancestors. They believed that Abraham and Sarah became missionaries and that Abraham instructed the men while Sarah instructed the women.

Feast of Tabernacles

However, perhaps we could also note that in the biblical passage under discussion, Abraham is seen as a semi-nomad. Later, Abraham's descendants were also to be semi-nomads when they came from the land of Egypt and travelled again to the land of Canaan which God had promised to them. In memory of the wandering of Abraham and more especially of the children of

Israel after their exodus from Egypt, the Jewish people keep a festival called the feast of Tabernacles. They construct huts made out of branches and other materials and they live in these for several days during the feast. They do this, not only to remind themselves of the history of their religious ancestors, but also to maintain the realization that this world is a land of pilgrimage to which we cannot become too greatly attached. They say that the huts should be fairly strong but preserve the character of a hut. It should not be more than ten feet high and not lower than ten hand-breadths. This is to teach men not to be too proud or to be too subservient. In a Jewish book called the *Book of Jubilees* which was composed before the time of Jesus, this feast was traced back to before the time of Abraham. However, this early date is most probably pious fiction.

The feast is also a feast of light and joy. In the days when the temple was still standing, the Jews used to have a great and beautiful ceremony in the court of women. Here people taught and expounded the law and then they danced in the light, even the scholars and the great men dancing together. It must have been an extraordinary sight. The feast is of interest to Christians because Jesus seems to have attended it just before he cured the blind man (see the Fourth Sunday in Lent). Moreover, it was perhaps on this feast that Jesus proclaimed that he was the light of the world. Here is a description of the feast.

At the termination of the first day of tabernacles, the priests, the Levites, and the people flocked to the temple court with its special sections for men and women. In a brilliantly illuminated court, there stood golden candelabra with four golden bowls on the top of each, and four ladders leading to each (since they were very high). Four youthful priests held jars of oil to feed the lamps. There was no courtyard in Jerusalem that was not illuminated by the lights which shone from the temple. Men of piety used to dance with torches in their hands and sing hymns and songs. And Levites without number, with harps, lyres, cymbals, trumpets, and other musical instruments, stood there upon the fifteen steps that lead from the court of the men to that of the women corresponding to the fifteen songs

54

of the ascents . . . in the Psalms. At each step they paused while one of these Songs of Degrees was chanted. At the other gate there stood two priests who sounded the Shofar [trumpet] as the singers ascended each step.[1]

This was an exquisite feast but it was not completely devoted to the Jewish people. It had a universal aspect because the celebrants remembered that God had promised through their ancestor, Abraham, that all nations of the world would be brought into the Light (see the third verse of this reading).

THE SECOND READING, II TIMOTHY 1: 8–10. THE CALL OF CHRISTIANS

Do not be ashamed then of testifying to our Lord, nor of me his prisoner, but take your share of suffering for the gospel in the power of God, who saved us and called us with a holy calling, not in virtue of our works but in virtue of his own purpose and the grace which he gave us in Christ Jesus ages ago, and now has manifested through the appearing of our Saviour Christ Jesus, who abolished death and brought life and immortality to light through the gospel.

The Context

Immediately before these two verses the author of this epistle mentions his sincere service toward God which he compares to that which his ancestors rendered (v. 3). Then he thanks God for the genuine faith of his readers which they received through their relatives (v. 5). After this he admonishes them to keep this faith and to put it into practice with courage and in a spirit of power, love, and self-control (see the characteristics of the sons of light, p. 53 above). The author has a sense of continuity with the past, an appreciation of those through whom

1. Translation from Y. Vainstein, *The Cycle of the Jewish Year,* Jerusalem, 1964, pp. 119–120.

the faith was transmitted, and a sense of responsibility in the present. He also knows that this responsibility entails sacrifice and suffering (see Abraham).

Holiness

There are several important words in this Scripture reading. The word "holy" (v. 9) denotes something more than "pure," "clean," or "set apart." It has a certain dynamic energy inherent in it when compared with such words as these. The holiness of God signifies the perfection of his being, and the holiness of his Name, Word and Spirit expresses the fact that he exists in a dimension different from all that is worldy or creaturely. However, this does not mean that he has no communication with mankind. Rather, in the Old Testament this holiness not only was revealed on Mount Sinai (Exod. 19: 7–25 and 24: 1–11), but was bestowed on Israel so that the people were brought into a special relationship with Yahweh. They became a people of grace and power, a people distinct from the nations who worshipped lifeless and ineffective idols. In the Old Testament the holiness of God has two dynamic elements. On the one hand, it can kill all that is false and unclean (see Exod. 19: 12–13), but, on the other hand, it can be the source of new and higher life to those who are dedicated to God. For example, Hosea says:

O Ephraim, what have I to do with idols? It is I who answer and look after you. I am like an evergreen cypress, from me comes your fruit. Whoever is wise, let him understand these things; whoever is discerning, let him know them; for the ways of the Lord are right, and the upright walk in them, but transgressors stumble in them. (Hos. 14: 8–9)

Glory

This Holiness, sometimes called the Glory of God, descended especially on the Tent of Meeting, the desert shrine (Exod. 40:

34–38), and later on the Temple in Jerusalem (I Kings 8: 10–11; II Chron. 5: 13–14). All who came into the vicinity of the Tent or Temple could be influenced by this Holiness.

The Appearing of Jesus

In the New Testament Jesus is seen as the Holy One of God who defeats all that is evil or unclean and brings the life-giving Holy Spirit to those who love him (see Luke 1: 35; Mark 1: 24; and Luke 4: 34). He makes others holy so that they may be the media of the Holy Spirit.

Thus the only calling of Christians is a dynamic calling (this is fully emphasized in v. 9 of our reading). It is not dependent on personal virtue or religious decision or speculation (v. 9), but upon the free and gracious election from God realized only in Jesus in whom the love of God is revealed. This love is manifested in the "appearing" (v. 10) of Jesus. The Greek word used for "appearing" denotes both divine intervention of a Saviour in a time of necessity and also the dawning of new light. The epistle uses the term meaning "bringing to light" (v. 10) in order to symbolize the new teaching about the knowledge of God and the nature of eternal life and especially the resurrection of Jesus (see II Tim. 2: 8; I Cor. 15: 51–56; and Acts 2: 27). Jesus and his followers bring to a climax the light and wisdom which Abraham first kindled. This intervention of Jesus conquers death, that which of all things on earth chains man down in fear. Through Jesus' resurrection life in the world to come becomes a concrete reality (v. 10).

THE THIRD READING, MATTHEW 17: 1–9. THE TRANSFIGURATION

And after six days Jesus took with him Peter and James and John his brother, and led them up a high mountain apart. And he was transfigured before them, and his face shone like the sun, and his garments became white as light. And behold, there appeared to them Moses and Elijah, talking with him. And Peter said to Jesus, "Lord, it is well that we are here; if you wish, I will make three booths here, one for you and one for Moses and one for Elijah." He was still speaking, when lo, a bright cloud overshadowed them, and a voice from the cloud said, "This is my beloved Son, with whom I am well pleased; listen to him." When the disciples heard this, they fell on their faces, and were filled with awe. But Jesus came and touched them, saying, "Rise, and have no fear." And when they lifted up their eyes, they saw no one but Jesus only.

And as they were coming down the mountain, Jesus commanded them, "Tell no one the vision, until the Son of man is raised from the dead."

The Idea of Glory

Among German scholars the transfiguration of Jesus is called the "glorification of Jesus." This title links the event with the important concept of *kabod* or "glory" in the Old Testament. *Kabod* or "glory" with regard to man meant his self, spirit, or innermost being, the things wherein his worth or essential being was believed to consist. *Kabod* with regard to God denoted the being or character of Yahweh revealed to man and this revelation was sometimes accompanied by physical phenomena by which his presence was made known. The chief physical phenomenon was one of light or radiance. In Jesus' glorification on the mount there was a revelation of his innermost character as a perfect human being and also a revelation of his nature as Son of God.

The revelation of glory in the Old Testament was associated especially with God's intervention in salvation history when he guided and delivered Israel. However, it was specifically associated with Mount Sinai where the Covenant and Law were given to Moses; and with the cloud that came upon the Tent of Meeting. This signified God's immanence in distinction from his transcendent nature above the earth.

58

A manifestation of glory was also expected to accompany the advent of the Messiah and was promised, too, to the righteous who would follow him.

Glory in Christ

The transfiguration indicated that the Glory of God was no longer limited to the Tent of Meeting or Temple but dwelt fully in Jesus and that he allowed this glory to overshadow his disciples. It showed that God had kept his word to dwell among his people. Peter saw the Glory of God shining through the Person of Jesus and wished to build three booths. He probably desired the experience to last.

The Transfiguration as the New Sinai

The description of Jesus on the Mount recalls a passage from a Jewish paraphrase of the Song of Songs.

My Beloved [Cant., v. 10]. Then Kennesseth [Assembly or Church of Israel] commences to engage in the praise of the Master of the Universe and speaks thus:
"It is my delight to worship God who wraps Himself by day in a robe white as snow and the glorious divine splendour, whose countenance shines like a flame by reason of the greatness of [His?] wisdom and thought, who delivers anew every day new traditions [decisions] which He has made known to His people on the Great Day, and whose array [or royal authority] extends over a myriad myriads of angels who serve before Him." [1]

Just as Yahweh revealed his Glory on Mount Sinai, so he revealed the Glory of his Son on the Mount of Transfiguration. It was a new Sinai. St. Matthew obviously meant one to see this resemblance between the two events. The people stayed at the

1. Cited by W. D. Davies, *Setting of the Sermon on the Mount,* Cambridge, 1964, p. 175; but not with reference to the transfiguration.

59

foot of the mountain (in one account of Sinai) and only three men, Aaron, Nadab, and Abihu, with seventy unnamed elders, accompanied Moses. Jesus was accompanied by only three diciples. Moses went up the mountain and after six days he saw the Glory of God, and when he returned to the people the skin of his face shone so that he was obliged to wear a veil. Six days are also mentioned with reference to the transfiguration, when Jesus appeared as the second and greater Moses, the new Teacher whose face shone, not with reflected glory, but with his own Divine Glory. However, whereas the face of Moses merely shone, St. Matthew tells us that Jesus' face was "transfigured." The Greek word used means that a profound change of form appeared. Elsewhere, it is used only in Romans 12: 2 and II Corinthians 3: 18 where it is used of the profound transformation in the being of a Christian. This is not without significance. The Glorification of Jesus prefigures the wonderful transformation of humanity.

The Figures of Moses and Elijah

Why did the two figures, Moses and Elijah, appear with Jesus? Perhaps it was because both held discourse with God on Mount Sinai (Exod. 33: 17ff. [Moses] and I Kings 19 [Elijah]). They represented the Law and the Prophets. They were both associated with eschatological expectation. Moses was more than a lawgiver, he was regarded as the prophet par excellence; and it was believed that another like him would come in the final days:

The Lord Your God will raise up for you a prophet like me [Moses] from among you, from your brethren—him you shall heed . . . (Deut. 18: 15)

Jesus fulfilled this prophecy.

Elijah was more than a prophet. He was expected to be the forerunner of the day of the Lord and to restore all things before its advent (see Malachi 4: 5–6).

In summary, we quote A. M. Ramsey:

Thus by appearing together Moses and Elijah sum up the entire drama of the old order from its beginning to its end: the one is the predecessor, the other is the precursor of the Messiah.[1]

Jesus in the Place of Yahweh

Yet there is one point which scholars do not appear to have remarked. They point to Jesus as the second Moses but here it would appear that he is even more than this. He stands in the position of Yahweh. As Yahweh spoke face to face with Moses and spoke with Elijah, so Jesus spoke with them. The cloud which overshadowed the disciples was the Cloud of Yahweh which overshadowed (the same word is used) the Tent and filled the Temple. Thus the transfiguration scene indicated that there was little doubt that the Father and Jesus were one. The voice was the same as the Voice at the Baptism and the words were similar, but to them were added the admonition "listen to him" (v. 5). What are the disciples to listen to? Perhaps the full Torah (revelation) or Wisdom given by Jesus, but perhaps also to the warning that the Son of man must suffer and die and rise again. They must not regard this as foolishness. One may compare I Corinthians 1: 23–24: "Christ crucified, a stumbling block to the Jews and folly to Gentiles, but to those *who are called* . . . the *power of God* and the *wisdom of God*" (see II Tim. 1: 8 and Matt. 17: 9–13).

The transfiguration looked toward the resurrection but also to the passion. As Adolf Schlatter says:

He who stood in glory with Moses and Elijah on either side will be crucified with evildoers on the right side and on the left; and the three disciples, who heard the Father's voice hail him as Son, will hear his voice in Gethsemane telling of his obedience to the Father's will. "They must learn the greatness of his offering—how

1. J. Jeremias in A. M. Ramsey, *The Glory of God and the Transfiguration of Christ,* New York, 1949, p. 114.

deep is his fellowship with the Father, and how great is the pain of his soul." [1]

The glorification was a light to encourage the disciples in the dark days of the passion. It was immediately after the glorification that Jesus spoke of the Son of man and especially about his suffering. The phrase "the Son of man" can mean either man in general, or the elect people of God, Israel, or a prophet, or an angel, or a supercelestial creature. Jesus appears to have used the title in the sense of a celestial creature. He had kept its full character hidden until now and even here he granted the disciples only a fleeting glimpse. The future revelation of this Son of man would come in Jesus' resurrection and ascension and then in the second coming. Then he would come on the clouds of heaven with the angels.

For us in Lent and especially on this Sunday we see the height to which man glorified in Christ will be raised, a glory more excellent than that of the first Adam, but this glory will not be acquired without suffering with the Son of Man (see II Timothy 1: 8).

Intercession

Second Sunday in Lent

The response is
Holy and Glorious Spirit of God, help us.

(1) For the gift of true wisdom and perfect knowledge, let us pray to the Lord.
(2) That all men and women may draw near to God with joy and love, let us pray . . .
(3) That we may be sons and daughters of light, let us pray . . .

1. A. M. Ramsey, *op. cit.,* p. 116.

(4) That God may restore to us the joy of his salvation and uphold us with a willing spirit, let us pray . . .

(5) That we may rejoice in thanksgiving for the redemption wrought by Christ and in the dynamic element of holiness, let us pray . . .

(6) For the gift of contemplative prayer wherein we may realize the Glory of Christ, let us pray . . .

(7) That we may learn to listen to the voice of the well-beloved Son of God, let us pray . . .

(8) That the reading of this gospel may cheer and encourage all who suffer or mourn, let us pray . . .

(9) That one day we may share Christ's glory, let us pray . . .

(10) For all who may be dying in ignominy or loneliness, let us pray . . .

The Third Sunday of Lent

Light and water are two symbols which dominate the paschal vigil. As the first reading from the vigil makes clear, they are meant to evoke the creation imagery of Genesis:

In the beginning God created the heavens and the earth. The earth was without form and void, and darkness was upon the face of the deep; and the Spirit of God was moving over the face of the waters. And God said, "Let there be light," and there was light.

(Gen. 1: 1–3 RSV)

The new life of the risen Lord is so radically new that it can only be described as a "new creation" or a "rebirth."

The prayer of the Church dramatizes this sense of newness, not only by using the symbols of light and water—symbols which are older than recorded human history—but also by incorporating a rich sexual imagery. The vigil views the baptismal font as a womb from which the new humanity emerges:

Send forth the spirit of adoption to regenerate the new people who are born at the font of baptism . . . May you, O Lord, who fill your city with joy by the flowing torrent of your grace, look mercifully upon your Church and multiply your acts of regeneration within her. Open the fonts of baptism all over the world for the renewal of the nations, so that under your majestic dominion they may receive from the Holy Spirit the grace of your only-begotten Son. May this water, prepared for the regeneration of man, be made fruitful. . . , so that a heavenly offspring, conceived in holiness and reborn into a new creature, may come forth from the spotless womb of this divine font; and may all regardless of distinction of

65

age or sex be brought forth into the same infancy by the mother-hood of grace. . . . May it be a font of life, a water of new birth . . . Here may the stain of all sin be washed away; may human nature created in your likeness and re-created to the glory of its maker, be cleansed from all the old defilement of man, so that everyone who receives this sacrament of regeneration may be born again into a new infancy of true innocence. (Blessing of the Font, *Missal,* pp. 197–205)

Inseparably linked to the themes of new creation and re-birth is the gift of the Spirit. Genesis describes the creation of the world by the agency of the breath (or Spirit) of God. Now the new creation emerges by the agency of the Spirit. The climax of the blessing of the font is the triple invocation of the Spirit upon the water. The new life of the risen Lord is the life of his own Spirit, the Holy Spirit of God.

The Third Sunday in Lent

The three points for meditation this Sunday are:
    (1) the Israelites' thirst for water in the desert;
    (2) the faith which saves Jew and Gentile;
    (3) the water of life, which is the Holy Spirit.

THE FIRST READING, EXODUS 17: 3–7. WATER FROM THE ROCK

But the people thirsted there for water, and the people murmured against Moses, and said, "Why did you bring us up out of Egypt, to kill us and our children and our cattle with thirst?" So Moses cried to the Lord, "What shall I do with this people? They are almost ready to stone me." And the Lord said to Moses, "Pass on before the people, taking with you some of the elders of Israel; and take in your hand the rod with which you struck the Nile, and go. Behold, I will stand before you there on the rock at Horeb; and you shall strike the rock, and water shall come out of it, that the people may drink." And Moses did so, in the sight of the elders of Israel. And he called the name of the place Massah and Meribah, because of the faultfinding of the children of Israel, and because they put the Lord to the proof by saying, "Is the Lord among us or not?"

The Thirst for Water

The Old Testament records three occasions when the Israelites in the desert murmured because they had no water. These accounts are found in Exodus 15: 22–27, Numbers 20: 2–13, and the present reading. However, they may be three versions of the same incident. The place where the murmuring occurred was called *Meribah* from the Hebrew word *rib,* which means quarrel. The name *Massah,* which signifies "testing," may be a later interpolation into the text.

Two Pious Reflections

However, Jewish commentators on the text added two pious reflections which may be of interest to Christian readers. Firstly, they inserted a reference to the law; thus, for example, they described *Rephidim* as "a place where their [the Israelites'] hands were idle in the commandments of the law," [1] and they said that the people were "empty of instruction." [2] They postulated that the name of the place was called *Massah* "because they tempted the Lord saying, 'Doth the glory of the majesty of the Lord [the Holy Spirit or Shekinah] truly dwell among us, or not?' " [3] Perhaps the Jewish writers wished to include a moral note, namely, that disregard for God's law and lack of faith in his protective care wrought—to their minds—catastrophe for the people.

Secondly, a legend about the rock was attached to the biblical account. The commentators said that it was a miraculous rock

1. J. W. Etheridge, *The Targums,* Ktav Press, New York, 1968.
2. *Ibid.,* p. 496.
3. *Ibid.,* p. 502.

which accompanied the Israelites, thus that "The water that flowed for them on this spot served not only as a relief for their present need, but on this occasion there was revealed to them a well of water, which did not abandon them in all their forty years' wandering but accompanied them on all their marches." [1] This well was called Miriam's Well because it was said that the miracles were wrought on account of the merits of the prophetess Miriam, the sister of Moses (*ibid.*). Thus, in contrast to the people's lack of faith, pious tradition stressed God's faithfulness and superabundant love.

St. Paul's Use of the Legend

St. Paul referred to this legend of the wandering well in I Corinthians 10:4:

> . . . and all drank the same supernatural drink. For they drank from the supernatural Rock which followed them, and the Rock was Christ.

Both these points will be taken up this Sunday. In the second reading there will be a reflection on the place of the ritual law in Christianity, and in the third reading Jesus will appear as the Well of Spiritual Living Water which transcends this ritual law.

THE SECOND READING, ROMANS 5: 1, 2, 5–8. JESUS, SAVIOUR OF THE "UNGODLY"

> Therefore, since we are justified by faith, we have peace with God through our Lord Jesus Christ. Through him we have obtained access to this grace in which we stand, and we rejoice in our hope of sharing the glory of God. . . . and hope does not disappoint us, because God's love has been poured into our hearts through the Holy Spirit who has been given to us. While we were yet helpless, at the right time Christ died for the ungodly. Why, one will

1. L. Ginzberg, *Legends of the Jews,* vol. III, Philadelphia, 1946, pp. 52f.

hardly die for a righteous man—though perhaps for a good man one will dare even to die. But God shows his love for us in that while we were yet sinners Christ died for us.

The Context

These verses follow St. Paul's discussion of the faith of Abraham and how he was saved by faith rather than ritual observance of the Law. He became the father of converts. In this reading St. Paul continues to stress our justification through faith, and this theme is especially apposite because of the gospel reading about the Samaritan woman. She was saved by belief in Jesus although her nation was regarded as *non-kosher*.

The Barrier Depriving Gentiles of Access to the Divine Presence

By advocating this concept of faith without ritual observance and the equality of Jew and Gentile, St. Paul was dealing a death-blow to all ultra-conservative Jewish racial pride. This insisted that men were not righteous without male circumcision and the observance of purificatory, dietary, and certain marriage laws. In Romans 5: 2 St. Paul speaks of "access." This signifies entry into the audience chamber of a monarch. The monarch for the Jewish people was Yahweh and the royal residence was the glory or radiance of the Shekinah or Holy Spirit. The most graphic verses in the New Testament which refer to the Gentiles gaining access to the royal-divine presence are Ephesians 2: 11–16:

Therefore remember that at one time you Gentiles in the flesh, called the uncircumcision by what is called the circumcision, which is made in the flesh by hands—remember that you were at that time separated from Christ, alienated from the commonwealth of Israel, and strangers to the covenants of promise, having no hope and without God in the world. But now in Christ Jesus you who once

69

were far off have been brought near in the blood of Christ. For he is our peace, who has made us both one, and has broken down the dividing wall of hostility, by abolishing in his flesh the law of commandments and ordinances, that he might create in himself one new man in place of the two, so making peace, . . .

Here St. Paul refers to a great wall or balustrade about four and a half feet high to prevent Gentiles from full access to the more sacred part of the Temple. On this wall at regular intervals stood slabs on which warnings were inscribed in Greek, and Latin about the laws of purification and saying that no foreigner was permitted to enter the holy place: the Roman government did not accept responsibility for their death if they did approach.[1]

In the gospel we see Jesus metaphorically breaking down this partition with respect to the Samaritans.

When this barrier is broken down Peace is established (see Rom. 5: 1). Peace is not merely lack of hostility or tranquility but complete spiritual well-being, namely, salvation. This well-being is experienced when the Holy Spirit is poured out (Rom. 5: 5). When St. Paul used the metaphor of "pouring out" he employed a common Oriental metaphor for spiritual refreshment and he may have had in mind the text of Isaiah 44: 3:

I will pour water upon him that is thirsty, and streams upon the dry ground: I will pour my Spirit upon thy seed.

THE THIRD READING, JOHN 4: 5–42. THE SAMARITAN WOMAN

So he came to a city of Samaria, called Sychar, near the field that Jacob gave to his son Joseph. Jacob's well was there, and so Jesus, wearied as he was with his journey, sat down beside the well. It was about the sixth hour.

There came a woman of Samaria to draw water. Jesus said to

1. See Josephus, *Jewish Wars,* V, 193, and *Antiquities,* 15:417.

her, "Give me a drink." For his disciples had gone away into the city to buy food. The Samaritan woman said to him, "How is it that you, a Jew, ask a drink of me, a woman of Samaria?" For Jews have no dealings with Samaritans. Jesus answered her, "If you knew the gift of God, and who it is that is saying to you, 'Give me a drink,' you would have asked him, and he would have given you living water." The woman said to him, "Sir, you have nothing to draw with, and the well is deep; where do you get that living water? Are you greater than our father Jacob, who gave us the well, and drank from it himself, and his sons, and his cattle?" Jesus said to her, "Every one who drinks of this water will thirst again, but whoever drinks of the water that I shall give him will never thirst; the water that I shall give him will become in him a spring of water welling up to eternal life." The woman said to him, "Sir, give me this water, that I may not thirst, nor come here to draw."

Jesus said to her, "Go, call your husband, and come here." The woman answered him, "I have no husband." Jesus said to her, "You are right in saying, 'I have no husband'; for you have had five husbands, and he whom you now have is not your husband; this you said truly." The woman said to him, "Sir, I perceive that you are a prophet. Our fathers worshipped on this mountain; and you say that in Jerusalem is the place where men ought to worship." Jesus said to her, "Woman, believe me, the hour is coming when neither on this mountain nor in Jerusalem will you worship the Father. You worship what you do not know; we worship what we know, for salvation is from the Jews. But the hour is coming, and now is, when the true worshippers will worship the Father in spirit and truth, for such the Father seeks to worship him. God is spirit, and those who worship him must worship in spirit and truth." The woman said to him, "I know that the Messiah is coming (he who is called Christ); when he comes, he will show us all things." Jesus said to her, "I who speak to you am he."

Just then his disciples came. They marvelled that he was talking with a woman, but none said, "What do you wish?" or, "Why are you talking with her?" So the woman left her water jar, and went away into the city, and said to the people, "Come, see a man who told me all that I ever did. Can this be the Christ?" They went out of the city and were coming to him.

71

Meanwhile, the disciples besought him, saying, "Rabbi, eat." But he said to them, "I have food to eat of which you do not know." So the disciples said to one another, "Has any one brought him food?" Jesus said to them, "My food is to do the will of him who sent me, and to accomplish his work. Do you not say, 'There are yet four months, then comes the harvest'? I tell you, lift up your eyes, and see how the fields are already white for harvest. He who reaps receives wages, and gathers fruit for eternal life, so that sower and reaper may rejoice together. For here the saying holds true, 'One sows and another reaps.' I sent you to reap that for which you did not labour; others have laboured, and you have entered into their labour."

Many Samaritans from that city believed in him because of the woman's testimony, "He told me all that I ever did." So when the Samaritans came to him, they asked him to stay with them; and he stayed there two days. And many more believed because of his word. They said to the woman, "It is no longer because of your words that we believe, for we have heard for ourselves, and we know that this is indeed the Saviour of the world."

The third lesson offers very rich material. It lies within the heart of St. John's teaching on the theology of baptism. It falls after the discussion of the baptism of John (John 1: 19–34); the discussion between Nicodemus and Jesus concerning regeneration with water and the Spirit, a rebirth from above, (John 3: 1–14); and a further dispute about purification (John 3: 25–36). This lesson speaks of inner life springing up within one, the life produced by the Holy Spirit.

The People of Samaria

On this occasion, Jesus entered a city of Samaria called Sychar (or Shechem). Samaria was a large tract of territory occupying about one-third of Palestine and dividing the North from the South. The residents were of Jewish origin, some wealthy and educated, others poor and ignorant with superstitious beliefs.

Some Jews regarded the Samaritans as true worshippers of Yahweh, while others looked upon them as almost pagan and refused to associate with them in any way. The Samaritans had built their own temple on Mount Gerizim. The ruins of this temple remain to this day, but it had been destroyed before the birth of Jesus in about 129 B.C. by a Jewish King and High Priest, John Hyrcanus. There was obvious rivalry between the priesthood of the Samaritan place of worship and the priesthood at Jerusalem.

Jesus entered the village and sat by an ancient well, discovered by the patriarch Jacob, a well which is still in use. He asked a Samaritan woman for a drink. This was an extraordinary thing to do for two reasons: firstly, because a man did not usually speak to a woman who was alone; and, secondly, because a strict Jew believed that the Samaritans were ritually defiled from their youth upwards. The strict Jew believed that if he drank from their vessels the very saliva of the Samaritan would defile him and he would be unable to attend temple services until he had cleansed himself in a ritual bath. This throws abundant light upon the problem of reconciling Jew and Gentile, which St. Paul and others were obliged to face.

The Arrangement of the Reading

St. John arranged this episode in five scenes:
1. (1) The meeting between Jew and Samaritan;
2. (2) The discussion of living water;
3. (3) The discussion concerning the worship of the Jews and the Samaritans;
4. (4) The discussion with the disciples about non-material food or sustenance which balances the talk about water;
5. (5) The episode about the acquaintances of the Samaritan woman and the declaration of Jesus as the Saviour of the world.

73

Jew and Samaritan

It is not facile to see Johannine symbolism in this section. Some scholars have suggested that the woman is a symbolic figure portraying the Samaritan people, her five husbands and five idolatrous beliefs or gods which the Samaritans mingled with their true Yahwist religion from about 721 B.C. It was then that their city and country was captured by the Assyrians and many of their people deported; further, it was a time when alien, idolatrous residents from Assyria came into their country bringing pagan influence into Samaria. Jesus symbolizes the true spiritual bridegroom of Samaria (see John 3: 29; St. John the Baptist referred to Jesus as "the bridegroom"). However, in the Old Testament it was God, Yahweh, who was represented as the bridegroom of Israel. Therefore, in the present context, Jesus is probably the bridegroom, the Son of God, reclaiming a portion of the Chosen People, the Samaritans, as his bride but purifying them with living water, that is, the Spirit, as they return to him.

The Living Water

St. John's Gospel is full of imagery: it is his practice to show spiritual truth through physical circumstances. Here St. John shows the ordinary happening of a thirsty and weary man, Jesus, asking for a drink from a well. It was unnatural for him to speak to a woman, yet it was a duty of hospitality to give water to strangers coming into a house or even passing by (see Gen. 24: 17, 43). If this duty was not fulfilled, dire hostility might result. One has an example in Exodus. The Israelites wished to pass through the territory of Edom, Ammon, and Moab, but the people there refused to give them water or money. Two hundred years later, this resulted in bitter warfare. Was the gentle request of Jesus a gesture on his part that he wished all rivalry between Jew and Samaritan to cease and

74

the hope that this could be done (partially at least) by the simple deed of loving kindness, that is, by the giving of a drink of water, and the sharing of a well discovered by a common ancestor, Jacob? We may compare Jesus' injunction in Mark 9: 40–41:

For he that is not against us is for us. For truly, I say to you, whoever gives you a cup of water to drink because you bear the name of Christ, will by no means lose his reward.

However, Jesus passed from the earthly realm of ordinary water to the idea of spiritual water. He himself symbolized the spiritual well who can give living water. If the woman knew the sacred Scripture, her thought would quickly have reflected upon the text of Jeremiah 2: 11–13:

> Has a nation changed its gods,
> even though they are no gods?
> But my people have changed their *glory,*
> for that which does not profit.
> Be appalled, O heavens, at this,
> be shocked, be utterly desolate, say the Lord,
> for my people have committed two evils:
> for they have forsaken *me,*
> *the fountain of living waters,*
> and hewed out cisterns for themselves,
> broken cisterns,
> that can hold no waters.

Idolatry, which is spiritual adultery, meant forsaking the Holy and Pure Spirit of Yahweh and depraving oneself with superstitions. The true living water, from the spiritual well, God, is the Holy Spirit. This is shown in the text of John 7: 37–39:

On the last day of the feast of Tabernacles, the great day, Jesus stood up and proclaimed, "If anyone thirst, let him come to me and drink. He who believes in me, as the scripture has said, 'Out of his heart shall flow rivers of living water.'" Now this he said about the Spirit, which those who believed in him were to receive; for as yet the Spirit had not been given, because Jesus was not yet gloried. (See the Second Sunday in Lent.)

75

Jesus offered the Samaritan nation in the person of this woman the Holy Spirit who would bring true life and true teaching. For water symbolized both the Holy Spirit and cleansing (compare Ezek. 36: 25) and also divine teaching and revelation (compare *Hag.* 3a, *B.M.* 84b; *Hor.* 14a: Ab. i. 2). When Jesus bade the woman to "call her husband" (v. 16), he was probably inviting her to spread the good news, become a "missionary" or disciple and teacher. Yet where was true teaching and the chief channel of the Holy Spirit found but in the worship of the true Jewish Church? It was natural, then, that the conversation turned to a discussion about the worship of Jews and Samaritans.

The Discussion Concerning the Worship of the Jews and the Samaritans

The woman perhaps inquired whether the Samaritan or the Jewish worship was correct and Jesus declared that salvation came from the Jews (v. 22). Yet he also asserted that "the hour is coming when neither on this mountain nor in Jerusalem will you worship the Father. You worship what you do not know; we worship what we know, for salvation comes from the Jews. But the hour is coming, and now is, when the true worshippers will worship the Father in spirit and truth, for such the Father seeks to worship him. God is spirit, and those who worship him must worship in spirit and truth" (vv. 21–24).

This was a truly ecumenical dialogue. The Samaritans were some of the other sheep which would be united to the one flock of which Jesus spoke in John 10: 16:

And I have other sheep that are not of this fold; I must bring them also, and they will heed my voice. So there shall be one flock, one shepherd.

There was an ancient belief among the Jews that the Shekinah or Holy Spirit could dwell only in a ritually clean land and that the special dwelling of the Shekinah was to be found only in the Temple at Jerusalem. This was to give place to something far greater. Jesus himself was the true Temple (John 2: 21–22), he was the true bearer of the Spirit, and after his resurrection the Holy Spirit would abide in a special manner in the Church which was his resurrected body. In that body there would be no discrimination against anyone but all would be one in the Spirit. This was confirmed by St. Paul, as in the following texts:

For as many of you were baptized into Christ have put on Christ. There is neither Jew nor Greek, there is neither slave nor free, there is neither male nor female; for you are all one in Christ Jesus. (Gal. 3: 27–28)

. . . put on the new nature, which is being renewed in knowledge after the image of its creator. Here there cannot be Greek and Jew, circumcised and uncircumcised, barbarian, Scythian, slave, free man, but Christ is all, and in all. (Col. 3: 10–11)

Yet one must note one further point. Jesus said that salvation came from the Jews, but on the other hand, in St. John's Gospel, in contrast to the other gospels, he declared openly that he was the Messiah. The Samaritan woman referred to the Messiah and Jesus answered, "I who speak to you am he" (v. 26). The Samaritan idea of the Messiah was not as politically oriented as that of the Jews. He was expected to be a person very like Moses but bringing with him the full revelation. Apparently Jesus thought it was safe to admit his identity in these surroundings. The Samaritans, although perhaps despised by many Jews, had cultivated expectations and truths, especially about the Messiah, which would be fulfilled by Jesus and transmitted to the Christian faith.

The Discussion of Spiritual Food

St. John introduced the discourse on non-material food (vv. 31–38) to balance the conversation about spiritual drink which

77

Jesus held with the Samaritan woman. The disciples came, as it were, from shopping, carrying with them material food, and they pressed Jesus to eat. But Jesus appears to have forgotten about his physical hunger and thirst as his contemplation passed to more important things, namely, spiritual food and drink. But once again, St. John has used an everyday occurrence, a material object, namely, bread, to introduce a deeply spiritual idea. When the disciples urged him to eat, Jesus replied, "I have food to eat of which you do not know" (v. 32b). Then he continued, "My food is to do the will of him who sent me, and to accomplish his work" (v. 34b). Jesus' words lead our thoughts back to the Temptation narrative. When Jesus told Satan that man does not live by bread alone but by every word which proceeds from the mouth of God, his quotation referred back to the Exodus narrative. We might also recall Mark 8: 14f., where Jesus spoke about bread and the disciples thought that he was speaking about ordinary bread; but rather he was referring to (1) spiritual teaching, namely, the leaven of the Pharisees, and (2) the theological implications of the miracle of the multiplication of the loaves. The multiplication of the loaves is closely associated with both the manna which God gave the Israelites in the desert, and also with the holy eucharist. One of many traditions among the Jewish people informs us that the manna in the wilderness was the *ziv* or radiance of the Shekinah which had taken on physical properties. They believed that in the world to come and even on this earth, if one were very saintly, one could be sustained by the radiance of the Shekinah or, as we would say, the Holy Spirit. Jesus regarded the accomplishment of the Father's will to be that which sustained his whole being. In one way, Jesus was independent and had no need for people to give him physical food, but by becoming incarnate he accepted this limitation and lived as other people did. On the other hand, he was entirely dependent upon the will of God, his mission was to complete the work of man's salvation. All the signs or miracles which St. John recorded in his gospel—for example, the transformation of water into wine, the healing of the sick people, the idea of raising a new temple, which would be his resurrected body— were all signs that Jesus was opening a new spiritual life to men. He gave this responsibility to his disciples. Jesus looked at the harvest of souls in this great tract of land called Samaria. He indicated that other missionaries had been working in that area, and indeed some scholars would suggest that there is good evidence that John the Baptist and his disciples worked in that district. Jesus and his disciples found the ground prepared for them when they came to Samaria. This may explain the proverb which Jesus cited: "One sows and another reaps. I sent you to reap that for which you did not labour; others have laboured, and you have entered into their labour." Later, as we learn in the eighth chapter of the Acts of the Apostles, Philip did missionary work here and Peter and John afterwards came down to confer the Holy Spirit upon those who had been converted.

Declaration of Jesus as Saviour

One might remark briefly upon a few salient points here. Firstly, the people of the Samaritan town believed, not because of miracles or persuasive argument, but simply on the testimony of the woman and then the words of Jesus himself (see the Epistle for today). Nicodemus, a Jewish teacher of Israel, could not understand Jesus' teaching on baptism and rebirth, but the Samaritans understood the Living Water. They declared Jesus "The Saviour of the World." This title goes far beyond mere Messiah. The Messiah was neither Redeemer nor Saviour. Only God—Yahweh, in the Old Testament—was declared Saviour (see Psalm 24: 5; Isaiah 12: 2; and in the New Testament Luke 1: 47). A fuller text is Isaiah 43: 11f:

"I, I am the Lord,
and besides me there is no saviour.
I declared and saved and proclaimed,

when there was no strange god among you;
and you are my witnesses," says the Lord.
"I am God, and also henceforth I am He;
there is none who can deliver from my hand;
I work and who can hinder it?"

The Samaritans may have realized Jesus' meaning when he said to the Samaritan woman, "I am he," words similar to the name which Yahweh revealed to Moses at the Burning Bush (Exod. 3: 14). That is, Jesus indicated his divinity which some of the Jews refused to acknowledge. This lesson contains abundant material for reflection on ecumenical movements within the Christian Church.

Intercession

Third Sunday in Lent

The response is
> *Faithful and loving Father, hear us.*

- (1) In thanksgiving for the gift of the sacrament of Baptism, let us pray to the Lord.
- (2) That we may trust in the providence of God and not put him to the test, let us pray . . .
- (3) For those who hunger and thirst like the Israelites, let us pray . . .
- (4) That we may have perfect hope and confidence in God's grace, let us pray . . .
- (5) That the Holy Spirit may heal within us all prejudice with regard to race, sex or class, let us pray . . .
- (6) That the Holy Spirit may heal all disunity within the Christian denominations, let us pray . . .
- (7) That we may thirst eagerly for the Living Water, which is the Holy Spirit, let us pray . . .

80

(8) For a deep realization of the labors of others into which we have entered, let us pray . . .

(9) For the rejected, despised or underprivileged that Christ may draw them to his loving Heart, let us pray . . .

(10) In memory of the Samaritan woman for all women missionaries and especially for deaconesses, let us pray . . .

THE FOURTH SUNDAY OF LENT

St. John's account of the healing of the man born blind was once the gospel for a day on which the Scrutinies were held. The Scrutinies were a formal admission to the final stage of the catechumenate, when an intense preparation for baptism began. Testimonies that the catechumens were living a good life were given by their sponsors. After exorcism, the candidates were officially ready to "hear the gospel," and as a sign of this, the beginning of each of the four gospels was read and explained to them. The creed and the Lord's prayer were "delivered" to them for the first time, with an explanation of their meaning. Since these prayers were known only by the faithful, this was in a real sense the first stage of the baptismal service. The story of the man born blind was read as a preparation for the actual baptismal service on Easter eve.

Throughout Lent, the liturgy recounts stories of deliverance and healing. Frequently there are miracles. The dead are raised, the dumb are made to speak, the blind see, the lepers are cleansed. To these situations, God responds with his saving power. He brings wholeness, fulfillment, the integration of the human person.

But sin, not physical suffering, is the root of the human plight. Our sinfulness isolates us from one another in our selfishness. It is sin which makes us alone, afraid, helpless, empty. The miracles of healing are signs of God's greater power to cure man's sinfulness. With the death and resurrection of Jesus, God's healing power is brought to mankind. In expectation of the deliverance which would finally come in Christ, the prophet Hosea could describe God's healing of his people:

I will heal their faithlessness; I will love them freely, for my anger has turned from them. I will be as the dew to Israel; he shall blossom as the lily, he shall strike root as the poplar; his shoots shall spread out; his beauty shall be like the olive, and his fragrance like Lebanon. They shall return and dwell beneath my shadow, they shall flourish as a garden; they shall blossom as the vine, their fragrance shall be like the wine of Lebanon. (Hos. 14: 4–7 RSV)

The healing of the blind man is an especially apt sign of salvation, because both the Old Testament and the New Testament commonly describe deliverance as a passage from darkness to light. Using the paschal candle as a symbol of the risen Lord, the Church incorporates the biblical imagery in her exaltation:

Rejoice, too, O earth; you are made brilliant by such splendor. Rejoice, for you have been illumined. Darkness everywhere has been overcome by the brightness of this everlasting King. Rejoice, O mother Church; you are made radiant by so great a light . . . This is the night on which the light of the pillar of fire destroyed the darkness of sin. This is the night which at this hour everywhere restores to grace and unites in holiness those who believe in Christ, separating them from worldly vice and the darkness of sin . . . It is of this night that Scripture says: "And the night shall be as bright as day. And the night shall light up my joy." (*Missal,* pp. 181–184)

Many early Christians were so imbued with this symbol that they described the sacrament of baptism as "illumination" or "enlightenment." It was entirely natural that the Church should choose the story of the healing of the blind man for its gospel on a day when the catechumens were examined as part of their preparation for baptism. They were looking toward their own passage from darkness to light.

Ritual gestures which indicated the passage from darkness to light were quickly developed. The baptismal candidates faced the west, the region of darkness, to renounce Satan, and then turned to the east, to the region of the rising sun, to make their profession of faith. Even the natural setting of the vigil suggested this passage. It began in darkness and ended with the light of the early dawn. The baptistery itself was located at the west side of the Church. The newly baptized would proceed from the baptismal pool to the brightly lighted Church for the paschal eucharist in a literal passage from darkness to light.

In faith, the baptized enter into the light of the risen Lord. The vigil in its celebration of the coming of light, anticipates the final destiny of the faithful:

And I saw no temple in the city, for its temple is the Lord God the Almighty and the Lamb. And the city has no need of sun or moon to shine upon it, for the glory of God is its light, and its lamp is the Lamb. By its light shall the nations walk; and the kings of the earth shall bring their glory into it, and its gates shall never be shut by day—and there shall be no more night there; they shall bring into it the glory and honor of the nations. (Rev. 21: 22–26 RSV)

The Fourth Sunday in Lent

The themes for the Fourth Sunday in Lent are:
  (1) the election of David as king; he is chosen for his interior disposition not his outward appearance;
  (2) the children of light whose characters are upright and genuine;
  (3) the healing of the blind man.

THE FIRST READING, I SAMUEL 16: 1B, 6–7, 10–13A. THE ANOINTING OF DAVID

Fill your horn with oil, and go; I will send you to Jesse the Bethlehemite, for I have provided for myself a king among his sons. (v. 1b)

When they came, he looked on Eliab and thought, "Surely the Lord's anointed is before him." But the Lord said to Samuel, "Do not look on his appearance or on the height of his stature, because

85

I have rejected him; for the Lord sees not as man sees; man looks on the outward appearance, but the Lord looks on the heart." (vv. 6–7)

And Jesse made seven of his sons pass before Samuel. And Samuel said to Jesse, "The Lord has not chosen these." And Samuel said to Jesse, "Are all your sons here?" And he said, "There remains yet the youngest, but behold, he is keeping the sheep." And Samuel said to Jesse, "Send and fetch him; for we will not sit down till he comes here." And he sent, and brought him in. Now he was ruddy, and had beautiful eyes, and was handsome. And the Lord said, "Arise, anoint him; for this is he." Then Samuel took the horn of oil, and anointed him in the midst of his brothers; and the Spirit of the Lord came mightily upon David from that day forward. (vv. 10–13a)

In the Old Testament there are two versions of David's introduction to Saul. In 1 Samuel 16: 14–23 he appears as a musician who calms the mentally disturbed king, but in I Samuel 17: 20–30 he is presented as a warrior of great prowess. The present reading concerning the anointing of David serves to associate him with the prophet Samuel and to present him, like Samuel, as a charismatic leader. There is a "political" anointing of David by the elders of Israel in II Samuel 2: 4 and 5: 3.

The present anointing is an idealized picture which forms a contrast to the preceding chapter (I Sam. 15). This chapter relates the story of Saul's victory over the Amalekites. Afterwards Saul disobeyed the prophetic injunctions from God (I Sam. 15: 1–3) by preserving the life of Agag, the king of the Amalekites, and keeping some of the best cattle. Samuel remonstrated with him. Saul took hold of Samuel's robe and it tore. Samuel accepted this as a sign that Saul's kingdom would be taken from him and given "to a neighbor of yours, who is better than you" (I Sam. 15: 28). God was free to choose whom he would. The neighbor was David, the least of his father's house. The biblical text says that God looked on the heart, not the external appearance, but it does not specify what was in David's heart. However, a psalm in the Greek version of the

Old Testament, supported now by a text from the Dead Sea Scrolls, gives us some idea. The psalm is a poetic commentary on I Samuel 16: 1–13. It suggests that David's greatest virtue lay in the fact that in his heart he gave glory to God and God saw and heard all David's deeds and words. Here are the pertinent stanzas:

> Smaller was I than my brothers
> and the youngest of the sons of my father,
> So he made me shepherd of his flock
> and ruler over his kids.
>
> My hands have made an instrument
> and my fingers a lyre;
> and [so] have I rendered glory to the Lord,
> thought I, within my soul.
>
> The mountains do not witness to him,
> nor do the hills proclaim;
> The trees have cherished my words
> and the flock my works.
>
> For who can proclaim and who can bespeak
> and who can recount the deeds of the Lord?
> Everything has God seen,
> everything has he heard and he has heeded.[1]

Later Jewish pious tradition attributed to David great tenderness of soul (*Exod. R.,* 2: 2), magnificent courage (see *Hagigah,* 13b), and the Spirit of prophecy (Josephus, *Ant.,* 6: 166; *T. B. Sanh.,* 93b). He is reported to have been a man of deep prayer and to have collected and composed psalms.

Josephus draws out the moral of this lesson when he represents God answering Samuel, ". . . I make not of the kingdom a prize for comeliness of body, but for virtue of soul, and I seek one who in full measure is distinguished by this, one

---

1. Quoted in J. A. Sanders, *The Psalms Scroll of Qumran Cave 11: Discoveries in the Judaean Desert of Jordan,* vol. 4, Oxford, 1965, pp. 55–56.

adorned with piety, justice, fortitude and obedience, qualities whereof beauty of soul consists" (Josephus, *Ant.*, 6: 160, Loeb translation).

THE SECOND READING, EPHESIANS 5: 8–14. THE SONS OF LIGHT

. . . for once you were darkness, but now you are light in the Lord; walk as children of light (for the fruit of light is found in all that is good and right and true), and try to learn what is pleasing to the Lord. Take no part in the unfruitful works of darkness, but instead expose them. For it is a shame even to speak of the things that they do in secret; but when anything is exposed by the light it becomes visible, for anything that becomes visible is light. Therefore it is said,
  "Awake, O sleeper, and arise from the dead,
  and Christ shall give you light."

The Context

This passage occurs in an exhortation to Christians to live pure lives free from immorality and idolatry. It should be compared with the idea of the sons of light and darkness (see p. 53 above). Light once again is a symbol of life, wisdom, and the Holy Spirit. In verse 9 some manuscripts read "Spirit," not "light." The fruits of the light are similar to the qualities of David's soul and also to the virtues of the Spirit which St. Paul lists in Galatians 5: 22–26.

Christ as Light

But the important point to observe is that it is Christ who overcomes the darkness (vv. 13–14). Among the Jewish traditions there was a belief that the Messiah would bring special light. Perhaps the most interesting example of this belief is found in a section of a Jewish work which is difficult to date but which is, perhaps, worthwhile quoting either as a possible background to Jesus as the Messiah, who brings light; or, if it is later than the time of Jesus, as a Jewish reflection upon the idea of the Messiah. This reflection would possibly have been borrowed from Christian works. The section reads as follows:

"In thy light we shall see light." What is this light which the congregation of Israel looks for? That is the light of the Messiah, as it is said, "God saw the light and it was good." God looked at the Messiah and his deeds before the world was created, and he hid the [primal or archetypal] light for his Messiah and for his generation under the throne of his glory. Then Satan said to God, "Lord of the world, for whom is this light which thou hast hidden under thy throne of glory?" God replied, "For him who will put thee to shame." When Satan saw him, he was appalled, and he fell on his face, and he said, "Verily, this is the Messiah who will cast me and all the princes [i.e., the angels] of the nations of the world into hell." [1]

This is a very intriguing quotation. If it could be established that it were pre-Christian, it would serve as an illuminating background to Jesus' discourse about the light of the world and to his healing of the blind man. However, one can say with confidence that the light brought by Jesus is truth. If one embraces this one attains the gifts of the Spirit, namely, wisdom, knowledge and understanding, goodness and purity, which the author mentions in this epistle.

In the third reading, the light or spiritual wisdom is offered both to the religious leaders at the time of Jesus and also to a layman but only one accepts the opportunity to know God. The Jewish people used to say, "Whosoever has a benign eye, a simple heart, and a humble spirit, or who is humble and pious, is a disciple of Abraham, but he who lacks kindness of heart is no true son of Abraham" (*J.E.,* under the entry "Abraham"). In the lesson from St. John the religious leaders have no such

---

1. *Pes. R.,* cited in C. G. Montefiore and H. Loewe, *A Rabbinic Anthology,* Philadelphia, 1963, pp. 584–586.

qualifications and so they fail to receive spiritual sight (see John 8).

A Note on Verse 14

This verse is difficult to explain. It might be an adaptation of Isaiah 60: 1:

> Arise, shine; for you light has come, and the glory of the Lord has risen upon you.

In this case Christ has the same attributes as Yahweh. However, it might be a baptismal hymn, perhaps associated with the fragment found in I Timothy 3: 16. The exalted Christ rouses men from the sleep of death or sin (see John 11: 11).

THE THIRD READING, JOHN 9: 1–41. THE MAN BORN BLIND

As he passed by, he saw a man blind from his birth. And his disciples asked him, "Rabbi, who sinned, this man or his parents, that he was born blind?" Jesus answered, "It was not that this man sinned, or his parents, but that the works of God might be made manifest in him. We must work the works of him who sent me, while it is day; night comes, when no one can work. As long as I am in the world, I am the light of the world." As he said this, he spat on the ground and made clay of the spittle and anointed the man's eyes with the clay, saying to him, "Go, wash in the pool of Siloam" (which means Sent). So he went and washed and came back seeing. The neighbors, and those who had seen him before as a beggar, said, "Is not this the man who used to sit and beg?" Some said, "It is he"; others said, "No, but he is like him." He said, "I am the man." (They said to him, "Then how were your eyes opened?" He answered, "The man called Jesus made clay and anointed my eyes and said to me, 'Go to Siloam and wash'; so I went and washed and received my sight." They said to him, "Where is he?" He said, "I do not know."

90

They brought to the Pharisees the man who had formerly been blind. Now it was a sabbath day when Jesus made the clay and opened his eyes. The Pharisees again asked him how he had received his sight. And he said to them, "He put clay on my eyes, and I washed, and I see." Some of the Pharisees said, "This man is not from God, for he does not keep the sabbath." But others said, "How can a man who is a sinner do such signs?" There was a division among them. So they again said to the blind man, "What do you say about him, since he has opened your eyes?" He said, "He is a prophet."

The Jews did not believe that he had been blind and had received his sight, until they called the parents of the man who had received his sight, and asked them, "Is this your son, who you say was born blind? How then does he now see?" His parents answered, "We know that this is our son, and that he was born blind; but how he now sees we do not know, nor do we know who opened his eyes. Ask him; he is of age, he will speak for himself." His parents said this because they feared the Jews, for the Jews had already agreed that if anyone should confess him to be Christ, he was to be put out of the synagogue. Therefore, his parents said, "He is of age, ask him."

So for the second time they called the man who had been blind, and said to him, "Give God the praise; we know that this man is a sinner." He answered, "Whether he is a sinner, I do not know; one thing I know, that though I was blind, now I see." They said to him, "What did he do to you? How did he open your eyes?" He answered them, "I have told you already, and you would not listen. Why do you want to hear it again? Do you too want to become his disciples?" And they reviled him, saying, "You are his disciple, but we are disciples of Moses. We know that God has spoken to Moses, but as for this man, we do not know where he comes from." The man answered, "Why, this is a marvel! You do not know where he comes from, and yet he opened my eyes. We know that God does not listen to sinners, but if anyone is a worshipper of God and does his will, God listens to him. Never since the world began has it been heard that anyone opened the eyes of a man born blind. If this man were not from God, he could do nothing." They answered him, "You were born in utter sin, and would you teach us?" And they cast him out.

91

Jesus heard that they had cast him out, and having found him he said, "Do you believe in the Son of man?" He answered, "And who is he, sir, that I may believe in him?" Jesus said to him, "You have seen him, and it is he who speaks to you." He said, "Lord, I believe"; and he worshipped him. Jesus said, "For judgment I came into this world, that those who do not see may see, and that those who see may become blind." Some of the Pharisees near him heard this, and they said to him, "Are we also blind?" Jesus said to them, "If you were blind, you would have no guilt; but now that you say, 'We see,' your guilt remains."

THE THEME OF LIGHT

The theme of Light runs through John 7 where the feast of Tabernacles, which we described above (pp. 53f.), is mentioned; through John 8 where Jesus declares that he is the Light of the World; and through John 9 where Jesus cures the man who was born blind. This episode is the dramatic climax.

BIBLICAL READINGS FOR THE FEAST OF TABERNACLES

It is thought that the biblical readings for the Jewish services at the time of this feast of Tabernacles would have been selected from Leviticus 13; II Kings 5; Deuteronomy 10; and II Kings 13. The first two lessons deal with the discovery of leprosy and the ritual performed when a leper is cleansed: II Kings 5 tells of Naaman, the leper who was cleansed by washing in the River Jordan. The lessons from Deuteronomy 10 and II Kings 13 are linked with God's love for the patriarchs on account of whom it was said that God would spare their rebellious descendants. All these four lessons form an excellent background for our New Testament reading. The descendants of Abraham, exemplified in the Jewish religious leaders, appear

92

to be rebellious toward Jesus; the blind man washes in the stream of Siloam, just as Naaman washed in the Jordan, and he makes his confession of Jesus as Naaman confessed the true God. There is some correspondence also between the leprosy of Naaman and the blindness of the Pharisees. Just as the leprosy of Naaman was transferred to the prophet's servant, Gehazi, so the Pharisees become spiritually blind, whereas the man with faith receives physical healing. Further, in Luke 4 Jesus is expelled from the synagogue when he preaches a sermon which seems to be based on these lessons. In a similar way in John 9 the blind man is excommunicated from the synagogue because of his belief in Jesus. This is understandable when one realizes that in the sermon in Luke 4 Jesus had said:

The spirit of the Lord is upon me, because he has anointed me to preach good tidings to the poor. He has sent me to proclaim release to the captives and recovery of sight to the blind, to set at liberty those who are oppressed, to proclaim the acceptable year of the Lord. (vv. 18–19)

Jesus made "extravagant" claims. But in John 9 he vindicates himself. He performed a great miracle, greater than any recorded in the Hebrew canon of the Bible. In the Old Testament we do not read of the healing of blindness, except in the case of Tobias, and he was not born blind. Yet in view of the lack of curing blindness in the Old Testament, one can see the full import of John 9: 32: "Never since the world began has it been heard that anyone opened the eyes of a man born blind." Jesus showed greater miraculous power than Elijah or Elisha.

THE DRAMATIC COMPOSITION OF JOHN 9

The dramatic composition of this chapter is brilliant. The episode illustrates the central theme of St. John's Gospel, namely, the conflict between spiritual light and spiritual darkness. Jesus

93

performs a symbolic act to show that he is the Light of the World, who comes into the darkness, and when he comes, those who thought they had light now find they have darkness. Curiously, however, St. John does not portray Jesus as a central figure in this drama. The whole discussion takes place between the cured man and Jesus' opponents, and Jesus appears only at the end, when he says dramatically, "For judgment I came into this world, that those who do not see may see, and that those who see may become blind" (John 9: 39). He is referring to the leaders who are culpably blind. (Unfortunately, this verse is omitted from the shorter lectionary reading.)

The story of the cure of the blind man is composed of a series of interrogations and during these interrogations either the faith or the disbelief of the speakers becomes increasingly apparent. On the one side the people ask the blind man concerning Jesus. First, he merely tells them that *"the man called Jesus"* (v. 11) cured him. Then, to the Pharisees, he admits that Jesus is *a prophet* (v. 17). Eventually, in the course of the final interrogation, he becomes a defender of Jesus' cause (vv. 24–34), and, lastly, when he sees Jesus with his newly opened eyes, he acknowledges him as *the Son of man* and worships him (v. 38). On the other hand, the Pharisees become harder and harder with reference to the truth about Jesus. First of all, they appear to accept the healing, but some are offended because it occurred on the sabbath day (v. 16); later they become more hostile, and come to doubt the miracle (vv. 18ff.). Finally, they lose all interest and try to trap the healed man (vv. 24–34). In fact, the court procedure falls into a disparagement of the witness, and the story ends with the Pharisees, who have judged Jesus, proven guilty by Jesus himself.

Pertinent to our discussion on the first two lessons is the fact that Jesus sought out the blind man (John 9: 35) just as wisdom is said to seek out those who are worthy of her. We read in the Wisdom of Solomon:

Wisdom is radiant and unfading, and she is easily discerned by those who love her, and is found by those who seek her. She hastens to make herself known to those who seek her. He who rises early to seek her will have no difficulty, for he will find her sitting at his gates [one sits at the gate to give judgment on cases]. To fix one's thought on her is perfect understanding, and he who is vigilant on her account will soon be free from care, because she goes about seeking those worthy of her, and she graciously appears to them in their paths, and meet them with all solicitude. (Wis. 6: 12–16)

Jesus, the Light of the World, is the personification and fulfillment of wisdom in the Old Testament. He looked into the heart of the blind man as God into the heart of David. He disqualified the leaders as Samuel disqualified Saul.

The Text and Its Relationship to Baptism

We should associate this narrative with the ceremony of baptism. In the early Church, a little time before actual baptism was administered, several scrutinies or examinations took place in which the candidates were asked concerning their belief in Jesus. When the examiners were satisfied, the service ended with a solemn reading of this gospel, and then the candidates pronounced the words of the blind man, "I do believe, Lord." After this they recited the creed.

Further, other associations with baptism are the anointing and the use of saliva (John 9: 6), both of which occur in the baptismal liturgy. Naturally, too, we should also see an allusion to baptism in the washing of the blind man in the pool at Siloam (John 9: 7) and in the very name of that pool, which means "one who has been sent." This was a phrase applied frequently by St. John to Jesus. Finally, we know that those who have been baptized were called those who had received light. Baptism, itself, was called enlightenment. For example, we read:

95

For it is impossible to restore again to repentance those who have been enlightened, who have tasted the heavenly gift, and have become partakers of the Holy Spirit, and have tasted the goodness of the word of God and the powers of the age to come . . . (Hebr. 6: 4–5)

We may refer also to two early Christian writers who associate the biblical lessons under discussion with the sacrament of baptism. St. Irenaeus writes:

It was not for nothing that Naaman of old, when suffering from leprosy, was purified upon his being baptized, but [it serves] as an indication to us. For as we are lepers in sin, so we are made clean by means of the sacred water and the invocation of the Lord, . . . being spiritually regenerated as newborn babes . . . *Adv. Haer.*, 5: 15, 3)

Then St. Ephraim, the Syrian, says:

Let him that is without eyeballs come to him that maketh clay and changeth it, that maketh flesh, that enlighteneth eyes . . . Gather ye together and come, O ye lepers, and receive purification without labor. For he will not wash you as Elisha, who baptized [Naaman] seven times in the river, neither shall he annoy you as the priests with their sprinklings. (Twelfth Rhythm on The Nativity)

The themes of these three readings should be especially meaningful as we look toward the Easter liturgical ceremonies, particularly the kindling of new fire and the proclamation, "Light of Christ."

Intercession

The Fourth Sunday in Lent

The response is

> *Christ, Light, Wisdom, Truth, hear us.*

(1) That, like God we may see the heart and not the outward appearance, let us pray to the Lord.

(2) For our leaders that they may tend the Church with gentleness, courage, and understanding, let us pray . . .

(3) For those who have not come to the light of the knowledge of Christ, let us pray . . .

(4) That we may not sleep through life, let us pray . . .

(5) For those who traffic in magic, superstition, or evil practices, let us pray . . .

(6) That we may really be sons and daughters of light and show the fruits of the Spirit, let us pray . . .

(7) In thanksgiving that God has brought us into the kingdom of his beloved Son, let us pray . . .

(8) For those who are blind or whose sight is failing, that they be healed, let us pray . . .

(9) That the eyes of our minds and souls may be opened to see and know God, let us pray . . .

(10) For those in religious authority that they may be docile to the Holy Spirit, let us pray . . .

The Fifth Sunday of Lent

Jesus' raising of Lazarus is a sign of his power over death. The Christian, sharing the risen life of the Lord, shares in that power. Physical death has no permanent hold on those who have risen with Christ, in baptism. The death of the Christian is charged with the hope of resurrection.

Recognizing this, the *Constitution on the Sacred Liturgy* declares that "The rite for the burial of the dead should express more clearly the paschal character of Christian death" (article 81). Already, new funeral rites are being used experimentally in some dioceses. Permission has been given to remove the *Dies Irae,* more charged with fear than with hope, from all funeral masses. Perhaps if funerals were celebrated with white vestments, we would see that even the service now in use is, above all, an Easter service.

"They shall rejoice in the Lord, the bones that are brought low in the dust" [1] is the refrain which accompanies the procession into the church. It suggests Ezekiel's vision of the valley of dry bones:

Behold, I will open your graves, and raise you from your graves, O my people; and I will bring you home into the land of Israel. And you shall know that I am the Lord, when I open your graves, and raise you from your graves, O my people. And I will put my Spirit within you, and you shall live, and I will place you in your own land; then you shall know that I, the Lord, have spoken, and I have done it, says the Lord. (Ezek. 37: 12–14 RSV)

1. *Collectio Rituum,* New York, 1964, p. 232; hereafter referred to as *Collectio.*

99

The Epistle has a similar vision:

. . . since we believe that Jesus died and rose again, even so, through Jesus, God will bring with him those who have fallen asleep . . . For the Lord himself will descend with a cry of command, with the archangel's call, and with the sound of the trumpet of God. And the dead in Christ will rise first . . . and so we shall always be with the Lord. (I Thess. 4: 14, 16, 17 RSV)

The Gospel is the account of the raising of Lazarus.

The final prayer before the burial service is similarly filled with hope:

May the angels take you into paradise: may the martyrs come to welcome you on your way, and lead you into the holy city, Jerusalem. May the choir of angels welcome you, and with Lazarus who once was poor may you have everlasting rest. (*Collectio,* p. 245)

But much of the burial rite seems to stand in contradiction to the hopeful, even joyous character of the major portions of the funeral mass. For the present burial rite is basically a penitential service. This part of the service developed at a time when the Church had severe difficulties with her penitential system, so that by the time of the peace of the Church, a severe penitential system had developed. Those guilty of serious public sins could be absolved only after a lengthy and rigorous public penance. After the peace of the Church, when the standards for membership had been considerably relaxed, the Church found that a large portion of her membership did not retain their baptismal innocence. In view of the rigorous demands of the penitential system, many sought absolution only on their death beds. Christian death became, for many, an admission to public penance. The funeral service thus became a penitential service. Now that a milder penitential system has long been in operation, we can expect a new burial rite which has a more hopeful character.

What is strangely missing from our present funeral service is the grounding of the Christian hope of resurrection in baptism.

In its memorial of the dead, the Roman Canon mysteriously speaks of those who are "marked with the sign of faith." The "sign of faith" is baptism; we are already marked for resurrection by our baptism. In baptism, the Christian has already passed from death to life. His baptism is a burial into the death of Christ. Mystically, sacramentally, he has shared in Christ's death. The early Christians saw the descent into the baptismal waters as a descent into the grave, and the pouring of water over the head or the immersion as a sign of burial into Christ's death. As he is buried into Christ's death, so also does the baptized Christian share in Christ's resurrection. The life-giving Spirit has already taken possession of him; he is already one with the risen Lord. The splendor of the risen Lord is a splendor which is already ours, although hidden and known only by faith.

The Fifth Sunday in Lent

This Sunday offers for our contemplation:
    (1) the Spirit of God which will raise the dead;
    (2) the same Spirit dwelling in our mortal bodies;
    (3) the raising of Lazarus from the dead.

THE FIRST READING, EZEKIEL 37: 12–14. THE VALLEY OF DRY BONES

. . . Therefore prophesy, and say to them, Thus says the Lord God: Behold, I will open your graves, and raise you from your graves, O my people; and I will bring you home into the land of Israel. And you shall know that I am the Lord, when I open your graves, and raise you from your graves, O my people. And I will put my Spirit within you, and you shall live, and I will place you in your own land; then you shall know that I, the Lord, have spoken, and I have done it, says the Lord.

101

The Context

These verses from Ezekiel should be seen in the context of the transformation of Israel which God promised to perform for the sanctification of his holy name: he promised to put a new heart and spirit into his people (Ezek. 36: 24–27). After this prophecy Ezekiel received a most dramatic vision of a battlefield strewn with dead bones. God showed him that the Spirit could put new life into these bones. However, this was not a prophecy concerning the resurrection of the body. This belief did not exist among the Jews at the time of the prophet Ezekiel. The vision symbolized new hope and life for the Jewish exiles living in Babylon at that time.

Before considering the second and third readings it would be advantageous to consider the growth of the belief in the resurrection of the dead.

Early Concept of "Immortality"

Until the second century B.C., the Hebrews had little or no concept of an after-life. There was only a vague belief in a shadowy, ghost-like existence in darkness and misery in a land of no return. A very good illustration is Psalm 88: 3ff. It speaks about the soul drawing near to Sheol or the place of darkness, the underworld.

> For my soul is full of troubles,
> and my life draws nearer to Sheol.
> I am reckoned among those who go down to the pit;
> I am a man who has no strength,
> like one forsaken among the dead,
> like the slain that lie in the grave,
> like those whom thou dost remember no more.
> for they are cut off from thy hand.
> Thou hast put me in the depth of the pit,

102

in the regions dark and deep.
Thy wrath lies heavy upon me,
and thou dost overwhelm me with all thy waves.
Thou hast caused my companions to shun me;
thou hast made me a thing of horror to them.
I am shut in so that I cannot escape;
my eye grows dim through sorrow.
Every day I call upon thee, O Lord;
I spread out my hands to thee.
Dost thou work wonders for the dead?
Do the shades rise up to praise thee?
Is thy steadfast love declared in the grave,
or thy faithfulness in Abaddon?
Are thy wonders known in the darkness,
or thy saving help in the land of forgetfulness?"

From this psalm we can see very vividly the thoughts of the Hebrews as they buried their dead and realized they would see them no more. For the Hebrew his only hope of "immortality" lay in the procreation of children. To the Jewish people and to all ancient people, children were exceedingly important. The Hebrews loved their children and wanted large families. By a play on words, because the words for builders and children are similar, they used to call their children builders because they thought of them as building the future of the family and, also, of the community. A childless person was accounted as one who was dead because he had not been able to perform the solemn duty which was given him by God in Genesis, namely, to "increase and multiply," and because his name would perish with him. To remain childless through one's own fault was regarded as a very serious offense. One may illustrate this from a legend about Hezekiah. When he lay dying, the prophet Isaiah came to him and warned him that he would be punished severely. He asked why, and the prophet replied, "Because you have not performed the duty of begetting children." This concept of "immortality" was to cede to the greater belief in the resurrection of the dead.

103

The Gradual Development of Belief in the Resurrection

A belief in the resurrection of the dead slowly developed, but for the Israelite it meant that there must be a direct intervention of Yahweh, who would contravene the laws of nature and bring the whole of man—body and soul were inseparable in Hebrew thought—back to life again. Perhaps this idea gained credence because people witnessed God restoring the sick, who were near to death, to health again, and they therefore realized that God was powerful enough to accomplish even greater things. First of all, the Jews accepted the belief that certain people would be raised from the dead; for example, the elect, so that God could give them salvation; or martyrs, as a reward for their fidelity; or sinners, so that God should punish them. And then, eventually, some accepted the concept of universal resurrection. God appears to have given the prophets Elijah and Elisha power to raise men from the dead (see I Kings 17: 17–23 and II Kings 4: 33 following), but a clear statement of belief in the resurrection of the dead does not occur until the Book of Daniel which was written in the second century B.C. In Daniel 12: 2, we read:

And many of those who sleep in the dust of the earth shall awake, some to everlasting life, and some to shame and everlasting contempt. And those that are wise shall shine like the brightness of the firmament; and those who turn many to righteousness, like the stars forever and ever.

Here we have at last a sure belief in the resurrection of the dead. We have another definite reference in II Maccabees 7: 9b:

But the King of the universe will raise us up to an everlasting renewal of life, because we have died for his laws.

And also, in the same chapter, verse 14:

And when he [that is, the fourth son] was near to death, he said,

104

"One cannot but choose to die at the hands of men and cherish the hope that God gives of being raised again by him. But for you there will be no resurrection to life!"

These quotations are from the Second Book of Maccabees, which describes the martyrdom of many Jewish people for their faith. They undergo martyrdom now with the hope of resurrection in the world to come. The sentiments of the mother of seven sons who were martyred forms a contrast to early Hebrew thought. The text reads as follows:

The mother was especially admirable and worthy of honorable memory. Though she saw her seven sons perish within a single day, she bore it with good courage because of her hope in the Lord. She encouraged each of them in the language of their fathers. Filled with a noble spirit, she fired her woman's reasoning with a man's courage, and said to them, "I do not know how you came into being in my womb. It was not I who gave you life and breath, nor I who set in order the elements within each of you. Therefore the creator of the world, who shaped the beginning of man and devised the origin of all things, will in his mercy give life and death back to you again, since you now forget yourselves for the sake of his laws."

This deep belief in the resurrection of the dead soon became quite widespread among the Jews from the second century B.C. It was held especially by the Pharisees and eventually they excommunicated people from the synagogue if they did not accept this belief. It is this concept which prepares us for the story of the raising of Lazarus which will be the third reading.

THE SECOND READING, ROMANS 8: 8–11. OUR PARTICIPATION IN THE RESURRECTION OF CHRIST EVEN ON THIS EARTH

. . . and those who are in the flesh cannot please God.
   But you are not in the flesh, you are in the Spirit, if the Spirit of

105

God really dwells in you. Any one who does not have the Spirit of Christ does not belong to him. But if Christ is in you, although your bodies are dead because of sin, your spirits are alive because of righteousness. If the Spirit of him who raised Jesus from the dead dwells in you, he who raised Christ Jesus from the dead will give life to your mortal bodies also through his Spirit which dwells in you.

This passage indicates that the Spirit of Christ does not wait until death and resurrection to be fully efficacious. He already dwells in those who are baptized into Christ. His dwelling is manifested by the fact that the ritual law has been superseded and Christians walk on a different dimension. In union with Christ they perform supernatural ministries similar to those which Christ performed in his earthly life. These ministries are listed in I Corinthians 12: 4–11 and Ephesians 4: 11–13. They comprise gifts of teaching, such as the utterance of wisdom and knowledge; prayer gifts, such as tongues and interpretation; community ministries, such as prophecy, healing, miracles, and discernment of spirits. But above all the indwelling of the Spirit is manifested by love (see I Cor. 13). In the Spirit a more than human aspect is revealed in the created world (see Rom. 8: 19). But the fullness of the Spirit will come with the fullness of resurrection (v. 11).

THE THIRD READING, JOHN 11: 1–45. LAZARUS RAISED FROM THE DEAD

Now a certain man was ill, Lazarus of Bethany, the village of Mary and her sister Martha. It was Mary who anointed the Lord with ointment and wiped his feet with her hair, whose brother Lazarus was ill. So the sisters sent to him, saying, "Lord, he whom you love is ill." But when Jesus heard it he said, "This illness is not unto death; it is for the glory of God, so that the Son of God may be glorified by means of it."

Now Jesus loved Martha and her sister and Lazarus. So when he

106

heard that he was ill, he stayed two days longer in the place where he was. Then after this he said to the disciples, "Let us go into Judea again." The disciples said to him, "Rabbi, the Jews were but now seeking to stone you, and you are going there again?" Jesus answered, "Are there not twelve hours in the day? If any one walks in the day, he does not stumble, because he sees the light of this world. But if any one walks in the night, he stumbles, because the light is not in him." Thus he spoke, and then he said to them, "Lazarus has fallen asleep, but I go to awake him out of sleep." The disciples said to him, "Lord, if he has fallen asleep, he will recover." Now Jesus had spoken of his death, but they thought that he meant taking rest in sleep. Then Jesus told them plainly, "Lazarus is dead; and for your sake I am glad that I was not there, so that you may believe. But let us go to him." Thomas, called the Twin, said to his fellow disciples, "Let us also go, that we may die with him."

Now when Jesus came, he found that Lazarus had already been in the tomb four days. Bethany was near Jerusalem, about two miles off, and many of the Jews had come to Martha and Mary to console them concerning their brother. When Martha heard that Jesus was coming, she went and met him, while Mary sat in the house. Martha said to Jesus, "Lord, if you had been here, my brother would not have died. And even now I know that whatever you ask from God, God will give you." Jesus said to her, "Your brother will rise again." Martha said to him, "I know that he will rise again in the resurrection at the last day." Jesus said to her, "I am the resurrection and the life; he who believes in me, though he die, yet shall he live, and whoever lives and believes in me shall never die. Do you believe this?" She said to him, "Yes, Lord; I believe that you are the Christ, the Son of God, he who is coming into the world."

When she had said this, she went and called her sister Mary, saying quietly, "The Teacher is here and is calling for you." And when she heard it, she rose quickly and went to him. Now Jesus had not yet come to the village, but was still in the place where Martha had met him. When the Jews who were with her in the house, consoling her, saw Mary rise quickly and go out, they followed her, supposing that she was going to the tomb to weep there.

Then Mary, when she came where Jesus was and saw him, fell at his feet, saying to him, "Lord, if you had been here, my brother would not have died." When Jesus saw her weeping, and the Jews who came with her also weeping, he was deeply moved in spirit and troubled; and he said, "Where have you laid him?" They said to him, "Lord, come and see." Jesus wept. So the Jews said, "See how he loved him!" But some of them said, "Could not he who opened the eyes of the blind man have kept this man from dying?"

Then Jesus, deeply moved again, came to the tomb; it was a cave, and a stone lay upon it. Jesus said, "Take away the stone." Martha, the sister of the dead man, said to him, "Lord, by this time there will be an odor, for he has been dead four days." Jesus said to her, "Did I not tell you that if you would believe you would see the glory of God?" So they took away the stone. And Jesus lifted up his eyes and said, "Father, I thank thee that thou hast heard me. I knew that thou hearest me always, but I have said this on account of the people standing by, that they may believe that thou didst send me." When he had said this, he cried with a loud voice, "Lazarus, come out." The dead man came out, his hands and feet bound with bandages, and his face wrapped with a cloth. Jesus said to them, "Unbind him, and let him go."

Many of the Jews therefore, who had come with Mary, and had seen what he did, believed in him; . . .

Lectionary Reading at the Time When Lazarus Was Raised From the Dead

When Jesus approached Bethany to raise Lazarus from the dead, it was at a time when the people who attended the synagogue would have heard readings from the Old Testament about the death of the patriarchs Jacob, Joseph, Moses, Joshua, Eleazar, David, and Elisha. The psalms which they would have recited would have been Psalm 88, which we have quoted above (pp. 102, 103), and other psalms concerning death and sickness, plague and Sheol. It is thought, for example, that some Jews recited Psalm 91, which we sing at compline, to exorcise demons and to bring health to people. So the death of Lazarus occurred at a very meaningful time. Moreover, although the names "Lazarus" and Bethany, the place where he lived, are not fictitious names, yet they have a symbolic meaning. Lazarus means "God helps" and Bethany means "house of affliction."

The Setting of the Scene

It was into this atmosphere of mourning and affliction that Jesus went, at the risk of his life, to help those whom he loved. Bethany was a place where he lodged when he came to Jerusalem and his friends, Martha, Mary, and Lazarus, and no doubt many other people. There were those whom he knew intimately and, indeed, for whom he felt deep human love. Into this homely scene he came and here he illustrated dramatically that he was the resurrection and the life. Like God in the Old Testament, he demonstrated power, not only over this earth, but over the nether world, over life and death. Those for whom he performed the miracle held the Pharisaic belief in the resurrection of the dead. In the synagogue, people would say the blessing "Thou, Lord, art mighty forever, thou quickeneth the dead, thou art mighty to save." But Jesus wished to go far beyond the expectations of this belief. He wished to perform this miracle of the raising of Lazarus "for the glory of God, so that the Son of God may be glorified by means of it." There is a certain parallel with the first miracle, which Jesus performed when at the request of a woman, his mother, when he changed water into wine at the marriage feast at Cana. St. John tells us that he performed this first sign "and manifested his glory; and his disciples believed in him" (John 2: 11b). So when Jesus drew to the end of his ministry and faced death, he performed perhaps his greatest miracle for the sake of two women whom he loved and in order to manifest his glory.

Martha Compared with Peter

Martha admitted that Lazarus would rise at the last day but Jesus turned to her and said quite simply, "I am the resurrection and the life; he who believes in me, though he die, yet shall he live, and who ever lives and believes in me shall never die. Do you believe this?" Martha was asked to make a supreme confession of faith, greater even than that of Abraham. She replied, "Yes, Lord; I believe that you are the *Christ, the Son of God,* he who is coming into the world." Martha made a confession very similar to that which Peter made at Caesarea Philippi (Matt. 16). Jesus had turned to the disciples and asked them who they thought the Son of man was. According to St. Matthew, Peter had replied, "You are the Christ, the Son of the living God" (16: 16). The phrase "the living God" really means the "God who gives life." After Peter's confession Jesus had demonstrated his glory in the transfiguration, and afterwards he predicted his passion and death. For Martha he demonstrated that he was the God who gave life, and he did this shortly before he faced death and resurrection itself.

Martha does not seem to have waited after her confession of faith, but to have gone almost immediately to her sister Mary, and called her to come to Jesus. Mary rose quickly and went to Jesus and, when she met him, fell at his feet: this is an attitude of adoration. Perhaps St. John wished to indicate that Mary also believed that Christ was the Son of God (see the blind man worshipping Jesus).

Unlike the miracle of the curing of the blind man, St. John goes into considerable detail about this miraculous event. Jesus saw Mary wailing and St. John tells us that he was "troubled." This is the word which Jesus was to use in his last discourses to his disciples when in John 14: 1 he said, "Let not your hearts be troubled: believe in God, believe also in me." He repeats this injunction again in the same discourse in verse 27: "Peace I leave with you; my peace I give to you; not as the world gives

110

do I give to you. Let not your hearts be troubled, neither let them be afraid." Perhaps the raising of Lazarus should have prevented their anxiety.

Jesus asked where they had laid the corpse and they invited him to come and see. Then he wept (the word is not "wail") and the Jews observed how he loved Lazarus. They recalled how he had opened the eyes of the blind man and they wondered why he did not keep Lazarus from death.

The Tomb

Then the evangelist describes Jesus, deeply moved, coming to the tomb. He describes this as a "cave" with a stone lying over it. If one goes to Israel, one is shown a tomb which was supposed to be the place where Lazarus was laid. Whether it is or not one cannot be sure, but what is interesting is that it is a very deep vertical tomb. One descends a flight of stairs, perhaps about fifteen to twenty in number, and then one takes a hairpin bend around a sharp corner and descends another fifteen to twenty steps. After that, one enters an antechamber which the Jews used for mourning, and then one goes right into the burial vault itself and finds the place where the corpse would have been deposited on a kind of shelf. If the tomb had been constructed in such a way, one can imagine the suspense in which the little crowd of friends were held as they waited for Lazarus to rise from the shelf, to go through the antechamber and ascend the stairs: it is no wonder, too, that Jesus cried "with a loud voice," for one would need a loud voice to allow the sound to travel down into the deep vault. The description is thus quite realistic and this is seen when one recalls that Martha reminded Jesus that by now the corpse would be decaying. She indicated the Jewish belief that the spirit of the corpse hovered around the body for about three days but after the third day it left and there would be no hope of resuscitation of the corpse. This was one more sign that the friends of Jesus realized that it would need a tremendous miracle for Jesus to raise this man from the dead. Perhaps it was for this reason that Jesus said to Martha, with a little reproach, "Did I not tell you that if you would believe you would see the glory of God?"

The Call of the Dead

They took away the stone and then Jesus lifted his eyes in prayer. He thanked the heavenly Father with confidence that he had heard his prayer and he remembered those standing by, hoping that they would believe that the Father had sent him into the world. Then he cried with a loud voice, and this word "cry" is significant. It only occurs eight times in the Greek translation of the Bible. Six of these incidents occur in St. John's Gospel. It is used of the crowds who shout for the crucifixion of Jesus, and thus perhaps there is a hint of irony in St. John's use of the word here. But more especially it is used in association with the resurrection of the dead from their graves. In John 5, after Jesus had cured the man who was paralyzed for thirty-eight years, he spoke about his work with his heavenly Father. In the center of that discourse occurred words which St. John surely meant his hearers to recall when they heard the gospel concerning the raising of Lazarus. In John 5 Jesus said:

For as the Father has life in himself, so he has granted the Son also to have life in himself, and has given him authority to execute judgment, because he is the Son of man. Do not marvel at this; for the hour is coming when all who are in the tombs will hear his voice and come forth, those who have done good to the resurrection of life and those who have done evil to the resurrection of judgment. (vv. 26–29)

Here the word "cry" is not used but we have references to (1) the voice of Jesus calling people from the grave, (2) the idea of Jesus as life, and (3) to tombs. Jesus fulfilled this "proph-

112

ecy" in John 11. Jesus called and the dead man came out with his feet still bound with the binding clothes and his face still wrapped in a cloth.

The miracle, however, was also a "prophecy in action."

The Parallel Between the Raising of Lazarus and Jesus

The significance of the raising of Lazarus as a prelude to the resurrection of Jesus is confirmed when one looks at the details of this miracle. First of all, it was Mary who was one of the Major figures in the Lazarus event, but it was also Mary who anointed Jesus in preparation for his burial (John 12: 1–8). Mary wailed both before Lazarus' and Jesus' tomb. In both incidents people, on the one hand Jesus concerning Lazarus, on the other hand Mary concerning Jesus, asked where the corpse had been laid. On both occasions a stone had to be rolled from the mouth of the tomb. In both cases the tomb was a "cave" and the same Greek word is used. In both incidents the details of the funeral clothes were mentioned. But, last of all, in both events, as we learn about the resurrection from St. Matthew's Gospel, some of the Jewish leaders took counsel. In one case they plotted to kill Jesus who had raised Lazarus. In the other case, they planned to keep the fact of Jesus' resurrection a secret so that people would not believe in him who had the power over life and death. The raising of Lazarus did, therefore, foreshadow the raising of Jesus.

Jesus Expected Disbelief Even After This Miracle

We should recall that Jesus once told a parable about a poor man, Lazarus, who died (Luke, 17: 19–31). This is the only parable of Jesus in which a character is given a name. The poor man died and went to heaven. He reclined on Abraham's bosom, that is, he was the guest of honor at the heavenly banquet. Then a rich man died and he went to eternal torment.

113

He looked up and asked Abraham to allow Lazarus to come and "to dip the end of his finger in water and to cool his tongue"; for he was in great anguish in the flame. Abraham reminded him that he received good things during his earthly life, but Lazarus suffered and there was a great chasm between the rich man and Lazarus, now that they were in the world to come. The rich man thought about his relatives who had not yet died and feared that they might come to the same place of torment as himself. He made another request of Abraham, namely, that he should send Lazarus to his father's house to warn his five brothers. However, Abraham replied, "They have Moses and the prophets; let them hear them." But the rich man, in his torment, said, "No, Father Abraham; but if someone goes to them from the dead, they will repent." To this Abraham responded, "If they do not hear Moses and the prophets, neither will they be convinced if someone should rise from the dead." Some scholars think that Jesus might well have told this parable on his way to raise Lazarus from the dead, in order to warn the disciples that, even though God should permit them to work great signs and wonders, yet people would still not believe. Yet there is a second message in this parable, namely, that even when Jesus rose from the dead, people would not believe. Jesus deliberately waited two days so that he could raise Lazarus on the third day, and it would seem that he expected the disciples to realize the clue, namely, that he himself would rise on the third day. This was possibly partially entertained by the disciples, for St. Luke records (Luke 24) that when Jesus met some disciples on the road to Emmaus, they spoke about Jesus who was "a prophet mighty in deed and word before God and all the people," and that the chief priests and rulers had delivered him up to death and crucified him; and they added, "But we had hoped that he was the one to redeem Israel. Yes, and besides all this, it is now the third day since this happened."

Even with all these careful preparations and the meticulous clues which Jesus dropped to his disciples, they still did not fully realize the full import and they were still frightened and disbelieving, even when he rose from the dead (see Mark 16: 8). So the great paradox of the story of Lazarus is that he who had come as the resurrection and the life and had shown this so dramatically in the raising of his friend from the dead should now himself be in imminent danger of death. Soon Martha and Mary would mourn once again, but not now over Lazarus, but over Jesus. But soon, too, these same women would rejoice again, when they had become the first witnesses to the resurrection.

Intercession

Fifth Sunday in Lent

The response is
> *Jesus, Life and Resurrection, hear us.*

(1) For those who are childless or desire more children, let us pray to the Lord.

(2) In thanksgiving for the hope of a future life with Christ, and that we may not mourn as those who have no hope, let us pray . . .

(3) For those who have no hope or comfort in bereavement, let us pray . . .

(4) For the bereaved, that even in the hour of sorrow they may feel the majesty of God and give him thanks for his manifold mercies, let us pray . . .

(5) For the departed, that their souls may rejoice "in the ineffable good that God has laid up for those who fear him," let us pray . . .

(6) That we may believe in the resurrection power of Jesus with greater conviction, let us pray . . .

(7) For all nations under oppression, that the Spirit of God may breathe new hope into them, let us pray . . .

(8) That we may use the ministries of the Spirit, let us pray . . .

(9) That we may truly realize that Jesus is deeply moved over our sorrows, let us pray . . .

(10) That we may commit no evil when others do mighty works for the glory of God, let us pray . . .

PALM SUNDAY

There seems to be a certain tension about Palm Sunday. On the one hand, there is the note of rejoicing. With procession and palms, the Church sings her hosannas to Christ the King. And on the other hand, the shadow of Holy Week and the death of Jesus is cast upon the celebration. The procession seems premature, anticlimactic. In view of the coming tragedy, there seems to be a bitter irony in the joyful hosannas.

If we are fully to understand what the liturgy of Holy Week has to say, we must understand the spirit in which the Church worships.

One of the great advantages of the Roman liturgy is the manner in which it celebrates the mystery of salvation through the course of a whole year. At Christmas, we bring our attention to bear on the incarnation, at Easter on the death and resurrection of Jesus, moving slowly to a consideration of the ascension, and to the sending of the Spirit at Pentecost. Advent is both a beginning and a finale—a beginning insofar as it looks backward to the yearning of mankind for salvation, a finale insofar as it looks with expectation to Jesus' coming in glory.

Our great temptation is to interpret this step-by-step consideration in such a manner that the liturgy becomes a kind of tableau, a series of "pictures" in word and rite. The unfolding of the liturgical year seems to be a series of "points" like those in a meditation book. From this perspective, the liturgy seems at best preoccupied with relating past events. At worst, there seems to be an air of unreality about the whole affair.

117

But such an interpretation does not do justice to the real spirit of the Roman liturgy. While there is a concentration on one event at a time, the liturgy is also conscious that in every celebration, the whole mystery of Christ is present. And the whole Christ is the risen Lord, who reigns in glory. Our faith compels us to see the events of his life from that perspective.

In the perspective of the resurrection, there is no tension in the celebration of Palm Sunday. The hosannas of the crowd are simply an echo of the faith of those who know that Jesus is risen. To the eyes of faith, the history of Jesus' death can only be bound up with the thought of his coming resurrection. His death is the beginning of his victory. For the unbeliever, the passion of Christ is simply a sordid tragedy, the killing of a wandering prophet in a rundown province of the Roman Empire. For the believer, it is the act by which God redeems his people. It is salvation, life, deliverance. The Preface of the Holy Cross summarizes the attitude of Palm Sunday and of Holy Week:

. . . for you ordained that the salvation of mankind should be accomplished upon the tree of the cross, in order that life might be restored through the very instrument that brought death, and that Satan, who conquered us through the tree, might also be overcome by it . . . (*Missal*, p. 66)

The Church centers her attention on Jesus' passion and death. But even here, she rejoices in the risen Lord, the Lord who "lives and reigns forever and ever." His passion is proclaimed as "gospel," "Good news":

. . . for thou wast slain and by thy blood didst ransom men for God from every tribe and tongue and people and nation, and hast made them a kingdom and priests to our God, and they shall reign on earth. (Rev. 5: 9, 10 RSV)

It is the present reality of salvation which is the real center of attention.

118

Passion Sunday or Palm Sunday

The three readings present:
(1) the obedience of the Servant of Yahweh;
(2) a very ancient Christian hymn which portrays the obedience of Christ;
(3) the Passion according to St. Matthew.

THE FIRST READING, ISAIAH 50: 4–7. THE SERVANT OF YAHWEH

The Lord God has given me
the tongue of those who are taught,
that I may know how to sustain with a word
him that is weary.
Morning by morning he wakens,
he wakens my ear
to hear as those who are taught.
The Lord God has opened my ear,
and I was not rebellious,
I turned not backward.
I gave my back to the smiters,
and my cheeks to those who pulled out the beard;
I hid not my face from shame and spitting.

For the Lord God helps me;
therefore I have not been confounded;
therefore I have set my face like a flint,
and I know that I shall not be put to shame; . . .

These verses comprise what is known as the third Servant Song in Isaiah. This Servant will be discussed in more detail for the Good Friday readings. It is sufficient to say here that the Servant probably represents the prophetic element in Israelite society which shows a faithful response to God's message

119

of salvation despite the humiliation of exile which Israel endured at that time.

The "tongue" mentioned in verse 4 is the tongue of the obedient disciple in the prophetic school who repeats his master's teaching aloud until it is fully committed to memory. It is also the tongue of the prophet who witnesses faithfully to prophecy and fulfillment despite derision and insult (vv. 6–7). The weary people whom he sustains with his speech are those who are lacking in divine strength because they do not possess the Word of God. The Servant's open ear (v. 5) symbolizes his readiness to receive the inspiration of God. It is a contrast to the spiritual deafness to which Isaiah refers in chapters 6: 9–10; 42: 19; and 43:8. This is a theme to which all the gospels and the Acts of Apostles return. Those who are taught (v. 4) are those who have divine insight into prophecy and its fulfillment.

In the second reading, Jesus is seen as the obedient Servant, and in the third reading St. Matthew shows insight into the divine mind and understanding of prophecy.

THE SECOND READING, PHILIPPIANS 2: 5–11. THE CHRISTOLOGICAL HYMN

Have this mind among yourselves, which was in Christ Jesus, who, though he was in the *form* of God, did not count equality with God a thing to be grasped, but emptied himself, taking the *form* of a servant, being born in the likeness of men. And being found in human form he humbled himself and became obedient unto death, even death on the cross. Therefore God hath highly exalted him and bestowed on him the name which is above every name, that at the name of Jesus every knee should bow, in heaven and on earth and under the earth, and every tongue confess that Jesus Christ is Lord to the glory of God the Father.

This hymn brings together many themes which we have already discussed, for example the theme of Adam, Jesus' temptation,

120

Jesus' glorification, Jesus' passion, and then a subject which will conclude our reflections, namely, the resurrection and ascension of Jesus.

Some Difficult Phrases

The words of this hymn might give rise to misunderstanding, and therefore it might be well to consider some of the difficult phrases and see how they are consonant with the Christian faith. We meet our first difficulty in the English translation "though he was in the *form* of God." This might suggest that Jesus had the outward form of God but that he was not really divine. However, the Greek word here is *morphē,* which can mean the unchanging form of a person or a thing. It is not quite equivalent to the Greek word for "essence," but nevertheless it does mean that the possession of the *morphē* involves participation in the essence also. Therefore, this phrase does not mean that Jesus was not truly the Son of God. In the same way, the phrase "taking the *form* of a servant" has the same Greek word for "form": Jesus is truly man as well. But the word *schema* is used in verse 8 (found in "*schema*" as a man). *Schema* usually refers to the outward and changing appearance or accidence of a thing. The *schema* of a thing may vary, but the *morphē* of a thing is immutable. So Jesus was always the Son of God, but he took upon himself human nature and became man.

This hymn uses also the phrase "being born in the likeness of men." This word "likeness" is ambiguous and might give rise to what is known as the Docetist heresy, namely, that Jesus had only a body or nature like men and that this body was a kind of phantom body. However, once again, if we look at the original Greek it need not suggest this Docetist idea. The Greek word can mean either similarity or *identity.* Therefore it suggests that Jesus was "born into the world as all men are

121

born." [1] Yet Jesus was unlike fallen man in that he possessed no sin (Rom. 8: 3).

Another difficult phrase is the one translated "but emptied himself." This does not mean that Jesus ceased to be God. When one offers an act of self-giving—and incarnation is the greatest act of self-giving—this does not mean that the selfhood ceases to exist. So Jesus, indeed, could remain God even though he took human nature, just as a man remains a man even though he is reduced to the status of slave. The Greek word here has given rise to the noun *kenosis*, which refers to this emptying which Christ performed. This *kenosis* indicates, so to speak, the complete "freedom" of God. It suggests that God is of such generosity that he is willing to accept the limitations of a human life, but in doing this he does not make himself *unlike himself*. It is a false notion to think that he cannot be "his true self" in the less glorious form of a servant, than in the surpassing glory of his transcendence. This is similar to the point which was noted with reference to Genesis 3: 1–7.

The innermost nature of God, if we may so express it, is not omnipotence and overawing majesty, but unchanging love and compassion or empathy in the deepest sense. This will be clear especially in the readings for Holy Thursday, when Jesus' last act to his disciples is to wash their feet, an extremely menial task. Such, then, is the meaning of the self-emptying of Jesus Christ, but we should add that while some scholars like to see this concept focused especially on the incarnation, others would like to see it especially related to the death of Jesus, the pouring out of his soul in death.

Three Themes in the Hymn

The next three points which we would like to make concern the three themes of this hymn: the theme of Adam; that of the suffering servant of Yahweh; and, lastly, the theme of the Lordship of Jesus.

1. F. W. Beare, *Epistle to the Philippians*, New York, 1959, p. 83.

Adam

Many scholars would feel that Jesus is represented here as the second or perhaps the last Adam, in contrast to the first Adam. Jesus himself is the exact image of God, in a sense infinitely more so than were Adam and Eve created in the image and likeness of God. But even with this surpassingly superior status, Jesus, unlike Adam, did not grasp or snatch violently the status of equality with God. In Genesis 3: 5, the serpent said to Eve that if she ate of the tree, she and Adam would become more like God. Both Adam and Eve were tempted because they wanted to be like God, and they sinned. As a consequence their highest possession, namely, their quality of being in the image of God, was greatly diminished. Jesus, who is the second Adam, did not perpetrate this "robbery," and therefore he remained faithful to the privileges which God had designed for Adam and Eve. Jesus atoned for Adam's disobedience by being obedient even to the ignominious death on the cross.

The result of Jesus' conduct was that God "highly exalted him," or rather perhaps we should translate "he did more than exalt him." Whereas Adam should have been Lord in his own capacity over the whole of creation to subdue and rule creation as the image of God, Jesus received a role which was even higher than this. He was given a name or rather "character" which was above every name and his role extended not only over the earth but over the heavens and things under the earth. Jesus, as true God and true man, having undergone the deepest experiences of mankind, showed mankind in the image and glory of God which Adam had failed to do.

The Suffering Servant

The first reading has referred to a figure in Isaiah who was the servant of the Lord and underwent grievous suffering even

123

though he was innocent. The Philippian hymn mentions Jesus taking "the form of a servant." Jesus, like the man in Isaiah, was obedient to God throughout his whole mission. The servant of Yahweh was numbered with transgressors (Isaiah 53: 12) or convicted even though he was innocent, and he appears to have undergone a very ignominious death. After this he was rewarded, but it is not clear at all that he was resurrected; rather his reward is expressed in these terms:

> Yet it was the will of the Lord to oppose him:
> he has put him to grief:
> when he makes himself an offering for sin,
> he shall see his offspring,
> he shall prolong his days;
> the will of the Lord shall prosper in his hand;
> he shall see the fruit of the travail of his soul and be satisfied:
> by his knowledge shall the righteous one, my servant,
> make many to be accounted righteous:
> and he shall bear their iniquities.
> Therefore I shall divide him a portion with the great,
> and he shall divide the spoil with the strong:
> because he poured out his soul to death,
> and was numbered with transgressors:
> yet he bore the sin of many,
> and made intercession for the transgressors.

The reward of the suffering servant in Isaiah is not as great as the exaltation of Jesus.

Jesus as Lord

The consequence of the obedience of Christ was his proclamation as Lord. This did not mean that Jesus was not Lord before he became man. Rather, it meant that he brought his human nature into a uniquely close relationship with God, and God conferred upon him the title of *Kyrios* which means full Lordship over everything. This title *Kyrios* or Lord is the designation of Yahweh in the Old Testament. This meant that Jesus was presented as the object of worship. Before he became man he was, indeed, equal with God, but after his death he was exalted to the right hand of God as Messianic sovereign. The words which St. Paul uses "at the name of Jesus every knee should bow, in heaven and on earth and under the earth, and every tongue confess that Jesus Christ is Lord," are words which were used with reference to Yahweh in the Old Testament.

> Turn to me and be saved,
> all the ends of the earth!
> For I am God, and there is no other.
> By myself I have sworn,
> for my mouth has gone forth in righteousness
> a word that shall not return:
> to me every knee shall bow,
> every tongue shall swear.
> Only in the Lord, it shall be said of me,
> are righteousness and strength;
> to him shall come and be ashamed,
> all who were incensed against him.
> In the Lord all the offspring of Israel shall
> triumph and glory. (Isaiah 45: 22–25)

The unique prerogative of Yahweh was now conferred on Jesus in his capacity both as God and man. This would be difficult for the monotheistic Jews to accept, for now in this hymn they were obliged to recognize that there were two persons in God, Jesus and the Father, and that these two persons were one in their essence as God. As the Christian revelation proceeded, people began to realize the still greater truth that there were three persons in the Godhead, the Father, Son, and Holy Spirit.

In conclusion, one should remark on the concept of the "glory of God." Many people concentrate upon the revelation of humanity which is found in Jesus' life. This, of course, is correct, but there is another side. This hymn reveals just as much about the nature of God as it does about the true nature of

125

man. Jesus knew that the true character of human-divine nature did not consist in grasping at honor, glory, and success. The political human Messiah (in contrast to the prophetical, non-messianic figure in Isaiah), which the Jewish people awaited, was expected to claim such things. For example, Psalm 72, which describes the ideal Kingship, does, indeed, show a King who is sensitive to the poor and to justice but it also reflects a King of great might:

> May he have dominion from sea to sea,
> and from the river to the ends of the earth!
> May his foes bow down before him,
> and his enemies lick the dust!
> May the Kings of Tarshish and of the isles
> render him tribute,
> May the Kings of Sheba and Seba bring gifts!
> May all Kings fall down before him,
> all nations serve him! (Psalm 72: 8–11)

Jesus did not appear like this. The more he denied worldly values, the more clearly men would see the values of God's kingdom. When Jesus became as nothing on the cross, his revelation of God was complete, for the true characteristic of God was not omnipotence and power, but love. Love itself is omnipotence, and is more persuasive than any other kind of power. Therefore, we betray the worldliness of our standards when we wish to surround Jesus with the panoplies of earthly kings and when we think of God in terms of scepters and crowns and thrones.

The self-emptying of Jesus shows us how God and man can be related, and that the nature of man is not alien to the nature of God. Jesus' self-emptying reveals a humanitarianism about God. This is well expressed by Donald G. Dawe.

Humanity is not a realm which excludes God by definition. Nor is divinity only thinkable by the exclusion of man. The humanity of God means that God does not cease to be himself when he enters human life. The inadequacies of the traditional doctrines of

126

God and man have created an insoluble problem. They have defined God and man in mutually exclusive terms. Having done this, traditional doctrine then proposes to describe how God and man can be related. But the true reality of man is given in Jesus Christ. In him we see that God and man are at one. There is an innate suitability of man for God and God for man. Kenosis reveals that there is a manward movement in the divine life. To become man is not something foreign to God. Kenosis says this in the most radical possible way. In Christ God did not become simply the sublime man, the hero; he became suffering and dying man.[1]

THE THIRD READING, MATTHEW 26: 36—27: 66. THE PASSION OF JESUS

As the passion narratives are long, the text has been divided into portions preceding the relevant commentary. The commentary on St. Matthew's passion is prefaced by a note on the interpretation of Scripture.

An Ancient Method of Interpreting Scripture

In I Corinthians 15: 3ff., St. Paul cites a short creed. It reads as follows:

For I delivered to you as of first importance what I also received, that Christ died for our sins *in accordance with the scriptures,* that he was buried, that he was raised on the third day *in accordance with the scriptures,* and that he appeared to Cephas, then to the twelve (1 Corinthians 15: 3–5)

Then in St. Luke 24, one reads that after Jesus' resurrection he walked with some disciples to a village called Emmaus and on the way he spoke to them as follows:

1. Donald G. Dawe, "A Fresh Look at the Kenotic Christologies," *Scottish Journal of Theology,* 15 (1962), pp. 337–49; the paragraph quoted is found on p. 349.

O foolish men, and slow of heart to believe all that the prophets have spoken! Was it not necessary that Christ should suffer these things and enter into his glory?" *And beginning with Moses and all the prophets, he interpreted to them in all the scriptures the things concerning himself.* (Luke 24: 25b–27)

These two quotations indicate that the scriptures foretold the passion, death, and the resurrection. In Jesus' time, many people did not take the scriptures merely in the literal sense but they used to search them so that they might be able to watch the signs of the times, and thereby recognize God's actions and the special people who would take a prominent part in the final stage of the drama of salvation. This is the prophetic insight which was implied in Isaiah 50: 4–7. To illustrate this, we may take two examples, which are found in the Jewish documents discovered near the Dead Sea from 1947 onwards. These are pre-Christian documents and among them are some biblical commentaries which show us how those Jewish scholars used to interpret the scripture. Following is part of a biblical commentary on Psalm 37; the italicized portion is the biblical text and the rest comprises the commentary.

But they that love the Lord shall be as him who is the glory of the lambs. This refers to the congregation of God's elect, who will become leaders and princes [among his people] like [lambs] among their flocks. *They shall vanish one and all like smoke.* This refers to the princess of the [heathen] realm who have oppressed God's holy people. *They shall vanish like the smoke of the hearth [in the wind].*[1]

The next example is from the biblical commentary on Isaiah 11: 1–4. We recall that this is the text which speaks of a descendant of David who will receive the spirit of the Lord, the spirit of wisdom and discernment, the spirit of counsel, might, knowledge, and the fear of the Lord. This text is well known

1. *Comm. on Ps. 137,* frag. a: col. 2, from T. Gaster, *The Dead Sea Scriptures in English Translation,* New York, 1964, p. 254.

128

to Christians. The explanation which we find in these documents is as follows:

[The reference is the scion of] David who will exercise his office at
the end [of days]. His [ene]mies [will be felled], but him will God
uphold [by bestowing upon him po]wer, a throne of glory, a h[oly]
crown and embroidered robes. A [shall be placed] in his hand,
and he shall bear sway over all the hea[th]en, and Magog [shall be
vanquished by him], and his sword shall wreak judgment upon all
the peoples. (*Commentary on the Book of Isaiah,* Chapter 11;
Gaster, p. 233)

These are two examples of some of the ways in which the
Jewish people before Jesus interpreted the scripture. Scholars
also collected proof texts, that is, texts which they thought
illustrated various characteristics of the messianic era. Among
these we find Deuteronomy 5: 25–26; 18: 18–19; Numbers
24: 15–17; Deuteronomy 33: 8–11; Joshua 6: 26; II Samuel
7: 10–14, and also some texts from the Psalms. In the same
way, the early Christians also collected and interpreted texts
which illustrated their beliefs about Jesus, his work, and
his character. We need not think that this was rather a foolish
way of interpreting scripture, because scripture is not like secu-
lar writings but is the Word of God, and it has more than a
literal meaning. One needed spiritual understanding to discern
this deeper meaning of scripture and to realize how Jesus
fulfilled all scripture. Even if this way of understanding scripture is alien to our culture, we must try to put ourselves in the
position of the early Christians and to understand scripture
in their way. When we examine St. Matthew's account of
Jesus' passion, we should pay special attention to the way in
which he has illustrated how Jesus fulfilled the scriptures which
we now call the Old Testament and also how Jesus fulfilled the
prophecies which he himself told his disciples concerning his
arrest, suffering, death, and resurrection. Apparently, he gave
three prophecies or predictions about these things.

The scriptures which St. Matthew saw to be especially ful-

129

filled in Jesus' passion are: (1) the portion of Isaiah which portrays the suffering servant of Yahweh; (2) some of the psalms, especially Psalm 22 and Psalm 69; (3) portions from Zechariah.

Gethsemane, Matthew 26: 36–56

Then Jesus went with them to a place called Gethsemane, and he said to his disciples, "Sit here, while I go yonder and pray." And taking with him Peter and the two sons of Zebedee, he began to be sorrowful and troubled. Then he said to them, "My soul is very sorrowful, even to death; remain here, and watch with me." And going a little farther he fell on his face and prayed, "My Father, if it be possible, let this cup pass from me; nevertheless, not as I will, but as thou wilt." And he came to the disciples and found them sleeping; and he said to Peter, "So, could you not watch with me one hour? Watch and pray that you may not enter into temptation; the spirit indeed is willing, but the flesh is weak." Again, for the second time, he went away and prayed, "My Father, if this cannot pass unless I drink it, thy will be done." And again he came and found them sleeping, for their eyes were heavy. So, leaving them again, he went away and prayed for the third time, saying the same words. Then he came to the disciples and said to them, "Are you still sleeping and taking your rest? Behold, the hour is at hand, and the Son of man is betrayed into the hands of sinners. Rise, let us be going; see, my betrayer is at hand."

While he was still speaking, Judas came, one of the twelve, and with him a great crowd with swords and clubs, from the chief priests and the elders of the people. Now the betrayer had given them a sign, saying, "The one I shall kiss is the man; seize him." And he came up to Jesus at once and said, "Hail, Master!" And he kissed him. Jesus said to him, "Friend, why are you here?" Then they came up and laid hands on Jesus and seized him. And behold, one of those who were with Jesus stretched out his hand and drew his sword, and struck the slave of the high priest, and cut off his ear. Then Jesus said to him, "Put your sword back into its place; for all who take the sword will perish by the sword.

130

Do you think that I cannot appeal to my Father, and he will at once send me more than twelve legions of angels? But how then should the scriptures be fulfilled, that it must be so?" At that hour Jesus said to the crowds, "Have you come out against a robber, with swords and clubs to capture me? Day after day I sat in the temple teaching, and you did not seize me. But all this has taken place, that the scriptures of the prophets might be fulfilled." Then all the disciples forsook him and fled.

Jesus in the Garden

When Jesus had kept the passover and instituted the holy eucharist, he and his disciples sang a hymn, possibly the Hallel, that is, Psalms 113–118 inclusive, and they went out to the Mount of Olives. On the way Jesus prophesied to them:

You will all fall away because of me this night, for it is written, "I will strike the shepherd, and the sheep of the flock will be scattered." But after I am raised up, I will go before you to Galilee. (Matthew 26: 31–32)

In predicting his capture and the flight of the disciples Jesus used the words of Zechariah 13. This chapter refers to a fountain which will be opened for the house of David and how the inhabitants of Jerusalem will cleanse themselves from all sin. All the false prophets will disappear from the land. Then the last part of the chapter reads as follows:

And if anyone asks him, "What are these wounds on your back?" he will say, "These wounds I received in the house of my friends."
>   Awake, O sword, against my shepherd,
>   against the man who stands next to me,
>   says the Lord of hosts.
>   Strike the shepherd, that the sheep
>   may be scattered; I will turn my hand
>   against the little ones.
>   In the whole land, says the Lord,
>   two thirds shall be cut off and perish,
>   and one third shall be left alive.

131

And I will put this third into the fire,
and refine them as one refines silver,
and test them as gold is tested.
They will call on my name,
and I will answer them.
I will say, "They are my people";
and they will say, "The Lord is my God."

(Zechariah 13: 6b–9)

Although this prophecy was not fulfilled in every detail, it did set the expectant atmosphere in which Jesus and his disciples walked into the Garden of Gethsemane for the last time. However, Jesus did not allow the atmosphere to be one of complete gloom, for he implied the resurrection when he said that he would go before the disciples in Galilee.

This scene in the garden of Gethsemane is somewhat reminiscent of two things in Jesus' life: (1) the transfiguration, and (2) the *Our Father*.

Gethsemane and the Transfiguration

Jesus takes the same disciples into the garden that he took onto the mountain when he was transfigured. Those who witnessed his glorification were also present to witness his agony. On both occasions, Peter comes to the foreground. On the mount of transfiguration, the disciples fell to their faces overawed by the magnificence of the form before them, but now it is Jesus who falls on his face in agonized supplication to the heavenly Father. On both occasions Jesus said "arise" to his disciples, on the first that they might arise from their prostration of wonder and worship, but on this occasion that they might arise from their sleep. From the cloud of the transfiguration came the voice of the Father expressing his love for Jesus, but now from the traitor's lips came the sign of kissing, which betrayed Jesus' love for all his disciples. In both cases, the transfiguration and the agony, Jesus is left alone: on the first occasion with the disciples' eyes fixed upon him, but on the second when all the

132

disciples have fled. Gethsemane appears as an antithesis to "Tabor."

Gethsemane and the Our Father

The second comparison pertains to the *Our Father*. It has been said that the best commentary on the *Our Father* was Jesus' own life, death, and resurrection. In the garden, Jesus addressed God as his Father, although St. Matthew, unlike St. Mark, does not use the form of *Abba,* which is a term of endearment used by Jesus to address his Father. Jesus said, "Thy will be done." Jesus was about to "eat the break of affliction" and to implement his own words that his food and drink was to do the will of him who sent him: "Give us this day our daily bread." Later Jesus put into practice the act for forgiveness which he had asked his disciples to make: St. Luke reports that when Jesus was crucified, he said, "Father, forgive them, they know not what they do" (Luke 23: 34). Further, it is in the garden of Gethsemane that Jesus advised his disciples to pray lest they enter into temptation; and he himself must have endured temptation from the evil one as he prayed in his agony. But his prayer was fulfilled, for he "was delivered from evil." Finally, it was through the passion that God's kingdom did come.

The Arrest of Jesus

When Jesus was captured it was the time of the Passover, so in the light of the full moon Jesus could see Judas and the crowd approaching him. The irony of the situation lies in the fact that Jesus, who had rejected military force, prestige, and success, was approached by a great crowd with weapons. But the pathos was increased when the betrayer kissed him. The Greek word used to describe this kiss suggests that it was an elaborate sign of affection and possibly not one kiss but many. Jesus answered Judas, "Friend, why are you here?" This word "friend" is used in the New Testament only by St. Matthew and always

133

in situations in which the person so addressed is in the wrong (compare, for example, 20: 13; 22: 12). This was a gentle reproach to Judas on the part of Jesus. The phrase "Why are you here?" is ambiguous. It may mean "Perform that for which you have come" or it may mean "Do you show me this sign of affection when you come with the purpose to betray me?" Without further ado, the crowd seized Jesus, and here St. Matthew adds a detail omitted by Mark and Luke. He reports that Jesus told one of his disciples to place his sword back into its sheath, and reminded him that he could call upon the Father for help from the angelic hosts. Once again, we find here a reflection of the temptation of Jesus. Just as Jesus had refused to throw himself from the temple and be rescued, so now he refuses to call upon the angels to assist him. Some scholars have suggested that the reference to a sword and to the fulfillment of scripture refers to Zechariah 13: 7 which we quoted above, and others have suggested that Jesus is quoting a proverb here. Perhaps a better suggestion has been made by Hans Kosmala.[1] He suggests that Jesus had in mind a text from Isaiah 50: 11. A translation of the Hebrew text of this verse reads:

Behold, all you [that] kindle a fire, [that] are armed with firebrands: walk in [or: go into] the flame of your fire and in [to] the firebrands you have lighted. From my hand you have this: you shall lie down in torment.

Dr. Kosmala, however, sugests that the quotation in St. Matthew's Gospel is closer to the Aramaic Paraphrase, which reads:

Behold, all you [that] kindle a fire, [that] take a sword: Go, fall into the fire which you have kindled, and into [or, by] the sword which you have taken. From my Memra you have this: you shall return to your destruction.

St. Matthew used that part of this citation which would apply to the occasion of Jesus' arrest. The Memra is the Word of

1. H. Kosmala, "A Quotation from the Targum," *Novum Testamentum*, IV (1960), pp. 3–5.

God, whom we now recognize as Jesus Christ. Jesus wished to remind those with him in the garden of God's will as it was revealed in the scriptures. The high priests and the elders of the people had sent out the crowd with swords and clubs and therefore this scripture applied to them, that they would perish and be destroyed.

Jesus' Condemnation by the Sanhedrin (Matthew 26: 57–68)

Then those who had seized Jesus led him to Caiaphas the high priest, where the scribes and the elders had gathered. But Peter followed him at a distance, as far as the courtyard of the high priest, and going inside he sat with the guards to see the end. Now the chief priests and the whole council sought false testimony against Jesus that they might put him to death, but they found none, though many false witnesses came forward. At last two came forward and said, "This fellow said, 'I am able to destroy the temple of God, and to build it in three days.'" And the high priest stood up and said, "Have you no answer to make? What is it that these men testify against you?" But Jesus was silent. And the high priest said to him, "I adjure you by the living God, tell us if you are the Christ, the Son of God." Jesus said to him, "You have said so. But I tell you, hereafter you will see the Son of man seated at the right hand of power and coming on the clouds of heaven." Then the high priest tore his robes, and said, "He has uttered blasphemy. Why do we still need witnesses? You have now heard his blasphemy. What is your judgment?" They answered. "He deserves death." Then they spat in his face, and struck him; and some slapped him, saying, "Prophesy to us, you Christ! Who is it that struck you?"

Jesus Before the Jewish Authorities

Jesus was brought before the Jewish authorities for trial. At first, they could not find witnesses to accuse him of crime, but at last a person came forward and asserted that Jesus had said

135

that he was able to destroy the temple of God and to build it in three days. Jesus had certainly wept over Jerusalem and predicted that she would fall and her house or temple be desolate (compare Matthew 23: 37–39). Further, on one occasion when he left the temple, his disciples appear to have been speaking about the buildings of the temple, but Jesus answered them:

You see all these, do you not? Truly, I say to you, there will not be left here one stone upon another, that will not be thrown down.

However, besides these statements St. John reports that when Jesus drove the animals and the businessmen out of the temple and insisted that his Father's house must not be a house of trade, the Jews asked him by what authority he did this. Jesus did not reply directly to them but said, "Destroy this temple, and in three days I will build it up." The Jews thought that he was speaking about the temple of Jerusalem but Jesus was speaking about his own body. It seems, therefore, that the accuser of Jesus at his trial had either misunderstood some statements or teaching of Jesus or that he had deliberately misrepresented them.

The Temple Not Made with Hands

We may feel that Jesus' teaching upon this point was rather ambiguous, but it is important to realize that at the time of Jesus certain Jews did not insist upon the importance of the temple in Jerusalem, and turned their thoughts to a temple which they said would be made up of human beings—not a temple of stone built with hands, but a temple consisting of men and women. This concept is found, for example, in the manuscripts from the area of the Dead Sea. One fragment reads:

[I will appoint a place for my people in Israel, and will plant them, that they may be settled there undisturbed;] and no son of perversity

136

shall oppress them any more, as has happened throughout the past, ever since that day when I commanded judges to be over my people Israel. (II Samuel 7: 10–11)

The explanation appended to this text from Samuel is as follows:

The reference here is to the house [which God will cause to be built for his abiding] in the last days, even as it is written in the book of the law; *a sanctuary,* O LORD, *have thy hands established, (whence) the* LORD *shall reign for ever and ever* [Ex. 15, 17–18]. It will be a house in which (as the scripture puts it) *neither Ammonite nor Moabite nor half-breed nor alien nor stranger shall ever enter.* [Deuteronomy 23: 3–4: Ezekiel 44: 9], but where (only) those shall be that are God's saints . . .

What (in fact) God here declares is that (in the future) there shall be built for him a sanctuary constitued out of mankind itself —a sanctuary in which performance of the things laid down in the law shall rank as equivalent of the (erstwhile) burning of incense in his presence.[1]

In view of this, perhaps Jesus' statements were not so ambiguous.

The Son of Man

Jesus did not answer to the charge against him and eventually the high priest was obliged to request him on oath to say whether he was the Christ, the Son of God. Jesus appears to have answered in the affirmative and he added that the son of man would be seen seated at the right hand of power and come on the clouds of heaven. The word "power" was a synonym for God, and it would be blasphemy for any mere man to say that he would have equal sovereignty with God. The clouds of heaven denote the glory of God. It is also possible that the title "son of man" is a euphemism or substitute for

1. Gaster, *op. cit.,* pp. 337–338.

137

the Son of God. The Jews often expressed sacred or sacrilegious terms by using words which had exactly the opposite meaning and there are several Jewish texts which apply the epithet "Man" to God. But even if this title were not a substitute for "Son of God" the high priest could still say that Jesus had blasphemed, for he had suggested that he would reign with God. The high priest would know that Jesus referred to a text in Daniel which mentions someone "like a son of man." The text reads:

> I saw in the night visions, and behold, with
> the clouds of heaven
> there came one like a son of man,
> and he came to the Ancient of Days
> and was presented before him.
> And to him was given dominion
> and glory and kingdom,
> that all peoples, nations, and languages
> should serve him;
> his dominion is an everlasting dominion,
> which shall not pass away,
> and his kingdom one
> that shall not be destroyed. (Daniel 7: 13–14)

This "one like a son of man" was not a mere human being. We know from other Jewish literature that the concept of "son of man" was one which depicted someone who was "supernatural," who was like an angel, who possessed the plenitude of wisdom, who would call people from their graves and, probably, also take a part in judging men. Jesus appears to have ranked himself with such a character. Therefore, the high priest could, perhaps, with reason say that Jesus had blasphemed.

Prophecy Fulfilled

We have found that the text of St. Matthew is impregnated with references back to the Old Testament and this passage

138

is no exception. The silence of Jesus in verse 63 may be paralleled with the servant of Yahweh in Isaiah 53: 7.

> He was oppressed, and he was afflicted,
> yet he opened not his mouth;
> like a lamb that is led to the slaughter,
> and like a sheep that before its shearers is dumb,
> so he opened not his mouth."

Likewise, we find a reflection to Isaiah 50: 6:

> I gave my back to the smiters,
> and my cheeks to those who pulled out the beard:
> I hid not my face
> from shame and spitting.

In Matthew 26: 67, Jesus was struck, spat upon, and slapped. This section ends once again with irony and violence, as Jesus' opponents said to him: "Prophesy to us, you Christ!" Yet Jesus, who possessed the power of prophecy and could use it for the glory of God, did not avail himself of this gift for his own sake. Once again, this recalls Jesus' attitude during his temptation.

Peter's Denial (Matthew 26: 69–75)

Now Peter was sitting outside in the courtyard. And a maid came up to him, and said, "You also were with Jesus the Galilean." But he denied it before them all, saying, "I do not know what you mean." And when he went out to the porch, another maid saw him, and she said to the bystanders, "This man was with Jesus of Nazareth." And again he denied it with an oath, "I do not know the man." After a little while the bystanders came up and said to Peter, "Certainly you are also one of them, for your accent betrays you." Then he began to invoke a curse on himself and to swear, "I do not know the man." And immediately the cock crowed. And Peter remembered the saying of Jesus, "Before the cock crows, you will deny me three times." And he went out and wept bitterly.

139

Peter's Boldness

This passage has often brought disrepute upon St. Peter. But perhaps one should recall that Peter and John alone of the disciples had the courage to follow Jesus to the high priest's residence. John apparently was related to some of the household of the high priest and perhaps he would have had some protection, but Peter had none. Yet Peter, with dogged loyalty, followed Jesus, as St. Mathew says in verse 58, "to see the end." Peter was not a weakling and perhaps he had hoped to keep his word to Jesus, "though they all fall away because of you, I will never fall away" (Matthew 26: 33). It was Peter, too, who according to St. John's Gospel cut off the ear of one of the servants of the high priest: Peter was trying to defend his Master. What is more important to realize is that Peter stayed with his Lord longer than anyone except St. John and the women. He broke down only after being asked three times whether he was with Jesus, and it would have been surprising if he had not broken down under these conditions. The evangelists possibly record this incident, not so much to portray Peter and his failure, but to show the fulfillment of the prophecy of Jesus, namely, "Truly, I say to you, this very night, before the cock crows, you will deny me three times."

The Petrine Confession and the Trial Scene

However, in St. Matthew's record of this incident, there is one more point to observe. The trial scene of Jesus which we have just discussed reflects the Petrine confession at Caesarea Philippi. At Caesarea Philippi, Jesus asked his disciples to identify the "Son of man." Peter replied that he was "the Christ, the Son of the living God." At the trial scene, the high priest asked Jesus, "Are you the Christ, the Son of the living God?" And Jesus replied, "Thou sayest . . . thou shalt see the Son of man . . ." The question which the high priest asked is very similar to the answer which Peter gave. When one considers this, the incident of Peter's denial is even more dramatic because Peter seems to have been sitting outside and listening to the discussion between Jesus and the high priest, and St. Matthew seems to show St. Peter reversing his role and denying rather than confessing the Son of God. Peter's threefold denial would be completely forgiven and forgotten when later he made his threefold confession of love in Jesus, which is recorded in John 21: 15–19.

Jesus' Delivery to Pilate and the Repentance of Judas (Matthew 27: 1–10)

When morning came, all the chief priests and the elders of the people took counsel against Jesus to put him to death; and they bound him and led him away and delivered him to Pilate the governor.

When Judas, his betrayer, saw that he was condemned, he repented and brought back the thirty pieces of silver to the chief priests and the elders, saying, "I have sinned in betraying innocent blood." They said, "What is that to us? See to it yourself." And throwing down the pieces of silver in the temple, he departed; and he went and hanged himself. But the chief priests, taking the pieces of silver, said, "It is not lawful to put them into the treasury, since they are blood money." So they took counsel, and bought with them the potter's field, to bury strangers in. Therefore that field has been called the Field of Blood to this day. Then was fulfilled what had been spoken by the prophet Jeremiah, saying, "And they took the thirty pieces of silver, the price of him on whom a price had been set by some of the sons of Israel, and they gave them for the potter's field, as the Lord directed me."

The Character of Pilate

The evangelists tell us that Jesus was taken to Pilate, the governor. Pilate is also mentioned by a Jewish historian, al-

141

most contemporary with Jesus, Flavius Josephus. In one of his books, entitled *Jewish Antiquities,* in Chapter 18, we read as follows:

About this time there lived Jesus, a wise man, if indeed one ought to call him a man. For he was one who wrought surprising facts and was a teacher of such people as accept the truth gladly. He won over many Jews and many of the Greeks. He was the Messiah. When Pilate, upon hearing him accused by men of the highest standing among us, had him condemned to death to be crucified, those who had in the first place come to love him did not give up their affection for him. On the third day he appeared to them restored to life, for the prophets of God had prophesied these and countless other marvelous things about him. And the tribe of the Christians, so called after him, have still to this day not disappeared.

Many scholars used to think that this description of Jesus was inserted by another hand into the text of Josephus, but nowadays more scholars are ready to accept it as genuine. We know also that Pilate was governor in Palestine from 26 to 36 A.D. From the text of Luke 13: 1, we learn that he appears to have killed some Galileans in the temple and mingled their blood with their sacrifices: this may have been why Herod, the tetrarch of Galilee, was not very friendly with Pilate (compare Luke 23: 12). From further sources, we gain the impression that Pilate had indulged in various acts of cruelty and injustice. Philo, another Jewish writer, nearly contemporary with Jesus, tells us that Pilate was "inflexible, merciless and obstinate" (*Leg. ad Gaium,* 38). Josephus also reports that Pilate attempted to put Roman insignia in the temple of Jerusalem but that the Jews obliged him to remove them; and also that he committed some atrocious crimes against the Samaritans (compare *Ant.* 18, 2, 2; 3, 1–4, 2; 6, 5; *JB* 2, 9, 2–4). These details show us a little of the character of the man who was responsible for allowing Jesus to be crucified.

142

The Character of Judas

Perhaps, in contrast to the figure of Pilate, we can see the character of Judas. In the passage under discussion he is shown to repent of his treachery and he appears not to have returned the money by dropping it, for example, in the chest provided for alms in the court of women. This passage implies that he went into the court of Israel, very near the altar of burnt offering, and in desperation threw the coins westwards into the door of the temple building. His action seems to have been visible to the priests. Once again, we see the irony of the situation. The priests feel they cannot use money given to take the life of a man, so they buy a field in which strangers may be buried if they die in Jerusalem—for example, when they come on a pilgrimage. For Matthew, however, this episode is interesting because once again it fulfills a prophecy found in the Old Testament. In Zechariah 11: 13, we read:

Then the Lord said to me, "Cast it into the treasury—the lordly price at which I was paid off by them. So I took the thirty shekels of silver and cast them into the treasury in the house of the Lord.

But St. Matthew has written Jeremiah instead of Zechariah. Perhaps he made this mistake because the suffering of Jeremiah and of Jesus were very similar.

Jesus Before Pontius Pilate (Matthew 27: 11–26)

Now Jesus stood before the governor; and the governor asked him, "Are you the King of the Jews?" Jesus said to him, "You have said so." But when he was accused by the chief priests and elders, he made no answer. Then Pilate said to him, "Do you not hear how many things they testify against you?" But he gave him no answer, not even to a single charge; so that the governor wondered greatly.

Now at the feast the governor was accustomed to release for

143

the crowd any one prisoner whom they wanted. And they had then a notorious prisoner, called Barabbas. So when they had gathered, Pilate said to them, "Whom do you want me to release for you, Barabbas or Jesus who is called Christ?" For he knew that it was out of envy that they had delivered him up. Besides, while he was sitting on the judgment seat, his wife sent word to him, "Have nothing to do with that righteous man, for I have suffered much over him today in a dream." Now the chief priests and the elders persuaded the people to ask for Barabbas and destroy Jesus. The governor again said to them, "Which of the two do you want me to release for you?" And they said, "Barabbas." Pilate said to them, "Then what shall I do with Jesus who is called Christ?" They all said, "Let him be crucified." And he said, "Why, what evil has he done?" But they shouted all the more, "Let him be crucified."

Release of Barabbas

In this passage, once again, the irony of the condemnation of Jesus is obvious. Pilate interviewed Jesus and asked him if he were the King of the Jews. Jesus appeared to have answered in the affirmative, but after that Jesus did not answer any of the charges against him and the governor "wondered greatly." So Pilate offered to release a prisoner in honor of the feast of the Passover and he asked the assembled people whether he should release Jesus who was called Christ, or a man whose name was Jesus Barbabbas: this is the name written in many manuscripts instead of Barabbas. The translation of this name would be "Jesus the son of the father." So a man who was a murderer and convicted for insurrection who bears the title "Jesus son of the father" is liberated and a "Jesus the messiah," the real Son of God, is condemned to death.

Pilate's Protestation of Innocence

Pilate seems to have given in to the request of the crowd because he feared a riot. But before he delivered Jesus over to

144

be killed, he performed a Jewish ceremonial action. He washed his hands before the crowd, and said, "I am innocent of this righteous man's blood." Deuteronomy 21: 1ff. describes this ceremonial. If a man was found slain, the people must declare themselves innocent of the murder thus:

And the priests the sons of Levi shall come forward, for the Lord your God has chosen them to minister to him and to bless in the name of the Lord, and by their word every dispute and every assault shall be settled. And all the elders of that city nearest to the slain man shall wash their hands . . . and they shall testify, "Our hands did not shed this blood, neither did our eyes see it shed. Forgive, O Lord, thy people Israel, whom thou hast redeemed, and set not the guilt of innocent blood in the midst of thy people Israel; and let the guilt of blood be forgiven them." So you shall purge the guilt of innocent blood from your midst, when you do what is right in the sight of the Lord.

Perhaps Pilate performed this action in mockery, knowing that the leaders of the Jews were guilty of innocent blood. After Pilate had done this the people said, "His blood be on us and on our children!" One must not read into this the responsibility of all the Jewish nation and all the Jewish generations for Jesus' death. This was the normal legal phrase which people used when they sincerely believed that in justice they had condemned a man who was guilty. It is obvious that many of the Jewish leaders did feel that Jesus was guilty of blasphemy and, therefore, that he did deserve death. They would have cried the same if Barabbas had been in the place of Jesus.

The Mocking of the King of the Jews (Matthew 27: 27–31)

So when Pilate saw that he was gaining nothing, but rather that a riot was beginning, he took water and washed his hands before the crowd, saying, "I am innocent of this man's blood; see to it yourselves." And all the people answered, "His blood be on us and on our children!" Then he released for them Barabbas, and having scourged Jesus, delivered him to be crucified.

Then the soldiers of the governor took Jesus into the praetorium, and they gathered the whole battalion before him. And they stripped him and put a scarlet robe upon him, and plaiting a crown of thorns they put it on his head, and put a reed in his right hand. And kneeling before him they mocked him, saying, "Hail, King of the Jews!" And they spat upon him, and took the reed and struck him on the head. And when they had mocked him, they stripped him of the robe, and put his own clothes on him, and led him away to crucify him.

Jesus as Mock King

This section in Matthew shows Jesus in the barracks of the soldiers where they indulge in coarse humor by mocking him. They robed Jesus in a scarlet soldier's cloak to represent the emperor's purple robe; they made him a crown of thorns in imitation of the crown with radiant spikes worn by the emperor and shown on coins of the period contemporary with Jesus; they placed a reed or staff in his hand to represent the scepter which the emperor held in his right hand as a symbol of his sovereignty; and they saluted Jesus saying, "Hail, King of the Jews" as they would salute the emperor saying, "Hail, Caesar." This scene fulfills the prediction of Jesus about his suffering which is found in Matthew 20: 18 following:

The Son of man will be delivered to the chief priests and scribes, and they will condemn Him to death, and deliver Him to the gentiles to be mocked and scourged and crucified, and He will be raised on the third day.

Many scholars nowadays say that this prediction must have been added by the evangelists and placed in the mouth of Jesus after the event described had occurred. These scholars do not appear to accept the validity of prophecy. One would imagine, however, that if this prediction had been composed by the evan-

146

gelists rather than spoken by Jesus, they would have added more precise details. Be that as it may, with the next passage from St. Matthew's Gospel one reaches a point where the evangelist sees Jesus fulfilling in reality much of what had been written in the psalms.

The Crucifixion of Jesus (Matthew 27: 32–44)

As they were marching out, they came upon a man of Cyrene, Simon by name; this man they compelled to carry his cross. And when they came to a place called Golgotha (which means the place of a skull), they offered him wine to drink, mingled with gall; but when he tasted it, he would not drink it. And when they had crucified him, they divided his garments among them by casting lots; then they sat down and kept watch over him there. And over his head they put the charge against him, which read, "This is Jesus the King of the Jews." Then two robbers were crucified with him, one on the right and one on the left. And those who passed by derided him, wagging their heads and saying, "You who would destroy the temple and build it in three days, save yourself! If you are the Son of God, come down from the cross." So also the chief priests, with the scribes and elders, mocked him, saying, "He saved others; he cannot save himself. He is the King of Israel; let him come down now from the cross, and we will believe in him. He trusts in God; let God deliver him now, if he desires him; for he said, 'I am the Son of God.' " And the robbers who were crucified with him also reviled him in the same way.

The Process of Crucifixion

The vertical shaft of the cross would possibly be in place when Jesus arrived and the usual method would be to lay Jesus upon the ground, stretch his arms upon the horizontal shaft, fix them there, and then lift him onto the cross itself. However, the evangelists only describe the crucifixion in two Greek words.

147

They do not elaborate at all upon Jesus' suffering. They have no need to describe the process of crucifixion, for this was a common punishment inflicted by the Romans. A man with a crossbeam laid upon his shoulders and his arms fastened to either end with ropes and driven, naked, under the whip to the place of crucifixion would be a common sight. One reads of thousands of crucifixions in the period of the Roman rule over Palestine. The upright beams of the cross were left permanently on the site of crucifixion, and when the man arrived he was lifted up onto one of these beams and the horizontal shaft was put into a groove at the top of the vertical shaft. His feet were fixed to the upright shaft in the same way as his hands with rope or nails. There does not seem to be any evidence for the footrest which appears on many of our crucifixes, but there does seem to have been a projection or seat half-way up the vertical shaft upon which the crucified man sat astride. The height of the crosses varied: sometimes the prisoner's feet were just above the ground but at other times they were more than a yard above. It might take several days for the victim to die, but on the other hand he might die within a few hours owing to the lost blood ensuing from the flogging or the nailing. If he remained upon the cross for some time he would be torn to pieces by wild animals or he might die from thirst, exposure, or very often from asphixiation. Frequently the Romans left the body upon the gallows to rot away or to be eaten by vultures.

The Dividing of the Clothing

When the soldiers had performed this dreadful task, they divided the clothes of the prisoners between them by casting lots. For the early Christians the scene would fulfill the verses of Psalm 22: 16–18:

> Yea, dogs are round about me;
> a company of evil-doers encircle me;

they have pierced my hands and my feet
I can count all my bones
They stare and gloat over me;
they divide my garments among them,
and for my raiment they cast lots.

But Matthew does not mention Jesus' friends until the very end. Instead he mentions the people who mocked Jesus. The passersby mocked him saying, "You who would destroy the temple and build it again." They mocked him as the devil did in the temptation, saying, "If you are the Son of God," come down from the cross. But Jesus did not condescend to perform a miracle for himself. The words of the passersby fulfilled Psalm 22: 6–8:

But I am a worm, and no man;
scorned by men, and despised by the people.
All who see me mock at me,
They make mouths at me, they wag their heads;
"He committed his cause to the Lord;
Let him deliver him,
let him rescue him, for he delights in him!"

The whole of Psalm 22 is interesting in relationship to the passion.

The Death of Jesus (Matthew 27: 45–50)

Now from the sixth hour there was darkness over all the land until the ninth hour. And about the ninth hour Jesus cried with a loud voice, "Eli, Eli, lama sabach-thani?" that is, "My God, my God, why hast thou forsaken me?" And some of the bystanders hearing it said, "This man is calling Elijah." And one of them at once ran and took a sponge, filled it with vinegar, and put it on a reed, and gave it to him to drink. But the others said, "Wait, let us see whether Elijah will come to save him." And Jesus cried again with a loud voice and yielded up his spirit.

149

The Darkness

We have remarked that the evangelists do not refer at all to the suffering of Jesus: the fulfillment of scripture is more important to them. When the darkness fell over the land for about three hours, they might well have reflected upon the darkness which was mentioned in Exodus 10: 22 on the night of the first Passover, for Jesus died around the feast of the Passover. This verse from Exodus reads: "There was thick darkness in all the land in Egypt three days." In the Exodus account, the darkness was the last plague which God inflicted on the land of Egypt before he allowed the death of the first-born; now darkness fell after the first-born, the Son of God, died upon the cross. The evangelists might well have recalled a text from the prophet Amos 8: 9:

And on that day, saith the Lord God, I will make the sun go down at noon, and darken the earth in the broad daylight.

For the early Christian this would not be a mere pious reflection. Then Jesus cried with a loud voice and, according to one text, cited the opening verse of Psalm 22, from which we have frequently quoted with reference to the crucifixion. This would read: "My God, My God why hast thou forsaken me?" This would, indeed, look like a cry of despair. However, Jesus may have tried to recite the whole Psalm in his agony. On the other hand, some manuscripts of Matthew read, "My God, my God, for this was I kept." If so, this was not a cry of despair but a cry of confidence. Some of the spectators thought that Jesus is calling on Elijah, because the Hebrew *"Eli"* is very close to the word "Elijah." In the Old Testament, we read that Elijah did not die but was assumed into heaven (II Kings 2: 9–12), and some believed that he would return to help those in distress.

150

The Signs After the Death of Jesus and the Burial of Jesus (Matthew 27: 51–66)

And behold, the curtain of the temple was torn in two, from top to bottom; and the earth shook, and the rocks were split; the tombs also were opened, and many bodies of the saints who had fallen asleep were raised, and coming out of the tombs after his resurrection they went into the holy city and appeared to many. When the centurion and those who were with him, keeping watch over Jesus, saw the earthquake and what took place, they were filled with awe, and said, "Truly this was the Son of God!"

There were also many women there, looking on from afar, who had followed Jesus from Galilee, ministering to him; among whom were Mary Magdalene, and Mary the mother of James and Joseph, and the mother of the sons of Zebedee.

When it was evening, there came a rich man from Arimathea, named Joseph, who also was a disciple of Jesus. He went to Pilate and asked for the body of Jesus. Then Pilate ordered it to be given to him. And Joseph took the body, and wrapped it in a clean linen shroud, and laid it in his own new tomb, which he had hewn in the rock; and he rolled a great stone to the door of the tomb, and departed. Mary Magdalene and the other Mary were there, sitting opposite the sepulchre.

Next day, that is, after the day of Preparation, the chief priests and the Pharisees gathered before Pilate and said, "Sir, we remember how that impostor said, while he was still alive, 'After three days I will rise again.' Therefore order the sepulchre to be made secure until the third day, lest his disciples go and steal him away, and tell the people, 'He has risen from the dead,' and the last fraud will be worse than the first." Pilate said to them, "You have a guard of soldiers; go, make it as secure as you can." So they went and made the sepulchre secure by sealing the stone and setting a guard.

The Veil of the Temple

Both St. Mark and St. Matthew tell us that the veil of the temple was torn in two. Within the temple, there was an inner sanctuary called the holy of holies. This was considered to possess the utmost degree of holiness and inaccessability: no one entered this except the high priest and he did so only once a year, on the Day of Atonement, to offer sacrifice. This holy of holies was divided from the rest of the temple by two curtains which stood about twenty inches apart. They separated the inner part from the outer room. They were richly made, and we read in the *Mishnah* that the inner curtain was one handbreadth (about three and a half inches) in thickness and was woven on seventy-two strands, and over each strand were twenty-four threads. This means the curtain was very heavy (compare *Shek.* 8: 5). St. Matthew and St. Mark represent this curtain being torn almost simultaneously with the death of Jesus. They wished to convey the idea that Jesus' body, which he had called the temple, had perished, and hence that with it had perished the sacrifices of the past: they had been fully superseded. Now a new way of access to God was offered to everyone, not to only one high priest once a year. We see this quite clearly from the Epistle to the Hebrews 10: 19ff.:

Therefore, brethren, since we have confidence to enter the sanctuary by the blood of Jesus, by the new and living way which he opened for us through the curtain, that is, through his flesh, and since we have a great priest over the house of God, let us draw near with a true heart in full assurance of faith, with out hearts sprinkled clean from an evil conscience and our bodies washed with pure water.

St. Matthew concludes his account of the crucifixion by referring to the women who were watching from afar. He may have seen this as a fulfillment of Psalm 38: 11: "My friends and companions stand aloof from my plague, and my kinsmen stand afar off." Then Joseph, the rich man from Arimathea, requested the body of Jesus from Pilate and buried it. The rabbis forbade one to bury one's kin where an executed man had been laid, so this was a generous act on behalf of Joseph.

Mary Magdalene and the other Mary sat opposite the sepulchre, for friends frequently watched in case the corpse revived. But St. Matthew may have another purpose in mentioning them here, for they were witnesses to the tomb in which Jesus was laid and later they would be witnesses, at this same tomb, that Jesus had risen and was on his way to Galilee. This was what Jesus had predicted. At the very beginning of the passion, as he and his disciples entered the garden at Gethsemane, he said, "But after I am raised, I will go before you to Galilee" (Matthew 26: 32). Thus St. Matthew represents the passion of Jesus as the fulfillment of many portions of scripture, and at this point he leaves Jesus buried in the tomb of the rich man. In Isaiah 53: 9, we read of the suffering servant of Yahweh:

> And they made his grave with the wicked
> and with a rich man in his death,
> although he had done no violence,
> and there was no deceit in his mouth.

But unlike the servant of Yahweh, Jesus would rise from the dead, and after his resurrection he would give the Holy Spirit, the Lord of life, to all those who believe in him.

Intercession

Passion Sunday

The response is
Jesus, courageous and humble of heart, hear us.

(1) That we may receive spiritual hearing and insight into prophecy, let us pray to the Lord.
(2) That we may be able to see the humanity of God, let us pray . . .
(3) That we may be able to see the Holy Spirit working in human nature, let us pray . . .

153

(4) That we may not grasp for worldly honor, let us pray . . .

(5) For those who have no worldly honor, let us pray . . .

(6) For rulers of nations that they may respect the sacredness of the human person, let us pray . . .

(7) For even more courage than St. Peter, let us pray . . .

(8) For the successor of Peter in the difficulties which he faces, let us pray . . .

(9) For biblical scholars that they may not yield to skepticism but apprehend the full truth of the scriptures, let us pray . . .

(10) For spiritual understanding of the scriptures, let us pray . . .

(11) For the growth of genuine prophecy in the Church, let us pray . . .

(12) For a true understanding of Jesus' passion, let us pray . . .

(13) For those suffering ignominous death, let us pray . . .

HOLY THURSDAY

The sequence of days from Holy Thursday to Easter can lead us to think that the liturgical celebration is a kind of tableau in which we follow Jesus step by step from the Last Supper to his appearance to the women in the garden (rather like a prolonged Stations of the Cross). But if we look at the liturgical texts, we find no such neat historical sequence of events. The eucharistic service for Holy Thursday omits all references to Jesus' night of agony and trial. The Good Friday service is charged with the sense of Jesus' resurrection victory (see p. 177). The Easter preface is particularly concerned with his redemptive death. If we are dealing with an historical sequence, it is a very untidy one.

But in reality, we are not dealing with a liturgical tableau. The three sacred days are a single festival. In each of the three services, we celebrate the whole paschal mystery. In fact, every Christian festival is, at its center, a celebration of Jesus' death and resurrection. Early Christianity was so struck by this truth that it abandoned all festival days. The primitive Church had only one festival—the weekly eucharist.

The Holy Thursday liturgy focuses on that central festival—the celebration of Jesus' death and resurrection in the eucharist. The service of the Word is particularly insistent that the risen Lord is present to form a people in love. Paul's solemn warning that the absence of love profanes the eucharist reinforces the message of the Gospel and the rite of footwashing. The latter is an acted parable, a demonstration of Jesus' declaration that his followers' love can have no reservations.

But for many centuries, the Church in Rome also drew attention to another aspect of the eucharist in its Holy Thursday celebration. Public sinners were reconciled to the Church on this day. There could be no more appropriate time for receiving sinners. For along with the severity of the Lord's demands, there is also the Lord's forgiveness, forgiveness which we receive in the eucharist itself. The Roman liturgy continually includes prayers for forgiveness in the eucharistic service. Yet how willing have we been to take seriously what the Gospels describe as Jesus' intent in instituting the eucharist:

> Take this, all of you, and drink from it:
> this is the cup of my blood,
> the blood of the new and everlasting covenant—
> the mystery of faith.
> It will be shed for you and for all men
> so that sins may be forgiven.*

We can come to the Lord's table rejoicing, because we are pardoned sinners. To sing, "Lord have mercy," or "Lamb of God, have mercy on us" is not a shamefaced admission that we really shouldn't be here. Rather, it is a confident acclamation of the Lord's forgiving love. It is the recognition that we are called to receive the Lord's mercy here and now.

The themes of love and forgiveness directly relate Holy Thursday to the paschal sacrament of baptism. Baptism appears in the Easter liturgy as an act of faith and repentance. As an act of faith, it is a response to the God who has first loved us, and who calls us to be one with him by becoming one with those he calls his own. As an act of repentance, it is the turning in confidence to the one who pardons all our infidelities. Holy Thursday evokes the baptismal commitment by summarizing the meaning of the Christian vocation: we are forgiven sinners, invited to live in love.

Every eucharist is an affirmation of the baptismal commit-

* Used by permission of the International Committee on English in the Liturgy, Inc.

156

ment, because each celebration is an invitation to renew our love and our gratitude. The recent introduction of new prefaces and eucharistic prayers in the Roman rite should help us to understand the paschal character of every eucharist. For every eucharistic prayer is a joyful summation of the Easter message. We do not gather to remember Jesus' farewell meal with his disciples, but to exult, "Christ has died, Christ is risen, Christ will come again!"

The meaning of the eucharistic banquet determines the function of the readings in the liturgy of the Word—not just at Easter time, but all through the year. The scriptures are a living word because they point to the risen Lord who is present among us. The past events of Israel's history or Jesus' ministry or the apostles' experiences are read to shed light on the character of the Lord who speaks *now*. If Holy Thursday is a time when Catholics can rejoice in their devotion to Christ's presence in the Blessed Sacrament, it should also be a time for sober reflection on our failure to develop a similar sensitivity to his presence in the proclaimed Word.

Holy Thursday

On Holy Thursday, we recall:
  (1) the Jewish Passover;
  (2) the Last Supper or eucharist which was instituted on the feast of the Passover;
  (3) Jesus' act of humility on the night that he was betrayed when he washed his disciples' feet.

THE FIRST READING, EXODUS 12: 1–14. THE HEBREW PASSOVER

The Lord said to Moses and Aaron in the land of Egypt, "This month shall be for you the beginning of months; which shall be

157

the first month of the year for you. Tell all the congregation of Israel that on the tenth day of this month they shall take every man a lamb according to their father's houses, a lamb for a household; and if the household is too small for a lamb, then a man and his neighbor next to his house shall take according to the number of persons; according to what each can eat you shall make your count for the lamb. Your lamb shall be without blemish, a male a year old; you shall take it from the sheep or from the goats; and you shall keep it until the fourteenth day of this month, when the whole assembly of the congregation of Israel shall kill their lambs in the evening. Then they shall take some of the blood, and put it on the two doorposts and on the lintel of the houses in which they eat them. They shall eat the flesh that night, roasted; with unleavened bread and bitter herbs they shall eat it. (Do not eat any of it raw or boiled with water, but roasted, its head with its legs and its inner parts. And you shall let none of it remain until the morning, anything that remains until the morning you shall burn.) In this manner you shall eat it: your loins girded, your sandals on your feet, and your staff in your hand; and you shall eat it in haste. It is the Lord's passover. For I will pass through the land of Egypt that night, and I will smite all the first-born in the land of Egypt, both man and beast; and on all the gods of Egypt I will execute judgments: I am the Lord. The blood shall be a sign for you, upon the houses where you are; and when I see the blood, I will pass over you, and no plague shall fall upon you to destroy you, when I smite the land of Egypt."

The Paschal Sacrifice

This passage of scripture describes the sacrificial meal, which, according to tradition, the children of Israel enacted before they left Egypt to pass to the promised land. The Israelites were about to pass from a land of darkness, slavery, and ignorance to a new life of freedom and a life wherein they could be united under one Lord, Yahweh.

The central purpose of the celebration of the meal both in Egypt and in the years when it is repeated was the voluntary dedication of each individual to Yahweh. This dedication was expressed vividly in the selection of the Passover victim, an animal chosen from the lambs or kids. The animal was required to be perfect, without a blemish, a male that was a year old. The offering, therefore, was one of peculiar sanctity. In the time of Jesus it was taken to the temple in Jerusalem and slaughtered about one-thirty or two-thirty in the afternoon. This part of the sacrifice was performed in the temple by laymen. The celebrants suspended the carcasses of the animals on hooks of iron fixed into the walls or the pillars, but if there was not sufficient room, the men placed staves on one another's shoulders and hung the victim upon this. The portions of the victim which were not to be eaten at the Passover meal were taken away and burned by the priests. The blood, which was the most important part of the animal and regarded as its life, was collected in bowls and thrown in one act or tossed against the base of the altar. The priests who were engaged in this action were dressed in red and stood in rows with bowls of silver or gold in their hands. They passed these along the line to the priest who was nearest the altar. One important precept was that the blood should not congeal, and for this purpose the basins had no bases lest the priests set them down and the blood clotted. Congealed blood was not considered *kosher*.

The Hallel Psalms

While all these rites were being performed, the Levites made music, with trumpets and flutes, and the Hallel Psalms were recited. These were Psalms 113 to 118 inclusive. The first psalm was one of praise containing the words:

> Blessed be the name of the Lord
> from this time forth and forever more!
> From the rising of the sun to its setting
> the name of the Lord is to be praised!"

(Psalm 113: 2–3)

159

The second psalm recalled Israel's exodus from Egypt and in this the mountains are described as skipping like rams and the hills like lambs. This verse would be especially pertinent:

> What ails you, O sea, that you flee?
> O Jordan, that you turn back?
> O mountains, that you skip like rams?
> O hills, like lambs?
> Tremble, O earth, at the presence of the Lord,
> at the presence of the God of Jacob . . .
>
> (Psalm 114: 5–7)

The third psalm contrasted the God of Israel with the graven images of the pagan nations. It began with a line attributing glory only to God:

> Not to us O Lord, not to us,
> but to thy name give glory,
> for the sake of thy steadfast love
> and thy faithfulness!
>
> (Psalm 115: 1)

The fourth psalm declared the psalmist's love for God because his cry was heard when the snares of death encompassed him and because, when he was brought very low, God saved him. It contained the verse:

> Return, O my soul, to your rest;
> for the Lord has dealt bountifully with you.
>
> (Psalm 116: 7)

It also spoke about the psalmist's fidelity or faithfulness, even when he was greatly afflicted. He said:

> What shall I render to the Lord
> for all his bounty to me?
> I will lift up the cup of salvation
> and call upon the name of the Lord . . .
> precious in the sight of the Lord
> is the death of his saints.
> O Lord I am your servant . . .

160

I will pay my vows to the Lord
in the presence of all his people . . .
in your midst, O Jerusalem.

(Psalm 116: 12–19)

Psalm 117 is a short psalm of praise to Almighty God. The last psalm 118, celebrates the steadfast love of God for his people Israel when they were grievously attacked by their enemies. In this psalm we find the sentence "the stone which the builders rejected has become the head of the corner." This verse was applied to Jesus by the New Testament writers; he, the stone, was rejected in Jerusalem, but later He became the head of the corner, that is, the chief person in the nation (see Matthew 21: 42). These psalms must have meant a great deal to our Lord when he celebrated his last Passover before his death.

The Paschal Meal

At one time the meal which completed the sacrifice was celebrated only by male adults from the age of twenty upwards, but by the time of Jesus it was a family meal which included women and also servants. On the occasion of the Last Supper, Jesus appears to have restricted the company to his twelve disciples, but other Passovers which he kept may well have included, for example, his mother, friends such as Lazarus, Mary, and Martha, and the women who attended to his needs and listened to his teaching. The pattern of the meal would be approximately as follows. There would be a preliminary course accompanied by the words of dedication, that is, the chief celebrant's blessing pronounced for the feast day over the first cup of wine. The first dish consisted of bitter herbs and a sauce made of fruit purée, probably of squeezed and grated fruits, such as figs, dates, raisins, apples, and also of almonds and spices; these spices were sold by the peddlers in Jerusalem. This course symbolized the bitter Egyptian slavery and the mortar used with the bricks with which the Israelites worked (see

161

Exodus 1: 8-14). Then the meal proper was served but not eaten immediately; a second cup of wine was mixed and set in its place but this was not drunk immediately either. Then came the recitation of the Passover narrative. This would comprise the story of the exodus from Egypt and the meaning of the feast and would be an extempore speech, not a formal recital. Hence the celebrant might well include some of his own interpretations of the symbolism of the ingredients of the meal. This would give Jesus an opportunity to explain the new covenant of his own blood, the full import of the eucharist, to point to the bread and say, "This is my body," and to the wine and say, "This is my blood." Next the first part of the Hallel was recited and the second cup of wine was drunk. Then followed the main meal with the grace recited by the celebrant over the unleavened bread, "the bread of affliction." The meal consisted of the Passover lamb, unleavened bread, bitter herbs, and wine. Each person was obliged to eat an olive's bulk of lamb.

The Blood

The sacrificial offering of the victim in the temple, and especially the pouring of the blood or the life upon the altar, symbolized surrender to and communion with God. Gathered at table the participants shared in the sacrificial meal which they had offered symbolically to God, and the four cups of red wine were possibly regarded as a substitute for the blood. Wine is often called the "blood of the grape," as for example in Genesis 49: 11b:

> He washes his garments in wine
> and his vesture in the blood of grapes;

and in Sirach 50: 14–15 which describes the great high priest, Simon, who was "the leader of his brethren and the pride of his people." He is described thus (probably on the Feast of Atonement):

162

Finishing the service at the altars,
and arranging the offering to the Most High, the Almighty,
he reached out his hand to the cup
and poured a libation of the blood of the grape:
he poured it out at the foot of the altar,
a pleasing odor to the Most High,
the king of all.

However, the shedding of blood, whether it was symbolized by the blood of the paschal lamb or the cups of wine, would be very significant to Jesus as he was about to pour out his own blood on the altar of the cross. It is thought that one of the scriptual texts read in the Passover service was from Isaiah 63: 1-9, which speaks of a man in glorious apparel coming to rescue Israel.

Who is this that comes from Edom,
in crimsoned garments from Bozrah,
he that is glorious in his apparel,
marching in the greatness of his strength?
"It is I, announcing vindication,
mighty to save."
Why is thy apparel red,
and thy garments like this that treads in the wine press?
"I have trodden the wine press alone,
and from the peoples no one was with me;
I trod them in my anger
and trampled them in my wrath;
their lifeblood is sprinkled upon my garments,
and I have stained all my raiment.
For the day of vengeance was in my heart,
and my year of redemption has come.
I looked, but there was no one to help;
I was appalled, but there was no one to uphold;
So my own arm brought me victory,
and my wrath upheld me.
I trod down the peoples in my anger,
I made them drunk in my wrath,
and I poured out their lifeblood on the earth."
I will recount the steadfast love of the Lord,

and the praises of the Lord,
according to all that the Lord has granted us,
and the great goodness to the house of Israel
which he has granted them according to his mercy,
according to the abundance of his steadfast love.
For he said, Surely they are my people,
sons who will not deal falsely;
and he became their Saviour.
In their affliction he was afflicted,
and the angel of his presence saved them;
in his love and in his pity he redeemed them;
he lifted them up and carried them all the days of old.

The Greek translation of this Hebrew text speaks not of an angel but of God himself who delivered the children of Israel. This Greek text is very close to a very old portion of the Passover service, which reads:

And YHWH brought up out of Misrayim (Egypt)
not by the hands of an angel
and not by the hands of a seraph
and not by the hands of an envoy
but the Holy One, blessed be he, in his Glory
and by himself . . .

Here we see clearly the belief that God himself redeemed Israel from the land of Egypt. On the Passover night, when Jesus instituted the eucharist and when the people of Israel anticipated the final redemption, which they expected to take place around the feast of Passover, Jesus like Yahweh was ready to be afflicted for his people and to become their Saviour. Not only was Jesus as man the personification of Israel and shed his blood in place of theirs, but he was God himself, who redeemed Israel and created life anew.

On the night of the exodus from Egypt, God slew the first-born of the Egyptians so that his children might attain freedom; and on the night of Jesus' Passover the first-born son of Mary and the only begotten Son of God was about to be slain so that

164

the blessings of the Spirit of Yahweh might be poured out, not only upon Israel, but upon the whole world.

We should make one more reflection. The first Passover was a night of vigil or watching, a watching for God to come to redeem his people. All other Passovers were also nights of watching, a watching for the future redemption. Those who celebrated the Passover were supposed to keep awake for a good portion of the night and this was why Jesus urged his disciples to keep awake in the Garden of Gethsemane. We conclude by citing an old Hebrew hymn: this hymn is much later than the time of Jesus, but as it expresses those sentiments which may well have been those of Jesus we cite it here.

O night of vigil, O witching hour,
When God rode forth from Egypt in his power!
The night shall come when he shall ride once more
As once he rode in those far days of yore.
But *we* with songs shall fill that eventide;
To *us* he comes a lover to his bride.

O night of vigil and O witching hour!
Tho' God with darkness all the world o'erpower,
Lo, in his hand is day as well as night,
And over us shall break his morning light;
For ne'er that other night shall be forgot
When Abraham led his men to rescue Lot.

O night of vigil, O witching hour!
As once when steers would his poor sheep devour,
The shepherd fought with them and lay them low,
So, as He rescued us so long ago,
He yet shall come, and this long night be done.
Deliverance comes with the rising sun.

O night of vigil and O witching hour!
Tho' dark the earth and tho' the heavens lower,
This is the hour when God his tryst shall keep
With his beloved, arouse her from sleep,

165

And, like a bridegroom leading home his bride,
Lead her in peace to Zion at his side." [1]

Our next commentary on St. John, the third reading, will introduce this theme of bride and bridegroom once again.

The Second Reading, I Corinthians 11: 23–29. The New Christian Passover or Eucharist

For I received from the Lord what I also delivered to you, that the Lord Jesus on the night that he was betrayed took bread, and when he had given thanks, he broke it, and said, "This is my body which is for you. Do this in remembrance of me." In the same way also the cup, after supper, saying, "This cup is the new covenant in my blood. Do this, as often as you drink it, in remembrance of me." For as often as you eat this bread and drink the cup, you proclaim the Lord's death until he comes. Whoever, therefore, eats the bread or drinks the cup of the Lord in an unworthy manner will be guilty of profaning the body and blood of the Lord. Let a man examine himself, and so eat the bread and drink of the cup. For anyone who eats and drinks without discerning the body, eats and drinks judgment upon himself.

In this text of St. Paul we have the oldest account of the eucharist. St. Paul says that he has "received" this tradition and "delivered" it to the recipients of his letter. These words are technical terms for transmitting special religious teaching and religious observances: St. Paul probably received this tradition about the eucharist from the disciples who accompanied our Lord whom he met after his conversion to Christianity.

We have suggested in the previous commentary that Jesus' passion and death took place on the Jewish feast of the Passover and that the eucharist would be instituted at the Passover meal held in the evening. The atmosphere would be one of

1. Translation from Theodor H. Gaster, *Festivals of the Jewish Year*, New York, 1964, p. 48.

earnest expectation, for the Jewish people expected the Messiah to come on Passover night, just as they believed God saved them from the bondage of Egypt on the first Passover night. There was an ancient saying, "In that night they [the Jews] were redeemed and in that night they will be redeemed" (Mek. Ex. 12: 42). Even the Christian writers remarked this, as for example when St. Jerome says, "It is a tradition of the Jews that the Messiah will come at midnight according to the manner of the time in Egypt when the Passover was [first] celebrated" (*Commentary on Matthew* 25: 6). It was on this night of expectation that Jesus instituted the eucharist. This was the messianic meal which anticipated the messianic banquet in the world to come. Pertinent to this messianic expectation is an interesting custom performed during the Passover meal and in all likelihood obtaining in the pre-Christian era. The celebrant of the Passover meal took the middle loaf of the three loaves lying before him and broke off a piece which was called the *aphikoman*. He hid this piece of bread until the end of the meal and then the guests consumed it when all the ceremonies were completed. It is thought that the name given to this piece of bread means "He that cometh" and that it symbolized the Messiah, who would be broken off from his people for a little while (compare John 16: 16-28) and then restored to them. The consummation of this little piece of bread symbolized that the nation would once again be complete and perfect when the Messiah returned.[1]

When Jesus took bread and said, "This is my body," it was probably the *aphikoman* which he used. Jesus probably recited the Jewish prayers which came before and then after the main dish of the Passover meal and appended his own words of interpretation concerning the bread and wine. But this would have been preceded by a meditation or discourse on the meaning of the Passover meal. It is important to realize this fact, because this would mean that the disciples were prepared for the words of interpretation and would not be surprised when

1. D. Daube, *He That Cometh*, October 1966, pp. 6–20.

Jesus identified himself with the piece of bread which symbolized the Messiah. Jewish tradition already regarded the different elements of the meal as symbols of events in redemption history. The celebrant would explain that the unleavened bread was the bread of affliction, which the Israelites "ate" in the land of Egypt. The bitter herbs, as we have already seen, symbolized the slavery which they underwent; the fruit purée resembled the clay which they used for making the bricks and the buildings of the Egyptians. The Passover lamb was a memorial of the fact that God passed over the houses of the Isralites and through the power of the blood of the lamb left their first-born sons immune from the plague which killed the first-born sons of Egypt.

Body and Blood

Consonant with this symbolism, then, Jesus would give a deeper meaning to the elements of the bread and wine. He interpreted the bread and wine to be his body and his blood. This expression "body and blood" has a double meaning: (1) it denotes man in contrast to God or supernatural powers; (2) it also denotes the component parts of the body, especially with reference to sacrificed animals, for in the animal sacrifices the blood was separated from the body. By using the phrase "body and blood," especially with its second meaning, Jesus was applying to himself technical language from the Jewish sacrificial ceremony. This is seen even more clearly from Mark 14: 24, who refers to Jesus' blood being "poured out." So "body and blood" denotes a killing wherein the blood is drained from the flesh. This means that Jesus spoke of himself as a sacrifice. At this Passover meal Jesus possibly also interpreted the Passover lamb to be a symbol of himself and his sacrifice on Calvary. We find this idea, for example, in I Corinthians 5: 7f., where Jesus is actually called the Passover lamb. So when Jesus said, "This is my [sacrificial] body," and, "This is my [sacrificial] blood,"

168

he was probably speaking of himself as the eschatological Passover lamb who represents the perfect fulfillment of the Egyptian Passover lamb and all the Passovers which were kept from that time onward until the time of Jesus. Further, when Jesus broke the bread, he symbolized the state to which his body would be subjected, and when the wine was poured out, the blood of the grape symbolized the outpouring of his own blood. At this Passover meal, then, Jesus, as it were, dramatized what was to happen on the morrow, Good Friday.

Blood of Isaac as the "Passover Lamb"

However, we must not forget that the Passover lambs were offered in memory of the sacrifice of Isaac. Through this connection they were held to have a redemptive power. In a Jewish commentary on Exodus, we read, "I [God] will see the blood of the Passover and make atonement for you" (*Ex. R.* 15, 12).

Jesus portrayed his death as the last redemptive Passover sacrifice which ushered in the new covenant. The new covenant was that of which Jeremiah the prophet spoke:

Behold, the days are coming, saith the Lord, when I will make a new covenant with the house of Israel and the house of Judah not like the covenant which I made with their fathers when I took them by the hand to bring them out of the land of Egypt, my covenant which they broke, though I was their husband, saith the Lord. But this is the covenant which I will make with the house of Israel after those days, saith the Lord; I will put my law within them, and I will write it upon their hearts: and I will be their God, and they shall be my people. And no longer shall each man teach his neighbor and each his brother, saying, "Know the Lord," for they shall all know me, from the least of them to the greatest, saith the Lord; for I will forgive their iniquity, and will remember their sin no more.

(Jeremiah 31: 31–34)

169

The "Last Testament" of Jesus

The new covenant could be regarded as the last will or testament of Jesus whereby we inherit his blessings. In Jewish tradition it was common to speak of a farewell meal enacted between father and son before the father was taken out of this world. One recalls, for example, Isaac and Jacob. When the meal had been consumed, the father gave his blessing to the son and this blessing could not be taken back. So at this last Passover meal, Jesus imparted the blessing of forgiveness of sins and the graces of redemption to his sons or disciples: they had a share in the redemptive power of his death. The disciples represented the new people of God or the new Israel, and through them Jesus' blessing was passed down to us. To participate in the redemptive death of Jesus and to become part of the new Israel is the greatest gift Jesus could have given on the night before he died.

Do This in Remembrance

We must now consider the injunction of Jesus, "Do this in remembrance of me." To the Hebrew, "remembrance" was no mere intellectual reflection. Memorial has a close association with the Hebrew concept of name which denotes a man's whole personality and power. When one remembers a person or a name, one, as it were, makes the person really present again. He becomes vitally alive to those who remember him and he influences them in a special way. When the priest and people remember Christ in the eucharist they experience an intimate relationship with him. But this remembrance takes on an even deeper significance when we realize that the phrase "Do this in remembrance of me" can also mean, "Do this that God may remember me [Jesus]." In remembering Jesus in the eucharist, one lifts the only begotten Son of God before his Heavenly Father, re-enacting, as it were, all that he did and said and

170

achieved in his earthly life and by his resurrection and ascension.

THE THIRD READING, JOHN 13: 1–15. JESUS WASHES THE DISCIPLES' FEET AND JUDAS BETRAYS JESUS

Now before the feast of the Passover, when Jesus knew that his hour had come to depart out of this world to the Father, having loved his own who were in the world, he loved them to the end. And during supper, when the devil had already put it into the heart of Judas Iscariot, Simon's son, to betray him, Jesus, knowing that the Father had given all things into his hands, and that he had come from God and was going to God, rose from supper, laid aside his garments, and girded himself with a towel. Then he poured water into a basin, and began to wash his disciples' feet, and to wipe them with the towel, with which he was girded. He came to Simon Peter; and Peter said to him, "Lord, why do you wash my feet?" Jesus answered him, "What I am doing you do not know now, but afterwards you will understand." Peter said to him, "You shall never wash my feet." Jesus answered him, "If I do not wash you, you have no part in me." Simon Peter said to him, "Lord, not my feet only but also my hands and my head!" Jesus said to him, "He who has bathed does not need to wash, except for his feet, but he is clean all over; and you are clean, but not all of you." For he knew who was to betray him; that was why he said, "You are not all clean." When he had washed their feet, and taken his garments, and resumed his place, he said to them, "Do you know what I have done to you? You call me teacher and Lord; and you are right, for so I am. If I then, your Lord and teacher, have washed your feet, you also ought to wash one another's feet. For I have given you an example, that you also should do as I have done to you."

The Dispute About Seating

St. John is the only evangelist who records this incident of Christ's washing of the disciples' feet. It appears to have taken place at the Last Supper and it may be associated with the dis-

171

pute which arose among the disciples which is recorded in Luke 22: 24-31:

A dispute also arose among them, which of them was regarded as the greatest. And he said to them, "The kings of the gentiles exercise lordship over them; and those in authority over them are called benefactors. But not so with you; rather let the greatest among you become as the youngest, and the leader as one who serves. For which is the greater, one who sits at table, or one who serves? Is it not the one who sits at table? But I am among you as one who serves. You are those who have continued with me in my trials; as my father appointed a kingdom for me, so do I appoint you that you may eat and drink at my table in my kingdom, and sit on thrones judging the twelve tribes of Israel. Simon, Simon, behold, Satan demanded to have you, that he might sift you like wheat, but I have prayed for you that your faith may not fail; and when you have turned again, strengthen my brethren." (Luke 22: 24–31)

The Lucan incident did occur just after Jesus had instituted the eucharist. The quarrel may have arisen because of the seating arrangements at the Last Supper (see Luke 14: 7-11). In all probability, Jesus and his disciples would be reclining on pillows, a symbol of the freedom acquired through the events of the first exodus. They would be lying on their left sides, leaning on their left arms with their feet stretched out toward the ground: each guest would occupy a separate couch or pillow. The couches would be arranged in the form of a long horseshoe, leaving one end of the table open to facilitate serving. The celebrant would be placed in the middle of one side, and we know from the Gospels that John was placed on the right-hand side of Jesus so that he would be at one end of the horseshoe shape. St. Peter appears to have been opposite him at the other end of the horseshoe, and Judas seems to have been on Jesus' left. Perhaps the very positions which they occupied gave rise to a discussion about their rank and honor. Jesus, as celebrant, would perform a ceremonial washing of his hands before the rest of the guests did so later on during the service. Perhaps it was at this preliminary washing of hands that Jesus performed this unusual gesture of washing the disciples' feet. This would have astonished the disciples, for according to Jewish custom even a Hebrew slave did not perform this menial task for his master. Neither did a disciple do this for his teacher. In the *Talmud* one reads:

Rabbi Joshua b. Levi ruled: all manner of service that a slave must render to his master a student must render to his teacher, except that of taking off his shoes. [Only a Canaanite slave performs this menial service, and a student performing it might be mistaken for such a slave.] Raba explained: this ruling [that a student would not assist his teacher in taking off his shoes] applies only to a place where he is not known but where he is known there can be no objection. R. Ashi: even where he is not known the ruling applies . . .[1]

By performing this humiliating and menial task Jesus showed that the Messiah himself took the form of a servant (compare Philippians 2). He put aside his lordship and worldly glory and, as it were, placed himself in the lowest social class. This was a fitting conclusion to his whole life, wherein he had comported himself as one who came to serve, not as one who came to be served. In the passage from St. Luke, Jesus indicated that the disciples had already shared some of his trials: they would share even more, but they would also participate in his glory. However, they must "empty" themselves, even as he had emptied himself and taken the form of a servant.

The Washing: A Symbol of Baptism and Priesthood

Some scholars have seen a symbol of baptism in the ceremony which Jesus performed. First, however, we should consider the priestly aspect of it. Among the lessons read around the feast of Passover was the following from Numbers 8: 6ff.:

1. Translation from W. D. Davies, *The Setting of the Sermon on the Mount,* Cambridge, 1964 p. 455.

Take the Levites from among the children of Israel and cleanse them. Sprinkle the water of expiation upon them, and let them wash, and cleanse themselves. And Aaron shall offer the Levites . . . that it may be theirs to do the service of the Lord. . . . For they are wholly given unto me from among the children of Israel. . . . I have sanctified them for myself . . . and the Levites purified themselves from sin, and they washed their clothes.

We know that there were no special laws for laymen with regard to washing feet, but that there was an obligation on behalf of the priests (see Exodus 30: 9-21). When Jesus said to Peter, "If I do not wash you, you have no part in me," he probably meant that St. Peter would have no portion in the priesthood of Christ unless he were washed in this way. As the Father had "given all things into his hands," Jesus by this priestly washing put all things into the hands of his disciples. According to Deuteronomy 14, the Levites had no worldly inheritance, for they were the Lord's portion; and in Deuteronomy 10: 8-9 we read:

. . . The Lord set apart the tribe of Levi to carry the ark of the covenant of the Lord, to stand before the Lord to minister to him and to bless in his name, to this day. Therefore Levi has no portion or inheritance with his brothers; the Lord is his inheritance, as the Lord your God said to him.

So the washing of the disciples' feet may symbolize their inheritance of the priesthood of Christ. This they showed especially when they performed the eucharist in memory of Jesus.

Yet we cannot neglect the allusions to the sacrament of baptism, to the priesthood of the laity, which appear to be implied in this text. One notices especially the words "washed" and "clean" in verse 10. These words call to mind the phraseology used in the early Church to designate baptism and its effect. One reads, for example, in Ephesians 5: 25-27:

Husbands, love your wives, as Christ loved the church and gave himself up for her, that he might *sanctify* her, having *cleansed* her by the *washing* of water with the word, that he might present the

174

church to himself in splendor, without spot or wrinkle or any such thing, that she might be holy and without blemish.

In some non-western rites, the washing of the feet of the bride had special significance. Jesus, the bridegroom, a synonym which we have had occasion to mention more than once, washed the feet of his bride, that is, the Church, before he died to ransom her. In this action, Jesus' great love was shown. This love will be more fully illustrated in the readings for Good Friday, when we see Jesus as the Suffering Servant of Yahweh: this role he began to play when he dressed as a servant and washed the disciples' feet.

Intercession

Holy Thursday

The response is

Jesus, meek and humble of heart, hear us.

(1) That we may truly have the mind of the Lord Jesus within us, let us pray to the Lord.
(2) That we may be prepared to pour out our lives for the Lord Jesus, let us pray . . .
(3) That we may celebrate the Holy Mass in the Spirit of Jesus at the Last Supper, let us pray . . .
(4) That we may fully realize the resurrected presence of Christ in the Eucharist, let us pray . . .
(5) That those confined to homes or hospitals may be able to receive the eucharist daily, let us pray . . .
(6) For all priests and bishops that they may celebrate the liturgy for God's glory and the edification of his people, let us pray . . .
(7) That we may refuse no menial or humiliating task for our neighbors, let us pray . . .
(8) For nurses and other people who give personal attention

175

to others that they may do this with the grace and love of Christ, let us pray . .

(9) For ordinands to the priesthood or diaconate that they may be prepared to share the sacrifices of Christ, let us pray . . .

(10) In jubilant thanksgiving for the eucharist, let us pray . . .

GOOD FRIDAY

We are accustomed to viewing Good Friday as a day for mourning the death of the Lord. The liturgy seems to reinforce the atmosphere of sorrow. The sanctuary is bare, the organ is silent. It is the single day in the year when there is no eucharistic celebration. At first glance, the Church seems to be prostrate with grief.

But if we begin to look at the words of the liturgy, it is clear that this is more than a service of mourning. The sober facts of Jesus' suffering and death stand at the center of the service in all their harsh reality. There is no attempt to mask or soften them. But these sad facts are not marshalled to evoke grief. They are seen in the perspective of Jesus' resurrection, of his victory over sin and death. His death has become a source of life for the world.

The cross indeed dominates the service, but the cross is a sign of victory. The readings portray Jesus' death as the act of deliverance which redeems mankind. The service of the veneration of the cross "translates" the readings into poetic terms. The reproaches are a plaintive acknowledgement that our sins have nailed Christ to the cross. But even this sad chant is charged with the sense that God's love has overcome our sin. The acknowledgement of Christ's triumph clearly emerges with the antiphon which concludes the reproaches:

We adore your cross, O Lord: we praise and glorify your holy resurrection. For behold, by reason of that wood, joy has come into all the world. (*Missal,* p. 163)

177

The refrain, *Crux Fidelis,* echoes the same theme:

> Faithful cross, O tree all beauteous!
> Tree all peerless and divine
> Not a grove on earth can show us
> such a flower and leaf as thine.
> Sweet the nails, and sweet the wood,
> laden with so sweet a load! (*Missal,* p. 163)

The veneration is concluded with the *Pange Lingua,* a victory hymn:

> Sing, my tongue, the Saviour's glory; tell his triumph far and wide . . . (*Missal,* p. 163)

The antiphons for the communion service are similarly charged with the sense of joy in the saving act of God:

> We adore you, O Christ, and we bless you, because by your holy cross you have redeemed the world.

> By a tree we were made slaves, and by the holy cross we are set free: the fruit of the tree seduced us, the Son of God has redeemed us.

> Saviour of the world, save us: you who by your cross and blood have redeemed us, help us, we implore you, our God. (*Missal,* p. 167)

The Good Friday service, then, is actually an Easter service. It is not without its sorrow, but that sorrow is transfigured by the joy of the resurrection. How much the Good Friday service is really an Easter liturgy can be seen most clearly by comparing the Good Friday hymns and readings with the Easter Preface:

It is truly right and just, proper and helpful toward salvation, that we always praise you, O Lord, but more especially so at this season, when Christ our Pasch was sacrificed. For he is the true Lamb who has taken away the sins of the world, who overcame death for us by dying himself, and who restored us to life by his own resurrection . . . (*Missal,* p. 222)

178

That preface is simply a brief summary of the passion according to John.

A problem remains: the physical atmosphere of the Church seems to contradict the spirit of the readings and prayers. What are we to make of the stripped sanctuary, the somber music, the unveiling of the crucifix, and, above all, the absence of a eucharistic celebration? Are these not tokens of mourning? In reality, they are not. Many features of the Good Friday service are very old. At the time of the origin of the Good Friday liturgy, all weekday services in Rome were similar to this one. The ancient Roman liturgy was particularly noteworthy for its stark simplicity. Roman churches had little decoration. The altar was left uncovered, except on days when there was a eucharist. There was strong resistance to the introduction of musical instruments (for a long time, the attitude of the Roman Church to the organ was rather like the attitude of some people today with regard to the guitar—it was viewed as a pagan instrument), and the chants were kept as simple as possible. For a long time, there were few eucharistic celebrations on weekdays.

Because of the importance of Good Friday, there was a reluctance to change the character of the service. If our Good Friday liturgy is rather somber, it is because the Church is Roman, not because the Church is sad.

While there was a reluctance to change the service, an important addition was made—the veneration of the cross was "imported" from Jerusalem. The cross which was unveiled was a jeweled cross, a symbol of victory. That the Roman Church saw no contradiction between her sober liturgy of the Word and the exuberant new rite from the East shows that the Good Friday service was understood as a celebration of Christ's triumph, not as a day of mourning.

Unfortunately, we are still left with a contrast between the setting of the service and its actual meaning. It seems dangerous to retrain the features of sixth-century Roman practice when those features hinder a full understanding of the liturgy. Surely we should celebrate the eucharist on this day. The eucharist, after all, is the divinely instituted way in which we "proclaim the death of the Lord until he comes." It has been suggested that Good Friday vestments should be red, as they are in the liturgy of Milan. Since red is the color for martyrs' festivals, it would seem appropriate to commemorate the paradigm of all martyrdom with red vestments. Also the practice of restricting parishes to one or two liturgies seems unnecessary. Good Friday is practically a public holiday in many places, and few parishes can accommodate all who can attend services in one or two liturgies. Such reforms could help to reveal the true character of Good Friday to us.

Good Friday

The readings for Good Friday present:
- (1) Jesus as the Suffering Servant;
- (2) the Day of Atonement;
- (3) Jesus as True King.

THE FIRST READING, ISAIAH 52: 13—53: 12. THE SUFFERING SERVANT

Behold, my servant shall prosper,
he shall be exalted and lifted up,
and shall be very high.
As many were astonished at him—
his appearance was so marred,
beyond human semblance,
and his form beyond that of the sons of men—
so shall he startle many nations;
kings shall shut their mouths because of him;
for that which has not been told them, they shall see,
and that which they have not heard they shall understand.
Who has believed what we have heard?

180

GOOD FRIDAY

And to whom has the arm of the Lord been revealed?
For he grew up before him like a young plant,
and like a root out of dry ground;
he had no form or comeliness that we should look at him,
and no beauty that we should desire him.
He was despised and rejected by men;
a man of sorrows, and acquainted with grief;
and as one from whom men hide their faces
he was despised, and we esteemed him not.
Surely he has borne our griefs
and carried our sorrows;
yet we esteemed him stricken,
smitten by God, and afflicted.
But he was wounded for our transgressions,
he was bruised for our iniquities;
upon him was the chastisement that made us whole,
and with his stripes we are healed.
All we like sheep have gone astray;
we have turned everyone to his own way;
and the Lord has laid on him
the iniquity of us all.
He was oppressed and he was afflicted,
yet he opened not his mouth;
like a lamb that is led to the slaughter,
and like a sheep that before its shearers is dumb,
so he opened not his mouth.
By oppression and judgment he was taken away;
and as for his generation, who considered
that he was cut off out of the land of the living,
stricken for the transgression of my people?
And they made his grave with the wicked,
and with a rich man in his death,
although he had done no violence,
and there was no deceit in his mouth.
Yet it was the will of the Lord to bruise him;
he put him to grief;
when he made himself an offering for sin,
he shall see his offspring, he shall prolong his days;

the will of the Lord shall prosper in his hand;
he shall see the fruit of the travail of his soul and be satisfied;
by his knowledge shall the righteous one, my servant,
make many to be accounted righteous;
and he shall bear their iniquities.
Therefore I shall divide him a portion with the great,
and he shall divide the spoil with the strong;
because he *poured out his soul to death,*
and was numbered with the transgressors;
yet he bore the sin of *many,*
and made intercession for the transgressors.

(The italicized portions are especially applicable to Jesus.)

The Interpretation of the Poem

This poem is contained in the second part of the Book of Isaiah, which was written much later than the first thirty-nine chapters. It reflects a period of history when the Jewish nation and Jerusalem had been conquered by the Babylonians and many of the inhabitants were in exile in Babylon. This was the occasion of a great crisis of faith for Israel. It must have been difficult for them to understand, after all of God's promises to them, why they should be conquered by heathen nations. The prophet appears to be encouraging them and opening up a new vista of hope: he shows that God is not only God of the Jewish nation but that he is a universal king and, therefore, that he is sovereign over every historical event, whether it be of the Jewish nation or of any other nation in the world.

However, the more detailed interpretation of this passage is very difficult and many different theories about it have been propounded. Some scholars think that Isaiah portrays the suffering of the whole nation of Israel; others suggest that the prophet himself suffered for the people and that one of his disciples wrote this description afterwards. Others think that the passage describes Moses or Jeremiah or Isaac or one of the kings of Israel, such as Jehoiachim. This king reigned in the sixth century and rebelled against his overlord, the king of Babylon. He was taken into exile, and some have suggested that the foreign king offered him as a sacrificial substitute for the people.

These theories are very complex, but the most important feature of the text is the idea of the servant undergoing vicarious or atoning suffering, perhaps not only for the Jewish nation but for other nations as well. The sharp antithesis between the individual and the community which is so familiar to our western minds was foreign to the people of the Old Testament and to the contemporaries of Jesus. So, without difficulty, they could think of this passage as referring both to an individual (prophet or king) and/or to the whole community of Israel. Although there seems to be very little evidence that the Jews expected the Messiah to suffer, they did realize the grace brought through the suffering of martyrs or prophets. There is, for example, a close parallel between the ideas found in Isaiah 53 and those found in Wisdom 5: 1-6a:

Then the righteous man will stand with great confidence
in the presence of those who afflicted him,
and those who make light of his labors.
When they see him, they will be shaken with dreadful fear.
and they will be amazed at his unexpected salvation.
They will speak to one another in repentance,
and in anguish of spirit they will groan, and say,
"This is the man whom we once held in derision
and made a byword of approach—we fools!
We thought that his life was madness
and that his end was without honor.
Why hath he been numbered among the Sons of God?
And why is his lot among the saints?
So it was we who strayed from the ways of truth,
and the light of righteousness did not shine on us, . . .

183

Further in Jewish writings the idea that suffering wins God's favor and makes atonement for men is quite frequent. Poverty and exile had atoning power. When men were dying or in danger, they were taught to say, "Let my death make atonement for all my sins" (*Ber.* 60a; *Sanh.* 6. 2). If this were true of ordinary death, how much more would it be true of a righteous man's death or of martyrs? In IV Maccabees 6 there is a description of Eleazar, a pious Jew, suffering martyrdom for his beliefs. The text reads, "He was about to give up the ghost, he lifted up his eyes to God and said, 'Thou, O God, knowest that though I might save myself I am dying by fiery torments for thy Law. Be merciful unto thy people, and let our punishment be a satisfaction in their behalf. Make my blood their purification, and take my soul to ransom their souls.' "

This passage from Isaiah, therefore, brings before us the efficacy of suffering and death, an idea which occupied an important place in the minds of people by the time of Christ.

This teaching must surely have been acceptable to Jesus, and he may have thought of his own mission in the terms of the Suffering Servant of Yahweh: at least we can say that the early Church described Jesus' work in this context. For example, when Philip met the Ethiopian in Samaria, the Ethiopian was reading from Isaiah and he asked Philip, "About whom, pray, does the prophet say this, about himself or about someone else?" (Acts 8: 34). So Philip showed him how Jesus had fulfilled the role of the Suffering Servant. We find another very clear reference to this in Luke 22: 37.

It was comparatively easy for the early Church to compare the servant of Yahweh and Jesus. If we read through the text of Isaiah, many details are common to both of them.

(1) In the beginning of the passage, it is said that the servant shall be "lifted up"; this means that he will be suspended or hung. The sentence does not necessarily refer to crucifixion, but neither does it exclude the idea. It portrays the corpse of the servant suspended on high and exposed to the wondering gaze

184

of the crowds. His appearance is marred, looking almost sub-human. The reaction of the crowd is to pucker up their mouths at the sight. The line which is translated, "So shall he startle many nations," should probably read, "So shall many nations despise him; kings shall shut their mouths at him."

(2) The phrase "He took our infirmities and bore our diseases" is quoted verbatim by Matthew, but in another context (Matthew 8: 17b). This verse suggests that the servant appeared to the people to be a sick man, probably a leper, but later the people come to the realization that their own illnesses, diseases, and deformities have been transferred to him, just as their sins were transferred to the scapegoat described in Leviticus 16. Isaiah seems to wish his readers to understand that the repulsive condition of the servant was a reflection of the almost sub-human conditions to which their sins had reduced them.

(3) The servant of Yahweh seems to have been pierced or stabbed (verse 5): Christians might see in this the piercing of Jesus' hands and feet.

(4) In this verse, too, there appears to be a reference to flogging.

(5) Further, the servant, like Jesus, remained silent like a lamb before the slaughter.

(6) Like Jesus, the servant was taken "by oppression and judgment." This appears to mean that he was not given an opportunity to prove his innocence by a judicial trial.

(7) In both cases, that of the servant and of Jesus, the promise of spiritual posterity recalls God's covenant with David of which we read in II Samuel 7: 16 and Ezekiel 37: 26. The servant could be presented as a royal figure of the Davidic line (see pp. 235–236 below).

(8) The servant's vicarious death is especially obvious in the sentence "he poured out his soul to death, and was numbered with the transgressors; yet he bore the sins of many . . ." The "many" may refer merely to Israel, but it is more likely that it

185

also embraces the Gentile nations. This recalls our Lord's words at the Last Supper. He took the cup, and he said, "This is my blood of the covenant, which is *poured out* for *many* for the forgiveness of sins" (Matthew 26: 28).

From the above brief discussion we can see that although the prophet Isaiah did not consciously direct his prophecy toward Jesus, and although Jesus himself may not have described his mission explicitly in the terms of the Suffering Servant of Yahweh, yet the early Christians would not find it difficult to apply this text especially to Jesus.

THE SECOND READING, HEBREWS 9: 11–15. THE BLOOD OF CHRIST CLEANSES US

But when Christ appeared as a high priest of the good things that have come, then through the greater and more perfect tent (not made with hands, that is, not of this creation) he entered once for all into the holy place, taking not the blood of goats and calves, but his own blood, thus securing an eternal redemption. For if the sprinkling of defiled persons with the blood of goats and bulls and with the ashes of a heifer sanctifies for the purification of the flesh, how much more shall the blood of Christ, who through the eternal Spirit offered himself without blemish to God, purify your conscience from dead works to serve the living God. Therefore he is the mediator of a new covenant, so that those who are called may receive the promised eternal inheritance, since a death has occurred which redeems them from the transgressions under the first covenant.

The background of this text is the ritual of the Day of Atonement when the high priest of the Jewish people entered alone into the holy of holies to offer sacrifice in expiation of the sin of Israel. This is a description of this particular part of the ritual for the Day of Atonement when the temple was standing.

He [the high priest] took the frypan [for incense] in his right hand and the ladle in his left hand. He walked through the sanctuary until he reached the space between the two curtains that separated

186

the sanctuary from the holy of holies, and between them was a cubit's space. . . . The outer one was folded up on the south side, and the inner one on the north side. He walked between them until he reached the north side; when he arrived at the north side he turned around to the south side walking around with the curtain until he arrived at the ark [or where the ark used to be]; when he reached the ark he set the frypan between the two bars [of the ark]; he heaped up incense on the burning coals and the whole compartment was filled with smoke; he came forth and went along by the way he entered, and in the other compartment he offered up a short prayer, but he did not prolong his prayer so as not to dismay the Jews [for fear lest he should have died in the holy of holies]. After the Ark was taken away a stone lay there from the time of the early prophets and it was called foundation . . . He took the blood from he who was stirring it; he went into the place where he had entered [the holy of holies] and stood in the place whereon he had stood, and tossed [or sprinkled] [the blood] from it once upwards and seven times downwards, and he did not attempt to toss up on high or below but as if wielding a whip. And thus he used to count, "one, one and one, one and two, one and three, one and four, one and five, one and six, one and seven." He came out and set it [the basin with the blood] down upon the golden stand in the sanctuary. (Yoma 5: 1)

All this ritual was superseded when Jesus died upon the cross and the veil of the temple is reported to have been rent in two. The ceremony sounds gory and repugnant. But blood to the Hebrew meant life, and the precious blood of Jesus means the life of Jesus which gives life, warmth, energy, color, beauty, and everything which is good and vital to his body, which is the Church. St. Catherine of Siena had a deep understanding of this idea of blood and she compared it to fire. She used to say, "The blood was sprinkled in the fire of love; there is no blood without fire, and no fire without blood. In the sprinkling of blood we receive the burning fire of love." Perhaps this is the way in which we should reflect upon the blood of Jesus which transfuses new spiritual life into us.

187

The Third Reading, John 18: 1—19: 42. The Passion of Jesus

The Arrest of Jesus in the Garden (*John 18: 1–14*)

When Jesus had spoken these words, he went forth with his disciples across the Kidron valley, where there was a garden, which he and his disciples entered. Now Judas, who betrayed him, also knew the place; for Jesus often met there with his disciples. So Judas, procuring a band of soldiers and some officers from the chief priests and the Pharisees, went there with lantern and torches and weapons. Then Jesus, knowing all that was to befall him, came forward and said to them, "Whom do you seek?" They answered him, "Jesus of Nazareth." Jesus said to them, "I am he." Judas, who betrayed him, was standing with them. When he said to them, "I am he," they drew back and fell to the ground. Again he asked them, "Whom do you seek?" And they said, "Jesus of Nazareth." Jesus answered, "I told you that I am he; so, if you seek me, let these men go." This was to fulfill the word which he had spoken, "Of those whom thou gavest me I lost not one." Then Simon Peter, having a sword, drew it and struck the high priest's slave and cut off his right ear. The slave's name was Malchus. Jesus said to Peter, "Put your sword into its sheath; shall I not drink the cup which the Father has given me?"

So the band of soldiers and their captain and the officers of the Jews seized Jesus and bound him. First they led him to Annas; for he was the father-in-law of Caiaphas, who was high priest that year. It was Caiaphas who had given counsel to the Jews that it was expedient that one man should die for the people.

Gethsemane According to St. John

When we considered the passion of Jesus according to St. Matthew, we paid special attention to the fulfillment of prophecy. Now, when we turn to St. John, we shall remark especially the concept of divine kingship. This was clearly shown as the life of

188

Jesus drew to a close. St. John reports that Jesus and his disciples entered a garden where Jesus often met with his followers, but John does not name the garden. Perhaps we are meant to be reminded of the Garden of Eden and to see Jesus as the second Adam. This idea is substantiated by the fact that St. John has told us that the devil entered Judas, (John 13: 2), and then took full possession of him (John 13: 27). The devil in Judas went to meet Jesus just as the devil, symbolized by the serpent in the Garden of Eden, faced Adam and Eve. St. John does not report the agony and anguish which Jesus endured in the garden: he has already intimated this in John 12: 27–36, but in the final stage of his drama, John wishes to convey the superb majesty of the second Adam, who will win a final victory over Satan. The Johannine picture of Jesus in the garden shows a man of supreme poise, purposefulness, and unparalleled courage. Jesus' utter calm contrasted strikingly with the militant band of soldiers who approached him. For St. John, it is no mere human adversary who approaches Jesus, but the power of supernatural wickedness; and Jesus is shown confronting this evil in a spirit of total acceptance of the will of God: for this acceptance he had prayed in John 12: 27–28. Judas and the soldiers approached, but no betrayal by a kiss is recorded. In fact, no conversation ensued between Judas and Jesus, and it seems that Judas' only function was to direct the party toward Jesus. Neither did Judas identify Jesus, but Jesus identified himself. Everyone seemed incapable of action in the presence of the divine Jesus. He asked them whom they sought and they answered, "Jesus of Nazareth." Jesus replied, "I am." These words had a double meaning; firstly, they meant "I am Jesus," but secondly they conveyed the idea of the divinity of Jesus. The phrase which we translate "I am" resembles the name of God which was revealed to Moses in the burning bush. When Moses asked God what his name was, he replied, "I am that I am." The Jews avoided using this Hebrew phrase, for they deemed it sacrilegious to pronounce the proper name of God.

189

Jesus used a phrase akin to the name of God and this, to the Jews, was blasphemy. When Jesus said, "I am," the soldiers drew back and fell to the ground. This was the characteristic gesture of people in the presence of the divine.

Jesus did not wish to use weapons and he requested Peter to sheath his sword, replying, "Shall I not drink the cup which the Father has given me?" This was the cup of the terrible judgments of God (see Rev. 16: 19), and St. John introduces it, not within a prayer pronounced by Jesus, that it might, if possible, pass from him, but in a simple sentence which showed a calm and purposeful acceptance. Jesus' suffering would be, not the force of circumstances, but the acceptance of the fulfillment of the work appointed him by his Father. Yet while accepting the suffering for himself, Jesus requested that his disciples be allowed to go away safely. The good shepherd preserved the sheep who had been given into his charge. This symbolized Jesus' perpetual love and care toward those who followed him. This is thrown into sharper relief when St. John records St. Peter's denial of the Master who showed so much concern for them. We notice that, whereas Jesus in the garden twice said, "I am," in contrast, St. Peter, on being interrogated concerning his association with Jesus, twice declared, "I am not." Once again we see St. John's artistry.

St. John's account of the scene in the garden differs in many points from the Synoptics, and is the prelude to his teaching about the divine kingship.

Jesus Before Pilate (John 18: 15–40)

Simon Peter followed Jesus, and so did another disciple. As this disciple was known to the high priest, he entered the court of the high priest along with Jesus, while Peter stood outside at the door. So the other disciple, who was known to the high priest, went out and spoke to the maid who kept the door, and brought Peter in. The maid who kept the door said to Peter, "Are not you also one of this man's disciples?" He said, "I am not." Now the servants and

190

officers had made a charcoal fire, because it was cold, and they were standing and warming themselves; Peter also was with them, standing and warming himself.

The high priest then questioned Jesus about his disciples and his teaching. Jesus answered him, "I have spoken openly to the world; I have always taught in synagogues and in the temple, where all Jews come together; I have said nothing secretly. Why do you ask me? Ask those who have heard me, what I said to them; they know what I said." When he had said this, one of the officers standing by struck Jesus with his hand, saying, "Is that how you answer the high priest?" Jesus answered him, "If I have spoken wrongly, bear witness to the wrong; but if I have spoken rightly, why do you strike me?" Annas then sent him bound to Caiaphas the high priest.

Now Simon Peter was standing and warming himself. They said to him, "Are you not also one of his disciples?" He denied it and said, "I am not." One of the servants of the high priest, a kinsman of the man whose ear Peter had cut off, asked, "Did I not see you in the garden with him?" Peter again denied it; and, at once, the cock crowed.

Then they led Jesus from the house of Caiaphas to the praetorium. It was early. They themselves did not enter the praetorium, so that they might not be defiled, but might eat the Passover. So Pilate went out to them and said, "What accusation do you bring against this man?" They answered him, "If this man were not an evildoer, we would not have handed him over." Pilate said to them, "Take them yourselves and judge him by your own law." The Jews said to him, "It is not lawful for us to put any man to death." This was to fulfill the word which Jesus had spoken to show by what death he was to die.

Pilate entered the praetorium again and called Jesus, and said to him, "Are you the King of the Jews?" Jesus answered, "Do you say this of your own accord, or did others say it to you about me?" Pilate answered, "Am I a Jew? Your own nation and the chief priests have handed you over to me; what have you done?" Jesus answered, "My kingship is not of this world; if my kingship were of this world, my servants would fight, that I might not be handed over to the Jews; but my kingship is not from the world." Pilate said to him, "So you are a king?" Jesus answered, "You say that I am a king. For this I was born, and for this I have come into the world,

191

to bear witness to the truth. Every one who is of the truth hears my voice." Pilate said to him, "What is truth?"

After he had said this, he went out to the Jews again, and told them, "I find no crime in him. But you have a custom that I should release one man for you at the Passover; will you have me release for you the King of the Jews?" They cried out again, "Not this man, but Barabbas!" Now Barabbas was a robber.

The King of the Jews Before the Roman Governor

St. John's account of Jesus' trial before the Jews is extremely short. Perhaps he wished our attention to be focused upon Pilate and Jesus and the antithesis between their respective authorities or kingships. The proceedings before the Roman authorities are described in far more detail and with a great deal more drama and subtlety than in the other gospels. Pilate appears as a figure of interest and authority and the Jewish leaders give the impression of guile and persistence. They even reach the point of turning their own political subjection to their own advantage: they know how to exploit Pilate's fears and weaknesses. The action and dialogue revolve around the idea of kingship. Indeed, the word is used twelve times in this passion narrative, whereas it is used only six times in Mark, and four times in Matthew and Luke. The case before the court was an examination of a person who is supposed to have followers who would fight to secure his sovereignty. When it transpired that Jesus' followers were not willing to have recourse to arms, Pilate brought Jesus before the Jewish authorities as a mock king. He called him "King of the Jews." The Jews reacted strongly to this and when Pilate attempted to release Jesus, they emphasized the political and military aspect of kingship. They accused Jesus of high treason against Caesar, so the accusation had to be decided upon this score.

St. John's irony is evident from the very beginning. He reports the fact that the Jews remained outside the praetorium. They wished to avoid ritual uncleanness in order to keep the

192

Passover festival. They persistently plotted to kill an innocent man, the Son of God, but they were meticulous about their religious observances. Yet reflection upon the matter suggests either that St. John had added this detail or that the Jewish authorities were going to extremes. Their ritual defilement could have been removed by a bath at the end of the day, or just a few of their number could have taken part in the case, and the rest have kept kosher for the Passover (compare *Pesahim* 7: 6).

King, One Who Witnesses to Truth

The discussion concerning Jesus' kingship ensues upon the affirmation of the Jewish authorities, rightly or wrongly, that it was not lawful for them to execute capital punishment. The evangelist explains that this was to fulfill a prophecy of Jesus which showed the death he was obliged to suffer, he was to be "lifted up," to suffer the Roman, not the Jewish penalty. There is a double meaning in this word, either "to be exalted" or "to be lifted up" on the cross. When Pilate inquired about Jesus' royalty, Jesus pleaded that a political aspirant would not have permitted himself to be captured without resource to arms. But to Pilate's question, "So you are a King?", Jesus replied, "You say that I am a King," that is, "You yourself have given me the title of King." Then Jesus proceeded to explain the nature of his kingship. It was a kingship with a teaching and witnessing magisterium. Jesus entered this world so that he could witness to the truth, that is, to eternal verities which exist over and above the visible things in this world; and, especially, to the non-political, spiritual, and everlasting kingdom of God, from whence all human authority took its origin and should take its model (John 19: 11). Jesus described his kingship in terms of missionary work, that is, to bring the truth to mankind. It obliged a man to make a decision, namely, whether to follow Jesus or to reject him. This is why Jesus said, "Every one who

193

is of the truth hears my voice." This statement reflected Jesus' discourse on the good shepherd: it is the sheep who are his own who hear the shepherd's voice (John 10: 3–4). They do not hear the voice of robbers or thieves. When one sees Pilate's rather cynical question, "What is truth?", against the background of the Good Shepherd discourse, it can be seen in a new light. In the passion of St. John, we see Pilate vacillating between whether he should hear the voice of the shepherd and release Jesus or whether he should join the thieves and robbers. The incident about the release of Barabbas should also be seen against this background. St. John adds the important note that Barabbas was a robber. In the discourse on the Good Shepherd (John 10), the robber is a figure who stands in sharp contrast to the Good Shepherd. So when the Jews reject Jesus and choose Barabbas, they are refusing to hear the voice of the Good Shepherd and joining the pack of robbers. At this point, the Good Shepherd, Jesus, is about to put down his life for his sheep (10: 11, 15, 17). Complete self-forgetfulness and self-surrender for the benefit of others is the central feature of Jesus' kingship.

The Coronation (John 19: 1–4)

Then Pilate took Jesus and scourged him. And the soldiers plaited a crown of thorns, and put it on his head, and arrayed him in a purple robe; they came up to him saying, "Hail, King of the Jews!" and struck him with their hands. Pilate went out again, and said to them, "Behold, I am bringing him out to you, that you may know that I find no crime in him."

Crowning of Jesus

However, this was not the end of the discussion of Jesus' kingship. The central scene in the passion of St. John is the crowning of Jesus as king. This is followed by the great scene,

194

"Behold, the man," which is peculiar to St. John's Gospel. The soldiers plaited a crown of thorns for Jesus and arrayed him in a purple robe, then they hailed him as King of the Jews. It is obvious that the evangelist wishes us to see this scene as an investiture of a king. St. John does not note the mockery of the soldiers, indeed he omits many details which are given in the other gospels and keeps only those which emphasize the kingship of Jesus: the crown, the purple garment, and the salutation of the soldiers. Further, St. John presents this scene before the actual condemnation of Jesus, whereas St. Mark places it after the condemnation. St. John shows Jesus in the vestments of a king, and he is presented twice to the Jews, presumably with Johannine irony, wearing these so that the Jews may have an opportunity of actually proclaiming him as king (John 19: 5, 13f.). This "proclamation" precedes the exultation of Jesus upon the cross.

Behold the Man (John 19: 5–16)

So Jesus came out, wearing the crown of thorns and the purple robe. Pilate said to them, "Here is the man!" When the chief priests and the officers saw him, they cried out, "Crucify him, crucify him!" Pilate said to them, "Take him yourselves and crucify him, for I find no crime in him." The Jews answered him, "We have a law, and by that law he ought to die, because he has made himself the Son of God." When Pilate heard these words, he was the more afraid; he entered the praetorium again and said to Jesus, "Where are you from?" But Jesus gave no answer. Pilate therefore said to him, "You will not speak to me? Do you not know that I have power to release you, and power to crucify you?" Jesus answered him, "You would have no power over me unless it had been given you from above; therefore he who delivered me to you has the greater sin."

Upon this Pilate sought to release him, but the Jews cried out, "If you release this man, you are not Caesar's friend; everyone who makes himself a king sets himself against Caesar." When Pilate heard these words, he brought Jesus out and sat down on the judg-

195

ment seat at a place called The Pavement, and in Hebrew, Gabbatha. Now it was the day of Preparation of the Passover; it was about the sixth hour. He said to the Jews, "Here is your King." They cried out, "Away with him, away with him, crucify him!" Pilate said to them, "Shall I crucify your King?" The chief priests answered, "We have no king but Caesar." Then he handed him over to them to be crucified.

The Proclamation

Then follows what is perhaps the most poignant scene in the whole gospel. The king Jesus was led out before the awaiting Jews and Pilate proclaimed, "Behold, the man." There is a double meaning running throughout this scene. Jesus, attired as a king, having claimed divine honors, was presented and announced as "the man." Pilate appeared to show both pity and contempt toward both Jesus and the Jews. Yet perhaps Pilate was saying more than he meant to. The title "the man" recalled Jesus' own title "the Son of man," with its connotation of a figure who had a supernatural origin and supernatural functions. It also suggested the second Adam, who did not snatch at equality with God and who claimed a different kind of kingship from that described in Ezekiel, chapter 28. But Pilate proclaimed Jesus, not only as the man (verse 5), but also as the Jewish King (verse 14). In both cases the Jews reacted in a similar way. They said, "Crucify him, crucify him" (verse 6) and "Away with him, away with him, crucify him" (verse 15). The two proclamations made by Pilate were climaxes in the whole scene of the trial and they were met on the side of the Jews, not with the acclamation of kingship toward Jesus, but, as it were, with the reverse of acclamation, that is, dethronement. Wayne Meeks has seen a striking comparison with a passage in the prophet Zechariah, 6: 11ff., which reads:

Take from them silver and gold, and make a crown, and set it upon the head of Joshua, . . . the high priest; and say to him, "Thus says the Lord of hosts, 'Behold, the man whose name is the Branch:

196

for he shall grow up in his place, and he shall build the temple of the Lord. It is he who shall build the temple of the Lord, and shall bear royal honor, and shall sit and rule upon his throne. And there shall be a priest by his throne, and peaceful understanding shall be between them both.' " [1]

The name Joshua is an alternative form of the name Jesus, and Joshua was to be crowned as both high priest and king. We reflect, of course, that Jesus was the Branch of David and that he built a temple of the Lord, not from stone, but from living stones of men and women. He reigned over them as both king and priest (compare I Peter 2: 4–10).

Pilate's proclamation of Jesus as "the man" and as "King of the Jews" was followed by another feature found in the order of the coronation of a king. In verse 13 we read that Pilate brought Jesus out, but it is not clear whether Pilate himself sat upon the judgment seat or whether he seated Jesus upon it. But St. John probably meant to present Jesus sitting enthroned as king and symbolically judging those who were not ready to accept him. Verse 14 tells us that Jesus was "enthroned" at the sixth hour on the eve of the Passover. The Jews who cried, "We have no king but Caesar," later, at their Passover service, would proclaim their allegiance to only one king, namely, God. At the conclusion of the Hallel (Psalms 113 to 118 inclusive), at the time of Jesus, there may well have been another hymn which included the lines:

> From everlasting to everlasting thou art God;
> Beside thee we have no king, redeemer, or saviour,
> No liberator, deliverer, provider
> None who takes pity in every time of distress and trouble.
> We have no king but thee.
>
> (Quoted by Meeks, page 77)

So the Jewish authorities rejected not only the Messiah but also God, who appeared in the person of his Son. This is emphasized by the fact that the Jews asserted that Jesus had claimed to be

1. W. Meeks, *The Prophet-King,* Leiden, 1967, p. 71.

the Son of God. When Pilate heard these words he was very afraid and questioned Jesus upon this. Jesus, who had consented to admit that he was king, did not answer Pilate directly when he was questioned concerning his divine Sonship.

The Enthronement (John 19: 17–24)

So they took Jesus, and he went out, bearing his own cross, to the place called the place of a skull, which is called in Hebrew Golgotha. There they crucified him, and with him two others, one on either side, and Jesus between them. Pilate also wrote a title and put it on the cross; it read, "Jesus of Nazareth, the King of the Jews." Many of the Jews read this title, for the place where Jesus was crucified was near the city; and it was written in Hebrew, in Latin, and in Greek. The chief priests of the Jews then said to Pilate, "Do not write, 'The King of the Jews,' but, 'This man said, I am King of the Jews.' " Pilate answered, "What I have written I have written."

When the soldiers had crucified Jesus they took his garments and made four parts, one for each soldier; also his tunic. But the tunic was without seam, woven from top to bottom; so they said to one another, "Let us not tear it, but cast lots for it to see whose it shall be." This was to fulfil the scripture,

> "They parted my garments among them,
> and for my clothing they cast lots."

The Title Over the Throne

The final stage in the coronation of Jesus as king is reached in the crucifixion. St. John merely states in verse 18 that Jesus was crucified. This was the "exaltation" or lifting up of Jesus of which he had spoken previously. But all the attention of St. John is focussed upon the title which Pilate fixed to the throne or the cross, namely, "Jesus of Nazareth, the King of the Jews." St. John gives a fuller title than St. Mark (Mark 15: 26). St. John wishes to emphasize three things. First of all, he stresses that

Jesus' kingship is universal (compare the passage from Isaiah read in the first lesson): this was implied by the three languages in which the inscription was written (verse 20). Secondly, in writing this title, Pilate implicitly rejected the repudiation of the high priests that Jesus was truly king of the Jews. Thirdly, and perhaps most important of all, Pilate refused to revoke his statement, and said instead, "What I have written I have written", an ironic but firm affirmation that Jesus is truly king forever. Jesus reigned from the throne of a cross.

The Kingship of Yahweh in Ezekiel 34

Jesus' teaching about the Good Shepherd can be understood principally from Ezekiel 34. In this chapter, God contrasts himself with the shepherds of Israel. The shepherds, or kings of Israel, had abused their authority by using the flock for their own advantage. Yahweh says, "You eat the fat, you clothe yourselves with the wool, you slaughter the fatlings, but you do not feed the sheep. The weak you have not strengthened, the sick you have not healed, the crippled you have not bound up, the strayed you have not brought back, the lost you have not sought, and with harshness you have ruled them." When Yahweh looked upon the disgraceful behavior of the shepherds, he pronounced himself against them and he averred that he would require the sheep from their hands. He himself would search out the sheep and fulfill the duties which the bad shepherds had failed to accomplish. He would perform judgment against these shepherds and would put over the sheep one shepherd, "my servant David," and this servant would feed the flock. This prophecy to the prophet Ezekiel was fulfilled in the kingship of Jesus, who died for his flock. Then according to John 21 the office of prophet-king and good shepherd was passed onto St. Peter.[1]

1. This section owes much to Wayne Meeks, *The Prophet-King,* Leiden, 1967.

199

The New Eve (John 19: 25–42)

So the soldiers did this. But standing by the cross of Jesus were his mother, and his mother's sister, Mary the wife of Clopas, and Mary Magdalene. When Jesus saw his mother, and the disciple whom he loved standing near, he said to his mother, "Woman, behold, your son!" Then he said to the disciple, "Behold, your mother!" And from that hour the disciple took her to his own home.

After this Jesus, knowing that all was not finished, said (to fulfill the Scripture), "I thirst." A bowl full of vinegar stood there; so they put a sponge full of the vinegar on hyssop and held it to his mouth. When Jesus had received the vinegar, he said, "It is finished"; and he bowed his head and gave up his spirit.

Since it was the day of Preparation, in order to prevent the bodies from remaining on the cross on the sabbath (for that sabbath was a high day), the Jews asked Pilate that their legs might be broken, and that they might be taken away. So the soldiers came and broke the legs of the first, and of the other who had been crucified with him; but when they came to Jesus and saw that he was already dead, they did not break his legs. But one of the soldiers pierced his side with a spear, and at once there came out blood and water. He who saw it has borne witness—his testimony is true, and he knows that he tells the truth—that you also may believe. For these things took place that the Scripture might be fulfilled, "Not a bone of him shall be broken." And again another Scripture says, "They shall look on him whom they have pierced."

After this Joseph of Arimathea, who was a disciple of Jesus, but secretly, for fear of the Jews, asked Pilate that he might take away the body of Jesus, and Pilate gave him leave. So he came and took away his body. Nicodemus also, who had at first come to him by night, came bringing a mixture of myrrh and aloes about a hundred pounds' weight. They took the body of Jesus, and bound it in linen cloths with the spices, as is the burial custom of the Jews. Now in the place where he was crucified there was a garden, and in the garden a new tomb where no one had ever been laid. So because of the Jewish day of Preparation, as the tomb was close at hand, they laid Jesus there.

200

The Office of Mary, the New Eve

The closing scene of the passion revealed those who were of the flock of Jesus and had, indeed, heard his voice. It is interesting to note that in the little group surrounding the cross of Jesus both sides of Jesus' family are represented. There is, of course, Mary, his mother, but also his maternal aunt, Salome, and his paternal uncle is represented by his niece, Mary, (or Mary may be the wife of Cleopas). Mary Magdalene represented Jesus' spiritual children brought from the darkness of sin to the light of grace. This group of people was an important link with the resurrection because they were witnesses in both cases. E. T. Bishop observes that Mary's witness was at first discounted by her father, but not for long. He continues, "May it not have been that in after years Mary, the mother of James and Joses, the daughter of Cleopas, was still young enough to relate to St. Luke the greatest of our resurrection stories, for she had been old enough to be an eyewitness of the mighty event, one of the first to believe the news too good to be true. Must she not have heard that narrative of the walk [to Emmaus] times without number and how he had been recognized by her father and the other traveler at the 'breaking of bread'?" [1]

This last scene has also been called "the hour of the mother." St. John shows that Jesus bequeathed Mary to the beloved disciple that he might take care of her. But this appears to be more than a juridical bequeathal, rather it has a messianic aspect, that is, it is brought into the economy of salvation. Had this been a mere juridical bequeathal, then Jesus need only have spoken to the man concerned. The fact that Jesus spoke first to his mother meant that he established a relationship which began, not with John, but with Mary. The fact that Jesus waited until the last moment, just before he died, to make this bequeathal means that Mary's maternity was associated with his

1. E. T. Bishop, *Expository Times,* 65 (September 1964), p. 382.

201

death. It was related to the mystical union of Jesus with the faithful, which is already depicted in this faithful little group around the cross. In saying to Mary, "Behold, your son," Jesus was demonstrating that the disciple and, in his name, the Church, took the place of Jesus himself as son of Mary. This idea must not be seen merely as a product of Catholic piety but in its full messianic import. The bequeathal lies in the heart of five episodes which have deep theological significance. These are (1) the title of the cross, which we have already discussed; (2) the dividing of the garments and, especially, the seamless robe of Jesus, which represents the high priestly robe which was woven without a seam; (3) these words to Mary; (4) the cry of Jesus, "I thirst," which fulfills both Psalm 68: 22 and the Johannine idea of spiritual thirst; and, lastly, (5) the words of Jesus, "It is finished." We notice that Mary is not addressed by her name, but called "Woman," just as she was called "Woman" at the marriage feast at Cana. There she was asked to relinquish her maternal concern that Jesus should use his miraculous powers to help his friends. Jesus told her that his hour had not yet come. Now Jesus' hour had come and he raised Mary's maternal solicitude onto a significantly higher spiritual plane. She became the mother of the whole Church. The title "Woman" may also signify that Mary is the new Eve, and in this way the episode recorded in St. John's Gospel may be associated with Genesis 3: 15:

> I will put enmity between you and the woman,
> and between your seed and her seed;
> he shall bruise your head,
> and you shall bruise his heel.

Mary had been associated as the new Eve in Jesus' victory over Satan which he finally accomplished on the cross.

When Jesus had accomplished these things, St. John tells us that he bowed his head and gave up his spirit. But the Greek text may also be translated, Jesus "handed on" or "transmitted" the spirit. Here again we may have a double meaning in the

202

words of St. John. If so, Jesus breathes the spirit upon this little group around the cross, and in so doing he copies his father, Yahweh, who breathed the breath of life into the first Adam. This is the new creation of the Church of God, the people of God. When Jesus' dead body was taken from the throne, it was placed with great care and reverence in a new tomb "where no one had ever been laid" in a garden near the place of crucifixion. The story of the first Adam had begun in a garden, the beginning of the passion of the second Adam had begun in a garden; and now this second Adam was laid in a new tomb, probably to symbolize the new aspect of death that came with the advent of Christianity.

THE EASTER VIGIL

In the Roman liturgy, the major festivals appear, not at the beginning of a cycle, but at the end of it. The liturgy reflects on a festival long before it arrives. If we wish to see the full meaning of Christmas, we must explore the Advent liturgy. In the same way, if we wish to see what the liturgy has to say about the Holy Spirit in the Church, we must begin with the Easter celebration, not with Pentecost. Our Pentecost celebration is simply the finale of the Pentecost season, the fifty days after Easter.

This pattern is especially true of the Easter celebration. The day of Easter is a finale, an act of rejoicing in the reality the liturgy has already celebrated through the Lenten season. "This is the day the Lord has made! Let us rejoice and be glad in it." Again and again this refrain is sung. In her Lenten eucharists, the Church has already lingered over the presence of the risen Lord in word and sacrament. Now her response is simply rejoicing. She welcomes her risen Lord, not as one who has been absent, but as one she has come to know more fully in her Lenten worship. Her message has been delivered. Now she can only cry, "Alleluia!"

In this perspective we can understand the Easter vigil. It presents nothing new. It is simply a grand summation of all the themes of the Lenten liturgy. It brings them to a climax in the baptismal affirmation of faith, and above all in the brief eucharistic service. It is the Amen to the Lenten liturgy.

For many who have participated in the Easter vigil, the preceding paragraphs are something less than the whole truth. All too often, the tiny handful of worshippers at the vigil stand in stark contrast to the crowded congregations of Holy Thursday and Good Friday. Even for the hardy souls who brave the late hour and the long service, the celebration can scarcely be described as enthusiastic, let alone ecstatic.

But have we, in any genuine sense, really restored the vigil? The mere "performance" of a rubrically correct paschal vigil is an insufficient guarantee of its vitality and popularity. As the texts and rite clearly indicate, the service is a baptismal vigil. An Easter vigil without *baptisms* is an abortive rite. The whole service celebrates the entry of new members into the life of the risen Lord. The critical need, then, is to see this service as the baptismal liturgy par excellence, the normative celebration of Christian baptism.

Ideally, this is the time for the baptism of converts, or for the reception of those already baptized into the communion of the Roman Catholic Church. The contemporary emphasis on Christian freedom is in the spirit of both the New Testament and the Roman liturgy. Nowhere is it more clearly affirmed than in the paschal vigil, when the adult convert freely chooses his life as a Christian. Any community which dares to call itself Christian should feel constrained to celebrate the most radical free decision a human being can make.

Much has been said about our new awareness of being God's people, our rediscovery of the corporate dimension of Christian life, our recognition that we are called to unity with one another in Christ and his Spirit. But we continually betray our lack of appreciation of this truth by receiving converts as privately as possible.

Similarly, we betray our lack of a corporate sense by failing to baptize infants at the Easter vigil. Do we not betray a serious misunderstanding of baptism when we continually reduce it to a quiet family affair?

The early Church viewed the eucharist as a consummation

of baptism. There is no reason why this aspect of the paschal celebration cannot be restored. Both the Holy Thursday liturgy and the paschal vigil are ideal occasions for the celebration of first communion. While a night vigil might not be the best occasion for the first communion of young children, the vigil would certainly be the time, not only for the communion of those newly received into the Church, but also for "late" first communicants. If we truly believe in the communal dimension of Christian life, then first communion is a matter of concern and celebration for the whole Church.

Present legislation makes baptisms and first communions possible within the context of the paschal liturgy. But along with the introduction of such practices, a new orientation of the believing community is necessary. We are generally quite careful to prepare converts and first communicants. Are we willing to be as careful to prepare the congregation to receive them? Only with this preparation can the paschal liturgy be restored in its fullness. At least from the beginning of Lent, the whole Church should be prepared to receive its new members.

Beyond the framework of present legislation, a number of adjustments in the present vigil also seem necessary. The length of the service and the lateness of the hour may contribute to the vigil's lack of popularity. These may not be insurmountable obstacles—witness the popularity of Christmas midnight mass. But there are a number of elements in the present vigil service which make the rite unnecessarily long and complex.

One of the problems is the baptismal rite itself. The giving of candles and the conferral of robes generally take longer than the actual baptisms, especially when there are several candidates. This is an unnecessary prolongation of the service. More seriously, it tends to overshadow the central significance of the water bath. A simpler solution would be to give the robes and candles in silence. A deacon or other minister could do this while the presiding celebrant prepares the congregation to renew their own baptismal promises. In the case of infants, such

207

practices seem unduly fussy, and might be omitted altogether. If real robes are not to be worn by adult candidates, a token "robe" trivializes the whole act. In such cases the giving of a candle would be quite sufficient. Also a "trimming" of the Litany of the Saints, in line with recent reforms of the calendar, would reduce the tedium of reciting the names of unknown worthies.

Another feature of the vigil which adds to its length without enhancing the celebration is the presence of two liturgies of the Word: one for the baptismal service and one for the eucharistic service. The latter could be omitted without doing violence to the vigil service. Surely the Word of God is adequately proclaimed in the baptismal service! And it would be all the more adequately proclaimed if there were time for a homily after the baptisms. And what is the Litany of the Saints, if not a Prayer of the Faithful? We suggest that the gifts should be brought up during or after the Litany of the Saints, and the eucharistic prayer begun after the Litany, when the gifts have been placed on the altar. Not only would the vigil service be shortened; it would also make the relationship between the baptism and the eucharist clear in our rite as well as in our doctrine. If the newly baptized brought up the gifts, the movement from font to table would be unmistakable.

Two other elements which could be incorporated easily without adding appreciably to the length of the service would be the confirmation of the newly baptized, and the extension of communion under both kinds to all present. Confirmation requires no more than a brief anointing and imposition of hands with prayer. With the bishop's permission, the sacrament could be administered by the pastor. The inclusion of confirmation in the paschal liturgy would fulfill the requirement of the *Constitution on the Sacred Liturgy* that the place of confirmation in Christian initiation must be restored. And if the vigil is to be a genuine communion festival, the fullest possible celebration of holy communion is necessary. Here, above all, we should keep the Lord's command: "Take this, *all* of you, and drink from it. This is the cup of my blood, the blood of the new and everlasting covenant." What are we celebrating, if not the Lord's new and everlasting covenant with us?

The first difficulty, then, of the "restored" Easter vigil is not that it is an old rite, but that it is only a partial restoration, a shadow of the ancient vigils. The second and more serious difficulty is that we have become excessively child-oriented in our instruction and liturgical practice. We have failed to grasp the importance of mature, adult Christian commitment. It is not only important that we be baptized and catechized as children. We must also freely choose the reality of our baptism, and understand it as adults. Until we accept our baptism, until we are all "converts," we are not really adult Christians. If our congregations are full of people for whom Christianity is "unfortunately true" who are present only to "fulfill their obligation," there can be no genuine paschal celebration. When people can rejoice in their own decision to be a Christian, then they can rejoice in the decision of others.

The new Preface for Lent indicates what should precede the paschal celebration:

> You bid your faithful people cleanse their hearts
> and prepare with joy for the paschal feast.
> More fervent in prayer,
> more generous in works of charity,
> more eager in celebrating the mysteries by which we are reborn
> may we come to the fullness of grace
> that belongs to the sons of God.
>   (International Committee on English in the Liturgy, Inc.)

As early as St. Paul, the Christian tradition has seen Christian baptism as a wedding festival: a celebration of the marriage between Christ and the Church. The baptismal robes came to be seen as wedding garments, the paschal eucharist as the marriage feast. Even if we find this imagery strange, there is still much that can be learned from it. What married person can attend a wedding without recalling something of his own? What happily married person can hear the marriage vows repeated without having the whole meaning of his marriage set before him? No wonder women cry at weddings: the celebration brings them face to face with the very center of their lives. The paschal liturgy was intended to be that sort of event—a recalling of the very center of Christian existence; a recalling, not in the sense of a vague remembrance, but in the sense of a re-evoking of all that it means to be a Christian.

No rite, however splendid, can evoke the sense of the meaning of Christian life when people are not adequately prepared. When they are so prepared, we can be sure that we will have a splendid rite.

The Easter Vigil

The readings for Holy Saturday offer the following points for reflection:

(1) the goodness of creation and mankind in the image and likeness of God; a prelude to life in the Holy Spirit;

(2) the sacrifice of Isaac; prefiguring the resurrection of Jesus;

(3) God's mighty deliverance of Israel at the Sea of Reeds, foreshadowing baptism;

(4) the covenant community of Yahweh, the future Church;

(5) spiritual nourishment for God's people; the background to John, Chapters 1, 4 and 6;

(6) pursuit after wisdom, the gifts of the Holy Spirit;

(7) cleansing of Israel and implanting a new spirit within her, looking toward Joel 3;

(8) renewal through the glory of Christ, a complement to the transfiguration of Christ and Christians;

210

(9) the resurrection, the center of the Christian message. These lessons draw together most of the themes which have been studied during Lent.

THE FIRST READING, GENESIS 1: 1—2: 1. CREATION

In the beginning God created the heavens and the earth. The earth was without form and void, and darkness was upon the face of the deep; and the Spirit of God was moving over the face of the waters.

And God said, "Let there be light"; and there was light. And God saw that the light was good; and God separated the light from the darkness. God called the light Day, and the darkness he called Night. And there was evening and there was morning, one day.

And God said, "Let there be a firmament in the midst of the waters, and let it separate the waters from the waters." And God made the firmament and separated the waters which were under the firmament from the waters which were above the firmament. And it was so. And God called the firmament Heaven. And there was evening and there was morning, a second day.

And God said, "Let the waters under the heavens be gathered together into one place, and let the dry land appear." And it was so. God called the dry land Earth, and the waters that were gathered together he called Seas. And God saw that it was good. And God said, "Let the earth put forth vegetation, plants yielding seed, and fruit trees bearing fruit in which is their seed, each according to its kind, upon the earth." And it was so. The earth brought forth vegetation, plants yielding seed according to their own kinds, and trees bearing fruit in which is their seed, each according to its kind. And God saw that it was good. And there was evening and there was morning, a third day.

And God said, "Let there be lights in the firmament of the heavens to separate the day from the night; and let them be for signs and for seasons and for days and years, and let them be lights in the firmament of the heavens to give light upon the earth." And it was so. And God made the two great lights, the greater light to rule the day, and the lesser light to rule the night; he made the stars also. And God set them in the firmament of the heavens to

211

give light upon the earth, to rule over the day and over the night, and to separate the light from the darkness. And God saw that it was good. And there was evening and there was morning, a fourth day.

And God said, "Let the waters bring forth swarms of living creatures, and let birds fly above the earth across the firmament of the heavens." So God created the great sea monsters and every living creature that moved, with which the waters swarm, according to their kinds, and every winged bird according to its kind. And God saw that it was good. And God blessed them, saying, "Be fruitful and multiply and fill the waters in the seas, and let birds multiply on the earth." And there was evening and there was morning, a fifth day.

And God said, "Let the earth bring forth living creatures according to their kinds: cattle and creeping things and beasts of the earth according to their kinds." And it was so. And God made the beasts of the earth according to their kinds and the cattle according to their kinds, and everything that creeps upon the ground according to its kind. And God saw that it was good.

Then God said, "Let us make man in our image, after our likeness; and let them have dominion over the fish of the sea, and over the birds of the air, and over the cattle, and over all the earth, and over every creeping thing that creeps upon the earth." So God created man in his own image, in the image of God he created him; male and female he created them. And God blessed them, and God said to them, "Be fruitful and multiply, and fill the earth and subdue it; and have dominion over the fish of the sea and over the birds of the air and over every living thing that moves upon the earth." And God said, "Behold, I have given you every plant yielding seed which is upon the face of all the earth, and every tree with seed in its fruit; you shall have them for food. And to every beast of the earth, and to every bird of the air, and to everything that creeps on the earth, everything that has the breath of life, I have given every green plant for food." And it was so. And God saw everything that he had made, and behold, it was very good. And there was evening and there was morning, a sixth day.

Thus the heavens and the earth were finished, and all the host of them.

The Biblical Idea of Image

The most important concept to note in this reading is man in the image of God. The biblical writer portrays the formation of the whole world, the heaven and earth, sea, vegetation, the celestial bodies, the fish, the birds and the animals. Yet when he speaks of mankind, he seems to pause, to enter into a new dimension. He denotes this by selecting a different and special word for the verb "create." This word is *bara*. He solemnly repeats it three times in verse 27. He has reached the zenith of all God's creativity, namely, man and woman. Their uniqueness lies in the fact that they are made in the image and likeness of God.

This concept of mankind's creation in the image of God is mentioned in only three texts of the Old Testament, in this text, in the Wisdom of Solomon 2: 23 and in Sirach (Ecclus.) 17: 3.

The Pagan Idea of Image

It is a concept which is difficult to explain, but a glance at the pagan idea of "image" and then at the more refined biblical meaning will serve to elucidate it. In the culture contemporary with the ancient Hebrews there was a belief that man was created by pouring clay into plastic models of the deities. Such an idea would be readily acceptable by those who venerated graven images, conceived the gods as deified heroes and heroines, and attributed to them "human" qualities such as mortality, procreation, emotion, rivalry, and caprice. However, by the time in which the three passages under consideration were written, the ancients had advanced beyond these primitive beliefs. They took this concept of "image" and created from it something far more sublime. The word "image" did not mean merely a secondary copy of something. It frequently meant the "real presence" and it was applied to the living person of a king who represented the deity. Even in a very ancient hymn concerning an Egyptian King, Thutmose III, we read as follows:

Put these words into the mouth of the god Amon: "I am come, I give you to walk on the princes of Djahi [the population of Phoenicia], I spread them out under your feet across their land, I cause them to see your majesty like that of a lord of glory, while you shine in their face like my own image." [1]

Adam was rather like this king. He lived in God's presence (see Sirach 17: 3ff.). He represented God by being King of the Universe over all the animals and the inanimate objects, and by being able to use all these in a resourceful and intelligent manner to bring glory to God. He was to bring the non-human part of the universe into a special relationship to God. The king-like character of the first man is illustrated in another part of the Bible, namely, Ezekiel 28, where we find another story rather like Genesis 1. This text represents the first man as a king who was full of perfection and wisdom and who possessed great riches. Unfortunately he misused all these talents and God reduced him to poverty.

Ruler Through the Spirit

Later Jewish writings show that men were deemed to rule by the inspiration of the Holy Spirit. This spirit gave them the wisdom, understanding, knowledge, and goodness to be able to fulfill the duties which God had committed to them. The bestowal of this spirit is suggested in the second account of the creation of man which is found in Genesis 2: 4–9 (see pp. 25–26 above). To the Hebrew, the breath of life mentioned in Genesis 2 was almost the same as the Spirit of God; it was the power of God which gave life to the whole person of man, both soul and body,

1. Cited by E. Jacob, *Theology of the Old Testament,* from J. de Savignac, "Interpretation du Psaume 110" in *Oudtestamentliche Studien,* IX, p. 111.

and when this Spirit was withdrawn, man died. The text in Genesis 2 is different from, but not inconsistent with, the first text in Genesis 1: 26–28, because in later Jewish writings, words "image," "likeness," and "majesty" are sometimes synonyms for the Spirit of God which Christians call the Holy Spirit.

The Bible portrays a lofty idea of man. He was created in the image and likeness of God. In principle this meant that he possessed, in a special way, the Spirit of God which enabled him to experience the presence of God as a living reality. Living in this presence, man was the intelligent, thinking, and speaking being created to rule over the whole universe, using its resources for the glory of God.

THE SECOND READING, GENESIS 22: 1–18. THE SACRIFICE OF ISAAC

After these things God tested Abraham, and said to him, "Abraham!" And he said, "Here am I." He said, "Take your son, your only son Isaac, whom you love, and go to the land of Moriah, and offer him there as a burnt offering upon one of the mountains of which I shall tell you." So Abraham rose early in the morning, saddled his ass, and took two of his young men with him, and his son Isaac; and he cut the wood for the burnt offering, and arose and went to the place of which God had told him. On the third day Abraham said to his young men, "Stay here with the ass; I and the lad will go yonder and worship, and come again to you." And Abraham took the wood of the burnt offering, and laid it on Isaac his son; and he took in his hand the fire and the knife. So they went both of them together. And Isaac said to his father Abraham, "My father!" And he said, "Here am I, my son." He said, "Behold, the fire and the wood; but where is the lamb for a burnt offering?" Abraham said, "God will provide himself the lamb for a burnt offering, my son." So they went both of them together.

When they came to the place of which God had told him, Abraham built an altar there, and laid the wood in order, and bound Isaac his son, and laid him on the altar, upon the wood. Then

215

Abraham put forth his hand, and took the knife to slay his son. But the angel of the Lord called to him from heaven, and said, "Abraham, Abraham!" And he said, "Here am I." He said, "Do not lay your hand on the lad or do anything to him; for now I know that you fear God, seeing you have not withheld your son, your only son, from me." And Abraham lifted up his eyes and looked and behold, behind him was a ram, caught in a thicket by his horns; and Abraham went and took the ram, and offered it up as a burnt offering instead of his son. So Abraham called the name of that place the LORD will provide; as it is said to this day, "On the mount of the LORD it shall be provided."

And the angel of the Lord called to Abraham a second time from heaven, and said, "By myself I have sworn, says the Lord, because you have done this, and have not withheld your son, your only son, I will indeed bless you, and I will multiply your descendants as the stars of heaven and as the sand which is on the seashore. And your descendants shall possess the gate of their enemies, and by your descendants shall all the nations of the earth bless themselves, because you have obeyed my voice."

The Rabbinic Interpretation

The second lesson narrates the sacrifice of Isaac by his father Abraham.

The non-biblical Jewish background to this sacrifice can be found in J. Massingberd Ford, *Wellsprings of Scripture* (New York, 1968, pp. 25-30), where the theology of what the Jews call *The Binding of Isaac* is summarized. By the time of Jesus, many Jews held the belief that Isaac offered himself as a voluntary sacrifice and ran with joy to the altar. Some rabbis even thought that he shed one-fourth of his blood and was, as it were, resurrected from the dead. They deemed God to be pleased with his sacrifice and bestowed, because of the generosity shown by Isaac, many blessings upon the Hebrew race—for example, their release from Egypt and their safe journey across the Red Sea. Isaac became the prototype of the martyr and the prototype of the resurrected man. Many Jews believed that through this sacrifice of Isaac the whole Jewish race was sanctified and people would be resurrected from the dead.

Christian Application

Here one may add that Jesus is the fulfillment of the type of Isaac, a concept emphasized very frequently by the early Christian writers. Thus St. John Chrysostom has written about the sacrifice of Isaac:

All these things were types of a cross. That is why Christ said: "Abraham rejoiced that he might see my day: he saw it, and was glad." How did he see it, considering he was born so many years before? In type and in shadow. A lamb was offered for Isaac, and a spiritual lamb was offered for the world. A reality had to be depicted beforehand in type. Consider, I beg you, to what extent everything had been told in advance. In both instances we have an only son; in both instances one who is greatly loved. The first was offered as a victim by his father, and so was the latter offered by his Father (Romans 8: 32). The type carries us a long way, but how much further does reality go.[1]

The Third Reading, Exodus 14: 15—15:1. The Crossing of the Red Sea

The Lord said to Moses, "Why do you cry to me? Tell the people of Israel to go forward. Lift up your rod, and stretch out your hand over the sea and divide it, that the people of Israel may go on dry ground through the sea. And I will harden the hearts of the Egyptians so that they shall go in after them, and I will get glory over Pharaoh and all his host, his chariots, and his horsemen. And the Egyptians shall know I have gotten glory over Pharaoh, his chariots, and his horsemen."

Then the angel of God went before the host of Israel moved and

1. *Hom. Gen.* 47, 3; translation from J. Daniélou, *From Shadows to Reality*, London, 1960, p. 129.

The Third Reading, Exodus 14: 15—15: 1. The Crossing of

went behind them; and the pillar of cloud moved from before them and stood behind them, coming between the host of Egypt and the host of Israel. And there was the cloud and the darkness; and the night passed without one coming near the other all night.

Then Moses stretched out his hand over the sea; and the Lord drove the sea back by a strong east wind all night, and made the sea dry land, and the waters were divided. And the people of Israel went into the midst of the sea on dry ground, the waters being a wall to them on the right hand and on their left. The Egyptians pursued, and went in after them into the midst of the sea, all Pharaoh's horses, his chariots, and his horsemen. And in the morning watch the Lord in the pillar of fire and of cloud looked down upon the host of the Egyptians, and discomfited the host of the Egyptians, clogging their chariot wheels so that they drove heavily; and the Egyptians said, "Let us flee from before Israel; for the Lord fights for them against the Egyptians."

Then the Lord said to Moses, "Stretch out your hand over the sea, that the water may come back upon the Egyptians, upon their chariots, and upon their horsemen." So Moses stretched forth his hand over the sea, and the sea returned to its wonted flow when the morning appeared; and the Egyptians fled into it, and the Lord routed the Egyptians in the midst of the sea. The waters returned and covered the chariots and the horsemen and all the hosts of Pharaoh that had followed them into the sea; not so much as one of them remained. But the people of Israel walked on dry ground through the sea, the waters being a wall to them on their right hand and on their left.

Thus the Lord saved Israel that day from the hand of the Egyptians; and Israel saw the Egyptians dead upon the seashore. And Israel saw the great work which the Lord did against the Egyptians, and the people feared the Lord; and they believed in the Lord and in his servant Moses.

Then Moses and the people of Israel sang this song to the Lord, saying,

> "I will sing to the Lord, for he
> has triumphed gloriously;
> the horse and his rider he has
> thrown into the sea."

218

The Situation

The Israelites were released from Egypt, but then suddenly the Egyptian tyrants appear to have changed their minds about this permission (see Exodus 12: 29-33). Perhaps they realized the injury to the slave trade which the Exodus would involve. They pursued the Israelites, and the fugitives seem to have found themselves in an impossible position. The Egyptian Etham fortress seems to have been behind them, Pharaoh's army was on the flank, and the Sea of Reeds before them. Only a miracle could save them in such a situation.

Miracle or Providential Sign

It was this "miracle" which the biblical narrator wished to throw into high relief. He wished to emphasize that God was fighting for his people, that this was a Holy War, that Israel must see the purpose of God behind every event and must realize the great faith of Moses. The people must imitate this faith.

Certain Jewish writers saw this incident as a "providential sign" rather than as a pure miracle. It is possible that high winds drove the water back—such winds enabled a Roman general, Scipio, to cross a lagoon and capture New Carthage; or that a hot wind dried the shallow Sea of Reeds. The heavier forces of the Egyptians with their chariots manned with two or three men might sink while the lightly equipped Israelites fled over.

However, what the biblical narrator wished to stress was that this was God's hour. In this reading there appears to be a conflation of three sources of traditions. In the earliest tradition the Lord allowed the pillar of cloud to stand between the Israelites and the Egyptian army to prevent a night encounter, and then he sent a strong east wind all night to drive back the waters. In a later source the angel of the Lord stood behind the host to guard

219

them and it was Moses' magic rod which caused the waters to recede for the Israelites and flow back again to engulf the Egyptians. In a still later source the waters stood like a wall on the right and left of the people.

This narrative may have been read at the Jewish feast of Passover, and hence it may have received various embellishments to increase the miraculous element in the story. One may compare Psalm 114, which portrays the incident in a very dramatic way, and Psalm 77: 16–20, which added the details of torrential rain accompanied by thunder and lightning and the crossing of God or his angel through the great waters:

> When the waters saw thee, O God,
> when the waters saw thee, they were afraid,
> yea, the deep trembled.
> The clouds poured out water;
> the skies gave forth thunder;
> thy arrows flashed on every side.
> The crash of thy thunder was in the whirlwind;
> thy lightnings lighted up the world;
> the earth trembled and shook.
> Thy way was through the sea,
> thy path through the great waters;
> yet thy footprints were unseen.
> Thou didst lead thy people like a flock
> by the hand of Moses and Aaron.

The Moral of the Event

The result of this providential sign was that the people were convinced of Yahweh's power and also of Moses' authority. They became deeply conscious of God's special protection. The prophets, who arose after the exodus, often referred to this event and found in it an assurance that God would deliver his people in the future.

St. Paul referred to the crossing in I Corinthians 10: 1–5 and described it as baptism into Moses.

220

The Symbolism of the Event

The Jewish liturgy commemorated the crossing of the sea with dance and song. The celebration occurred near the feast of Passover. On the same night, Christians appear to have practiced baptism. The early Christian writers saw the three days' journey in the desert as a type of the three days between Christ's death and resurrection and the mystery on the third day, namely, the crossing of the sea, as a type of baptism. Hippolytus of Rome in his Passover homily prayed, "give us the gladness to sing the victorious Song of Moses" (Exodus 15: 16–18).

THE FOURTH READING, ISAIAH 54: 5–14. THE COVENANT COMMUNITY OF YAHWEH

For your Maker is your husband,
the Lord of hosts is his name;
and the Holy One of Israel is your Redeemer,
the God of the whole earth he is called.
For the Lord has called you
like a wife forsaken and grieved in spirit,
like a wife of youth when she is cast off,
says your God.
For a brief moment I forsook you,
but with great compassion I will gather you.
In overflowing wrath for a moment
I hid my face from you,
but with everlasting love I will have
compassion on you,
says the Lord, your Redeemer.

For this is like the days of Noah to me:
as I swore that the waters of Noah
should no more go over the earth,
so I have sworn that I will not be angry with you
and will not rebuke you.

221

For the mountains may depart
and the hills be removed,
but my steadfast love shall not depart from you,
and my covenant of peace shall not be removed,
says the Lord, who has compassion on you.

"O afflicted one, storm-tossed, and not comforted,
behold, I will set your stones in antimony,
and lay your foundations with sapphires.
I will make your pinnacles of agate,
your gates of carbuncles,
and all your wall of precious stones.
All your sons shall be taught by the Lord,
and great shall be the prosperity of your sons.
In righteousness you shall be established;
you shall be far from oppression,
for you shall not fear;
and from terror, for it shall not come near you."

Different Biblical Images

This lesson draws together many different biblical images with reference to the covenant which God made with his people Israel.

(1) The beginning of the chapter reflects God's promise to Abraham and his special intervention on behalf of Sarah, Rachel, and Rebecca to give children to these barren women.

(2) Verses 5–8 combine the concept of Yahweh as creator with that of husband, covenant partner in the bond of marriage. The husband motif is especially prominent in Hosea 1–2 where the prophet in his own life dramatically symbolizes the love of Yahweh. He takes back his wife, who has been unfaithful to him. In the same way Yahweh was ready to accept the idolatrous Israel once again. In Isaiah 54: 7 the "overflowing wrath" must symbolize Israel's exile in Babylon. She suffered this on account of her disloyalty to Yahweh.

(3) Verses 9–10 refer to the covenant with the whole earth

222

which God made with Noah. The renewal of the covenant will be unbreakable like the Noachic one.

The Building up of the Community

Verses 11–14 prophesy the building up of the community: there is a play on the words "sons" and "builders" as these words are very similar in Hebrew. The individuals of the community are to be the embodiment of righteousness as precious as jewels. The Dead Sea Scrolls have a very interesting interpretation of these verses which is worth quoting.

Behold, I will set your stones in antimony. This refers to the fact that . . . all Israel like antimony around the eye [?].

. . . *and lay your foundations with sapphires.* This refers to the fact that they have founded the deliberative council of the community out of priests and laity—a veritable congregation of God's elect—like a sapphire among gems.

And I will make your pinnacles of agate. This refers to the twelve . . . who shine after the manner of the Urim and Thummim. Even the more inferior of them were like the sun in all its radiance and like . . .

. . . *and your gates of carbuncle.* This refers to the heads of the tribes of Israel . . . each man [filling] his assigned role, (together constituting) the rotas of . . .[1]

THE FIFTH READING, ISAIAH 55: 1–11. THE NOURISHMENT OF THE POOR AND THE ETERNAL COVENANT OF GOD

Ho, every one who thirsts, come to the waters; and he who has no money, come, buy and eat! Come, buy the wine and milk without money and without price. Why do you spend your money for that which is not bread, and your labor for that which does not satisfy? Hearken diligently to me, and eat what is good, and delight yourselves in fatness. Incline your ear, and come to me; hear, that your

1. T. H. Gaster, *The Dead Sea Scriptures in English Translation*, New York, 1964, p. 235.

soul may live; and I will make with you an everlasting covenant, my steadfast, sure love for David. Behold, I made him a witness to the peoples, a leader and commander for the peoples. Behold, you shall call nations that you know not, and nations that knew you not shall run to you, because of the Lord your God, and of the Holy One of Israel, for he has glorified you.

Seek the Lord while he may be found, call upon him while he is near; let the wicked forsake his way, and the unrighteous man his thoughts; let him return to the Lord, that he may have mercy on him, and to our God, for he will abundantly pardon. For my thoughts are not your thoughts, neither are your ways my ways, says the Lord. For as the heavens are higher than the earth, so are my ways higher than your ways and my thoughts than your thoughts.

For as the rain and the snow come down from heaven, and return not thither but water the earth, making it bring forth and sprout, giving seed to the sower and bread to the eater, so shall my word be that goes forth from my mouth; it shall not return to me empty, but it shall accomplish that which I purpose, and prosper in the thing for which I sent it.

The Christian Interpretation

The fifth lesson speaks of spiritual water and spiritual food, which we discussed for the lessons read for the Third Sunday in Lent. Jesus is the one who gives this spiritual water, and he is also the Word which comes from the mouth of God and does not return to God empty, but accomplishes that which he purposed.

The Pre-Christian Interpretation

However, the pre-Christian interpreters would see in this passage three motifs:

    (1) an exodus theme;

    (2) the covenant;

    (3) a wisdom motif.

224

(1) Yahweh's invitation to the people to accept nourishment without price would recall the gratuitous gift of manna, quails and water, which the Israelites received in the desert. It would also reflect Hosea's insistence that Israel's sustenance found its only source in Yahweh, her husband (see p. 222 above). Further, the exodus motif is very clear in verse 12, "you shall go out in joy."

(2) The second theme is the eternal covenant (v. 3). David is mentioned only here in Isaiah 40–55. An eternal covenant with David is recorded in II Samuel 7: 11–16 and in Psalm 89: 28–37. In Isaiah 55, Israel is promised the titles given to David (see Pss. 72: 9; 89: 24–27) and she is to rule, not by political dominion, but by communicating faith in Yahweh to the nations (see the kingship of Jesus, pp. 192ff. above). The personified word of Yahweh (vv. 10–11) will accomplish its mission and Israel is destined to be witness to this (v. 4).

(3) The wisdom theme is noticeable because of the affinity between this passage and Proverbs 9: 1–6 and Canticles 5: 1. In Proverbs, wisdom issues an invitation to a joyous banquet consisting of nourishment which provides full spiritual vitality. The wisdom theme is especially clear in the Aramaic translation of this text, which reads:

Ho, every one that wishes to learn, let him come, and learn, and he that hath no money; come ye, and hear, and learn; come, hear, and learn, without price and without money, instruction that is better than wine and milk. . . . Incline your ear, and hearken unto my Memra; hear, and your soul shall live: and I will make an everlasting covenant with you, *even* the sure mercies of David.

This reading furnishes an excellent background to much of St. John's theology, such as John 1, 4, and 6.

THE SIXTH READING, BARUCH 3: 9–15, 32—4: 4. WISDOM LEADS TO LIFE

Hear the commandments of life, O Israel:
give ear, and learn wisdom!

225

Why is it, O Israel, why is it that
you are in the land of your enemies,
that you are growing old in a foreign country,
that you are defiled with the dead,
that you are counted among those in Hades?
You have forsaken the fountain of wisdom.
If you had walked in the way of God,
you would be dwelling in peace for ever.
Learn where there is wisdom,
where there is strength,
where there is understanding,
that you may at the same time discern
where there is length of days, and life,
where there is light for the eyes, and peace.
who has found her place?
And who has entered her storehouses?

But he who knows all things knows her,
he found her by his understanding.
He who prepared the earth for all time
filled it with four-footed creatures;
he who sends forth the light, and it goes,
called it, and it obeyed him in fear;
the stars shone in their watches, and were glad;
he called them, and they said, "Here we are!"
They shone with gladness for him who made them.
This is our God;
no other can be compared to him!
He found the whole way to knowledge,
and gave her to Jacob his servant
and to Israel whom he loved.
Afterward she appeared upon earth
and lived among men.

She is the book of the commandments of God,
and the law that endures for ever.
All who hold her fast will live,
and those who forsake her will die.
Turn, O Jacob, and take her;

226

walk toward the shining of her light.
Do not give your glory to another,
or your advantages to an alien people.
Happy are we, O Israel,
for we know what is pleasing to God.

This lesson is especially apposite to the baptismal theme of Easter, for the seven gifts of the Holy Spirit, of which wisdom is the chief, are given in this sacrament. Wisdom is symbolized in the salt placed upon the tongue of the candidate.

The poem is a wisdom hymn celebrating the law as wisdom.

The Context

In Baruch 3: 1–8, the Jewish exiles in Babylon cry to God to forgive their sin and those of their fathers. They promise to remove from their hearts all iniquity. To this prayer the poet replies. Wisdom, who was created by God, was given to Israel and is the law. The exiles who are dead in sin (vv. 10–11) are invited to receive life by accepting the law, that is, wisdom (see the fall of mankind, p. 29 above).

The Idea of Wisdom

The Old Testament has a lofty idea of wisdom. She is personified as a woman in Proverbs 8: 22–31 and Sirach 24: 1–21, and she stands in sharp contrast to folly, who is also personified as a woman (Prov. 9: 13–18). Wisdom was created by God and came forth from the mouth of the Most High (Sir. 24: 1). In Wisdom 7: 22 she is even described as an emanation of God's might and glory. By wisdom, God creates and governs the world, and by her mankind can live on a higher level of existence. However, she is a gratuitous gift of God unattainable by merely human endeavors. The nourishment which she offers to the men of the Old Testament is the Mosaic law (Sir. 24: 22).

227

In the New Testament one finds a certain disparagement of human wisdom (as in I Cor. 1: 17–29). True wisdom is still the gift of God (I Cor. 12: 8; Eph. 1: 8f., 17f.); it is no longer the law, but Christ himself (I Cor 1: 30).

The points mentioned above are reflected in the present reading. Verse 12 speaks of the fountain of wisdom, that is, God; verse 14 mentions several gifts of the Spirit—strength, understanding, discernment, and peace. These may be compared to Isaiah 11: 1ff. Verse 32 re-emphasizes the fact that wisdom comes only from God. "Afterward she appeared upon earth and lived among men" (v. 37) was understood by early Christian writers to refer to Christ's incarnation, but modern scholars suggest that it may be an interpolation. Nevertheless, the teaching on wisdom in the Old Testament sheds abundant light upon both the person of Christ and the characteristics which should be realized in the Christian soul.

THE SEVENTH READING, EZEKIEL 36: 16–28. THE CLEANSING OF ISRAEL AND THE IMPLANTING OF A NEW SPIRIT WITHIN HER

The word of the Lord came to me: "Son of man, when the house of Israel dwelt in their own land, they defiled it by their says and their doings; their conduct before me was like the uncleanness of a woman in her impurity. So I poured out my wrath upon them for the blood which they had shed in the land, for the idols with which they had defiled it. I scattered them among the nations, and they were dispersed through the countries; in accordance with their conduct and their deeds I judged them. But when they came to the nations, wherever they came, they profaned my holy name, in that men said of them, "These are the people of the Lord, and yet they had to go out of his land." But I had concern for my holy name, which the house of Israel caused to be profaned among the nations to which they came.

Therefore say to the house of Israel, Thus says the Lord God: It is not for your sake, O house of Israel, that I am about to act, but for the sake of my holy name, which you have profaned among the nations to which you came. And I will vindicate the holiness of my great name, which has been profaned among the nations, and which you have profaned among them; and the nations will know that I am the Lord, says the Lord God, when through you I vindicate my holiness before their eyes. For I will take you from the nations, and gather you from all the countries, and bring you into your own land. I will sprinkle clean water upon you, and you shall be clean from all your uncleannesses, and from all your idols I will cleanse you. A new heart I will give you, and a new spirit I will put within you; and I will take out of your flesh the heart of stone and give you a heart of flesh. And I will put my spirit within you, and cause you to walk in my statutes and be careful to observe my ordinances. You shall dwell in the land which I gave to your fathers; and you shall be my people, and I will be your God!

The Context

The prophet reproached Israel for breaking the covenant law and also for indulging in idolatry. Her condition was like that of a menstrous woman who would not be permitted to approach anything which was holy (see Lev. 12: 1–8 and 15: 16–33). In a similar way Yahweh did not permit Israel to dwell in the Holy Land. He sent her into exile to Babylon.

However, the exile was likely to bring reproach upon Yahweh's Name or character because the nations might accuse him of the violation of his covenant with Israel. Therefore, for his own sake, Yahweh would restore his people and show that he did keep the covenant.

The Transformation

He would perform for them the ritual bath obligatory for cleansing after defilement (see Ex. 30: 17–21; Lev. 14: 52; and Num. 19: 7, 9). However, more than the external rite of purification was necessary. A total transformation and inner

229

renewal had to be effected. Therefore, Yahweh promised them not only a "new spirit" (v. 26) but his own spirit (v. 27). It was the bestowal of the Spirit of Yahweh which effected a permanent change of heart, an abiding power, and enabled the people to live on a new level of life.

In this passage there is a high concept of the relationship between the Mosaic law and the life of the spirit which was to be developed by St. Paul in the new dispensation. In the present context the promise looks forward to the realization of the prophecy of Joel 3: 1ff. (see Acts 2: 1–21), and emphasizes the fact that the covenant relationship between Yahweh and his people is based on the gift of the Spirit. It is the Spirit which enables the people to live a life of wisdom, that is, abiding by God's precepts and covenant. The covenant motif is reflected in verse 28, "you shall be my people, and I will be your God" (see Ex. 6: 7; Hosea 2: 23; and Jeremiah 31: 31–34).

The sprinkling with clean water and the implantation of the new spirit looked forward to Pentecost and the ingathering of the people for baptism after it.

THE EIGHTH READING, ROMANS 6: 3–11. PARTICIPATION IN THE DEATH AND RESURRECTION OF JESUS

Do you not know that all of us who have been baptized into Christ Jesus were baptized into his death? We were buried therefore with him by baptism into death, so that as Christ was raised from the dead by the glory of the Father, we too might walk in newness of life.

For if we have been united with him in a death like his, we shall certainly be united with him in a resurrection like his. We know that our old self was crucified with him so that the sinful body might be destroyed, and we might no longer be enslaved to sin. For he who has died is freed from sin. But if we have died with Christ, we believe that we shall also live with him. For we know that Christ being raised from the dead will never die again; death no longer has dominion over him. The death he died he died to sin, once for all,

230

but the life he lives he lives to God. So you also must consider yourselves dead to sin and alive to God in Christ Jesus.

This reading develops the ideas in the previous one. It occurs in the context of St. Paul's discussion of the Christian relationship to the Mosaic law. The controversy about the law and the gospel was the most lively issue in the early Church. In Romans 6–8 the apostle shows that a Christian's attitude must not be one of defiance or scorn toward the law, but neither must he be a servant of the law. Many of the ritual requirements had to be regarded as non-obligatory and some superseded after the advent of Christ—for example, purification of women and lepers. They merely foreshadowed Christ's work or filled a need until he came. But on the other hand, the grace of Christ gave the power to fulfill the moral requirements and even to go beyond these, in the excess of love which is found in Christ.

In Romans 6: 1–2, St. Paul rejects absolutely the idea that the grace of Christ brings with it a liberalism which condones sin. The Christian must adopt an attitude completely contrary to this. In Christ the old self with its sin has died, being "drowned," as it were, in baptism wherein one experiences Christ's crucifixion and the new self comes up out of the bath as one experiences new life in Christ. The Jews already saw baptism as an emergence from death to life or a rebirth: they called the convert one risen from the grave or a new-born babe. This was a symbol, but in Christian baptism the reality was present. This reality was present on account of Christ's resurrection. In the Old Testament the miracles of the exodus (Ex. 15: 7, 11; etc.) were performed through the glory of God, (see pp. 217ff., 225 above). This same glory performed the miracle of the resurrection of Christ (Rom. 6: 4). The power of this glory was communicated through the risen, glorified Christ to those who accepted him in baptism, that is, to those who were immersed in his glory, his name, or his character. This is illustrated very clearly in II Corinthians 3: 4–18 where the new grace in Christ is contrasted with the lesser

231

glory of the Mosaic law. Here St. Paul speaks of Christians changing into Christ's likeness, passing from one degree of glory to another through the power of the Lord "who is the Spirit" (*ibid.*, v. 18). In view of these privileges, sin should no longer charm man who dwells in Christ (Rom. 6: 9–11). All of this applies to Christians today.

The Gospel, Matthew 28: 1–10. Christ's Resurrection

Now after the sabbath, toward the dawn of the first day of the week, Mary Magdalene and the other Mary went to see the sepulchre. And behold, there was a great earthquake; for an angel of the Lord descended from heaven and came and rolled back the stone, and sat upon it. His appearance was like lightning, and his raiment white as snow. And for fear of him the guards trembled and became like dead men. But the angel said to the women, "Do not be afraid; for I know that you seek Jesus who was crucified. He is not here; for he has risen, as he said. Come, see the place where he lay. Then go quickly and tell his disciples that he has risen from the dead, and behold, he is going before you to Galilee; there you will see him. Lo, I have told you." So they departed quickly from the tomb with fear and great joy, and ran to tell his disciples. And behold, Jesus met them and said, "Hail!" And they came up and took hold of his feet and worshipped him. Then Jesus said to them, "Do not be afraid; go and tell my brethren to go to Galilee, and there they will see me."

Prophecy of the Resurrection in St. Matthew

The resurrection of Jesus should have caused no surprise, for Jesus appears to have indicated this when he said:

For as Jonah was three days and three nights in the belly of the whale, so will the Son of man be three days and three nights in the heart of the earth. (Matt. 12: 40)

Further, St. Matthew reports that the Jewish authorities said to Pilate, "Sir, we remember how that imposter said, while he

232

was still alive, 'After three days I will rise again' " (Matt. 27: 63).

The Women Did Not Expect the Resurrection

Yet the women who had watched around the cross and before the grave do not seem to have expected the resurrection. After the Sabbath they went to anoint the corpse of Jesus. The lack of expectation with reference to the resurrection is further illustrated by the testimony of St. Mark. It is thought that St. Mark's Gospel originally ended at verse 8. He records that the women came to the tomb wondering who would roll away the stone for them, and when they arrived they saw a young man who told them that Jesus had risen. The young man added, "But go, tell his disciples and Peter that he is going before you to Galilee; there you will see him, as he told you." However, the women were filled with fear and trembling, and St. Mark's Gospel apparently ended with the dramatic verse:

And they went out and fled from the tomb; for trembling and astonishment had come upon them, and they said nothing to anyone, for they were afraid. (Mark 16: 8)

St. Matthew elaborated the Marcan account but he did not add fanciful details such as are found in the Gospel of Peter, which was rejected by the Church as inauthentic. St. Matthew mentions an earthquake, just as he mentioned this at the death of Christ. Possibly by this symbolism he wished to emphasize that a great act of God had taken place. We recall that the manifestation of God in the Old Testament was sometimes described as accompanied by similar cosmic phenomena. St. Matthew also describes the angel. Here he wished to recall his description of the transfiguration of Jesus, where the appearance of Jesus was similar to the appearance of this angel: "His face shone like the sun, and his garments became white as light [or snow]" (Matt. 17: 2b). The transfiguration was a

233

preparation or prelude to the resurrection. In Matthew's account, too, the effect of the apparition on the guards is to immobilize them. This is not unlike the effect on the soldiers which St. John describes in the garden of Gethsemane. The angel bade the women not to be afraid, in Mark he bade them not to be amazed. They were told to take the glorious message to the disciples and Matthew tells us that they performed this commission with alacrity, fear, and great joy. In contrast to St. Mark, St. Matthew stresses this Easter joy, which was emphasized so much by the early Church. In addition, he shows Jesus meeting the women; and, at his salutation, they approached him, took hold of his feet, and worshipped him. The incident corresponds to the Magi, about whom St. Matthew spoke at the beginning of his gospel.

Resurrection in the Early Church

For the early Church, the resurrection of Jesus was the touchstone of the Christian faith. This mighty act of God is referred to frequently in the early sermons in the Acts of the Apostles, as for example: Acts 2: 24, 32–36; 3: 13–16; 5: 30ff. It is assumed in the First Epistle to Timothy:

> Great indeed, we confess, is the mystery of our religion:
> He was manifested in the flesh,
> vindicated in the Spirit,
> seen by angels,
> preached among the nations,
> believed on in the world,
> taken up in glory.

(I Timothy 3: 16)

The resurrection meant the end of the *kenosis* or self-emptying of Jesus and it was the divine seal upon his mission. It inaugurated his reign in glory, and won for him the title of *Kyrios* or

234

Lord. When Jesus was taken up in glory, man received an obligation to acknowledge him and to worship him. St. Matthew shows the women beginning this homage.

In the early Church, there was frequently little distinction between the resurrection, ascension, and exaltation of Jesus at the right hand of the Father. This is seen, for example, in Acts 2: 22–36. This is part of the speech of St. Peter on the day of Pentecost. (This section of the address should be distinguished from Acts 2: 14–21, which refers chiefly to the outpouring of the Holy Spirit.) In verse 34 the resurrection is seen as an ascension or assumption, and in verse 33 it is intimately associated with the enthronement of Jesus at the right hand of the Father and the giving of the Holy Spirit.

Jesus as Davidic King

In this early strata in the speech of Peter, Jesus is seen as the Davidic king, who is superior to David himself. In Jesus, God fulfilled the covenant which he made to David and to his descendants in II Samuel 7: 12 (see p. 225 above). David ascended an earthly throne, but Jesus was enthroned on high. This aspect of the resurrection of Jesus was seen to be predicted in three psalms, namely, Psalm 16: 8–11; Psalm 110: 1; and Psalm 132: 11. Therefore, just as Jesus' passion fulfilled certain concepts found in the psalms, so does his resurrection. The ancients considered the psalms to have been written by David. They believed that he had received the gift of prophecy and expressed this in the psalms which he wrote. The early Christians, then, presented the resurrection of Jesus as the fulfillment of a prophecy told by David, namely, the Holy One, whom God had chosen, who would not see corruption but would inherit the everlasting dynasty of David. They used the phrase "raised up," which was seen in two senses—to raise up children as successors to the throne of David, and in

235

the sense of "to resurrect from the dead." Once an heir to the throne had obtained immortality, there was no further need for successors.

However, the resurrection of Jesus was not only the resurrection of an individual: the whole house or nation of David participated in the success of their king. This was another aspect of the idea of solidarity of peoples and nations. In the Dead Sea Scrolls to which we have referred, the commentary on II Samuel 7 reads as follows:

This is a branch of David who will arise with the seeker of the Law and who will sit on the throne of Zion at the end of days; as it is written, I will raise up the tabernacle of David which is fallen. This tabernacle of David which is fallen is he who will arise to save Israel.[1]

Here the tabernacle of David is a person, probably the Messiah. The passage is akin to Jesus' teaching that he himself is the temple. The resurrection of this temple, his body, involved the resurrection of all Christians. The Jews believed that the sacrifice of Isaac had conferred blessing upon the Jewish nation:

By Isaac's unique example God conferred upon human nature its true dignity, the dignity of a divinely required and freely offered self-sacrifice. The blessing resulting from it would extend to all men forever, and they would understand that they possess the same humanity which was made holy by Isaac's sacrifice.[2]

The Christians saw this to be true, indeed, of the resurrection of Jesus. Jesus, as the new Adam, became a life-giving spirit and his newly resurrected humanity was victorious over death for every individual Christian. The Church became a temple of living men and women who had the character and power of the Lord Jesus. They still reproduce, in their own lives, the life,

1. Translation from John H. Hayes, "The Resurrection as Enthronement and the Earliest Church Christology," *Interpretation*, 22 (July 1968), no. 3, pp. 333–345.
2. G. Vermès, *Scripture and Tradition in Judaism, Leiden*, 1961, p. 201.

death, resurrection, and missionary activity of Jesus. In this new temple of which Jesus spoke to the Samaritan woman, there was no distinction between Jew or Gentile, slave or free, man or woman, for they were all one in Jesus (Gal. 3: 27–28). Hence the resurrection scene in St. Matthew's Gospel is really a prelude to the end of his gospel, where Jesus commands the disciples to "make disciples of all nations." They are to communicate the faithfulness of Yahweh and Jesus to these nations and tell them that Jesus "by dying did away with our own death, and by rising again restored our life . . ." (The Easter Preface). The restoration of life is life in the Holy Spirit.

SELECTED BIBLIOGRAPHY

Books

W. C. Allen. *St. Matthew*, I.C.C. Edinburgh, third edition, 1947.

C. K. Barrett. *The Gospel According to St. John*. London, 1962.

M. Black and H. H. Rowley, editors. *Peake's Commentary on the Bible*. London, revised edition, 1962.

Raymond E. Brown. *The Gospel According to St. John*, I–XII, The Anchor Bible Commentary. New York, 1966.

Raymond E. Brown, S.S., Joseph A. Fitzmyer, S.J., Roland E. Murphy, O.Carm., editors. *The Jerome Biblical Commentary*. Englewood Cliffs, N.J., 1968.

Dominic Crossan, O.S.M. *The Gospel of Eternal Life, Reflections on Theology of St. John*. Milwaukee, 1967.

Jean Daniélou, S.J. *From Shadows to Reality*. London, 1960.

W. D. Davies. *Paul and Rabbinic Judaism*. London, 1962.

W. D. Davies. *The Setting of the Sermon on the Mount*. Cambridge, England, 1964.

C. H. Dodd. *Historical Tradition in the Fourth Gospel*. Cambridge, England, 1963.

C. H. Dodd, *The Interpretation of the Fourth Gospel*. Cambridge, England, reprint, 1968.

A. M. Dubarle. *The Biblical Doctrine of Original Sin*. New York, 1964.

A. Dupont-Sommer. Trans. G. Vermès. *The Essene Writings from Qumran*. Cleveland, 1962.

Alfred Edersheim. *The Life and Times of Jesus the Messiah*, two volumes. New York, fifth edition, 1886.

J. W. Etheridge. *The Targums of Onkelos and Jonathan Ben Uzziel on the Pentateuch with the Fragments of the Jerusalem*

Targum. London, 1865. Facsimile of the original produced in 1967 by microfilm-xerography by University Microfilms, Ann Arbor, Michigan.

J. C. Fenton. *St. Matthew, The Pelican Gospel Commentaries.* Baltimore, reprint, 1966.

J. Massingberd Ford. *The Spirit and the Human Person.* Dayton, 1969.

J. Massingberd Ford. *Wellsprings of Scripture, A Thematic and Rabbinic Introduction.* New York, 1968.

Jean de Fraine, S.J. Trans. Daniel Raible, C.Pp.S. *Adam and the Family of Man.* New York, 1965.

Theodor H. Gaster. *The Dead Sea Scriptures in English Translation.* New York, revised and enlarged edition, 1964.

Theodor H. Gaster. *Festivals of the Jewish Year, A Modern Interpretation and Guide.* New York, second printing, 1964.

L. Ginzberg. *Legends of the Jews.* Seven volumes. Philadelphia, 1946.

J. van Goudoever. *Biblical Calendars.* Leiden, second revised edition, 1961.

Aileen Guilding. *The Fourth Gospel and Jewish Worship.* Oxford, 1960.

Alexander Heidel. *The Gilgamesh Epic and Old Testament Parallels.* Chicago, fifth impression, 1965.

Jean Héring. *The First Epistle of St. Paul to the Corinthians.* London, reprint, 1966.

Jean Héring. *La Seconde Épître de Saint Paul aux Corinthiens.* Paris, 1958.

M. D. Hooker. *Jesus and the Servant.* London, 1959.

John C. Hurd, Jr. *The Origin of 1 Corinthians.* London, 1965.

Edmond Jacob. Trans. A. W. Heathcote and P. J. Allcock. *Theology of the Old Testament.* London, third impression, 1964.

J. C. Kirby. *Ephesians, Baptism and Pentecost.* London, 1968.

A. R. C. Leaney. *The Gospel According to St. Luke.* London, second edition, 1966.

R. H. Lightfoot. *St. John's Gospel.* Edited by C. F. Evans. Oxford, 1960.

J. Louis Martyn. *History and Theology in the Fourth Gospel.* New York and Evanston, 1968.

John L. McKenzie, S.J. *Myths and Realities: Studies in Biblical Theology.* Milwaukee, 1963.

239

John L. McKenzie, S.J. *Second Isaiah, The Anchor Bible.* New York, 1968.

Wayne A. Meeks. *The Prophet-King, Moses Traditions and the Johannine Christology.* Leiden, 1967.

C. G. Montefiore and H. Loewe. *A Rabbinic Anthology.* Philadelphia, 1963.

André Parrot. *The Flood and Noah's Ark.* London, 1955.

H. H. Rowley. *The Servant of The Lord and Other Essays on the Old Testament.* Oxford, second edition, revised, 1965.

J. B. Segal. *The Hebrew Passover from the Earliest Times to A.D. 70.* New York, 1963.

J. F. Stenning. *The Targum of Isaiah.* Oxford, 1949.

Yaacov Vainstein. *The Cycle of the Jewish Year.* Jerusalem, second revised and enlarged edition, 1964.

Marvin R. Vincent. *The Epistles to the Philippians and to Philemon.* Edinburgh, first impression, 1955.

Selected Articles

L. Alonso-Schökel. "Sapiential and Covenant Themes in Genesis 2–3." *Theological Digest,* 13 (1965). Pages 3–10.

Anon. "New Thinking on Original Sin." *Herder Correspondence,* 4 (1967). Pages 135–141.

C. J. Armbruster. "The Messianic Significance of the Agony in the Garden." *Scripture,* 16 (1964). Pages 111–119.

N. B. Baker. "The Cry of Dereliction." *Expository Times,* 70 (1958). Pages 54–55.

W. Barclay. "Great themes of the New Testament: Philippians 2: 1–11." *Expository Times,* 70 (1958). Pages 4–7, 40–44.

W. Barclay. "Great themes of the New Testament: Romans 5: 12–21." *Expository Times,* 70 (1959). Pages 132–135, 172–175.

T. Barosse. "The Relationship of Love to Faith in John." *Theological Studies,* 18 (1957). Pages 538–539.

P. Benoit. "The Holy Eucharist." *Scripture,* 8 (1956). Pages 97–108.

E. F. F. Bishop. "Mary of Clopas and her Father." *Expository Times,* 73 (1962). Page 339.

E. F. F. Bishop. "Scripture Says." *Evangelical Quarterly,* 37. Pages 218–220.

J. Blenkinsopp. "The Unknown Prophet of the Exile." *Scripture*, 14 (1962). Pages 81–90, 109–118.

J. Bligh. "Jesus in Samaria." *Heythrop Journal*, 3 (1962). Pages 329–346.

B. Botte. "Le texte du 4me évangile et le papyrus Bodomer II." *Bible et Vie Chrétienne*, 24 (1958). Pages 96–107.

D. J. Bowman. "The Resurrection in Mark." *The Bible Today*. Pages 709–713.

S. G. F. Brandon. "In the beginning." *History Today*, 11 (1961). Pages 380–387.

K. L. Carroll. "The 4th gospel and the exclusion of Christians from the synagogues." *Bulletin of John Ryland's Library*, 40 (1957). Pages 19–32.

J. J. Collins. "Bulletin of the New Testament: The Pauline Epistles." *Theological Studies*, 17 (1956). Pages 531–548.

B. Cooke. "The Hour of the Temptation." *The Way*, 2 (1962). Pages 177–187.

F. J. Cwiekowski. "Biblical Theology as Historical Theology." *Catholic Biblical Quarterly*, xxiv, no. 4 (October 1962). Pages 404–411.

W. J. Dalton. "The 4th Song of the Servant of Jahveh." *Scripture*, 10 (1958). Pages 1–10.

D. Daube. *He That Cometh*. Published by the Council of the Christian-Jewish Understanding, 9 Amen Court, London, E.C. 4, England. October 1966.

R. Davidson. "Universalism in Second Isaiah." *Scottish Journal of Theology*, 16 (1963). Pages 166–185.

H. Dean. "Christ's True Glory." *Expository Times*, 71 (1960). Pages 189–190.

Roger Le Déaut, C.S. "Actes 7:48 et Matthieu 17:4 (par.) à la lumière du Targum Palestinien." *Recherches de Science Religieuse*, 52 (1964). Pages 85–90.

P. Doble. "The Temptations." *Expository Times*, 72 (1960). Pages 91–92.

A. M. Dubarle. "Le péché originel dans les livres sapientaux." *Revue Thomiste*, 56 (1956). Pages 597–619.

R. Dunkerly. "Was Barabbas Also called Jesus?". *Expository Times*, 74 (1963). Pages 126–127.

J. Dupont. "L'Arrière-fond Biblique du récit des tentations de Jésus." *New Testament Studies*, 3 (1957). Pages 287–304.

J. J. Enz. "The Book of Exodus as a literary type for the Gospel of John." *Journal of Biblical Literature,* 76 (1957). Pages 208–215.

W. G. Essame. "Matthew 27: 51–54 and John 5: 25–29." *Expository Times,* 76 (1964). Page 103.

J. Massingberd Ford. "The Pact of the Pieces." *Continuum,* vol. 6, no. 2 (summer 1968). Pages 205–213.

Pierre Grelot. "L'Exégèse messianique d'Isaie LXIII. 1–6." *Revue Biblique,* 70 (1963). Pages 371–380.

Pierre Grelot. "Une tosephta targoumique sur Zacharie II. 14–15." *Revue Biblique,* 73 (1966). Pages 197–211.

D. R. Griffiths. *"Harpagmos & Eauton Ekenosen* in Philippians 2: 6–7." *Expository Times,* 69 (1958). Pages 237–239.

Martin Hopkins, O.P. "The Temptations as Jesus' Identity Crisis." Unpublished Paper read at the Catholic Biblical Association, August 1968.

D. F. Hudson. "A further note on Philippians 2: 6–11." *Expository Times,* 77 (1965). Page 29.

H. B. Huffman. "The Exodus, Sinai and the Credo." *Catholic Biblical Quarterly,* 27 (1965). Pages 101–113.

Hvidberg. "The Canaanite background of Genesis 1–3." *Vetus Testamentum,* 10 (1960). Pages 285–294.

V. Keisch. "Hypostatic and Prosopic Union in the exegesis of Christ's temptation." *St. Vladimir Seminary Quarterly,* 9. Pages 118–137.

H. A. Kelly. "The Devil in the desert." *Catholic Biblical Quarterly,* 26 (1964). Pages 190–220.

Anthony Kenny. "The Transfiguration and the Agony in the Garden." *Catholic Biblical Quarterly,* 19 (1957). Pages 444–452.

Hans Kosmala. "A quotation from the targum." *Novum Testamentum,* 4 (1960). Pages 3–5.

G. Lafont. "Sur l'interpretation de Romans 5." *Recherches de Science Religieuse,* 45 (1957). Pages 481–513.

W. G. Lambert. "New Light on the Babylonian Flood." *Journal of Semitic Studies,* 5 (1960). Pages 113–25.

J. Leveen. "Yzh in Isaiah 52: 15." *Journal of Jewish Studies,* 7 (1956). Page 93.

C. Lindhagen. "The Servant of the Lord." *Expository Times,* 67 (1955). Pages 279–283.

N. Lohfink. "Genesis 2–3 as Historical Etiology." *Theological Digest,* 13 (1965). Pages 11–17.

R. A. F. MacKenzie, S.J. "The Concept of Biblical Theology." *Proceedings of the Catholic Theological Studies Association* (1955). Pages 48–73.

R. A. F. MacKenzie, S.J. "The Divine Soliloquies in Genesis." *Catholic Biblical Quarterly,* 17 (1955). Pages 277–286.

A. Mahoney. "A new look at an old problem: John 18: 12–14 and 19–24." *Catholic Biblical Quarterly,* 27. Pages 137–144.

Bruce Malina. "Some Observations on the Origin of Sin in Judaism and St. Paul." *Catholic Biblical Quarterly,* 31 (1, 1969). Pages 18–34.

F. Martin. "And therefore God raised him on high." *The Bible Today.* Pages 694–700.

J. P. Martin. "History and Eschatology in the Lazarus Narrative." *Scottish Journal of Theology,* 17 (1964). Pages 332–343.

R. P. Martin. *"Morphe* in Philippians 2: 6." *Expository Times,* 70 (1959). Pages 183–184.

N. J. McEleney. "The translation of Isaiah 41: 27." *Catholic Biblical Quarterly,* 19 (1957). Pages 441ff.

D. Mollat. "La guérison de l'aveugle-né." *Bible et Vie Chrétienne,* 23 (1958). Pages 22–31.

J. Morgenstern. "The Suffering Servant: a new solution." *Vetus Testamentum,* 11 (1961). Pages 292–320, 406–431.

R. H. Mounce. "Continuity of the primitive tradition. Some pre-pauline elements in 1 Corinthians." *Interpretation,* 13 (1959). Pages 417–424.

J. Muilenburg. "Abraham and the Nations." *Interpretation,* 19 (1965). Pages 387–398.

R. C. Nevius. "A reply to Dr. Dunkerly." *Expository Times,* 74 (1963). Page 255.

O. A. Piper. "Unchanging Promises: Exodus in the New Testament." *Interpretation,* 11 (1957). Pages 3–23.

W. Powell. *"Harpagmos . . . Eauton Ekenose." Expository Times,* 71 (1959). Page 88.

W. Powell. "The Temptation." *Expository Times,* 72 (1961). Page 248.

A. F. Sava. "The Blood and the water from the side of the Christ." *American Ecclesiastical Revue,* 138 (1958). Pages 341–345.

P. Smulders, "Evolution and Original Sin." *Theological Digest,* 13 (1965). Pages 172–176.

E. A. Speiser. "Mesopotamian Motifs in the early chapters of Genesis." *Expedition,* 5 (1962). Pages 18–19, 43.

D. M. Stanley. "Bulletin of the New Testament: The Johannine Literature." *Theological Studies,* 17 (1956). Pages 516–531.

D. M. Stanley. "The passion according to John." *Worship,* 33 (1959). Pages 210–230.

P. Staples. "The Kingdom of God has come." *Expository Times,* 71 (1959). Pages 87–88.

H. S. Stern. "The knowledge of Good and Evil." *Vetus Testamentum,* 8 (1958). Pages 405–418.

M. Strange. "Temptations." *Worship,* 36 (1962). Pages 227–234.

M. H. Sykes. "The Eucharist as Anamnesis." *Expository Times,* 71 (1960). Pages 115–118.

F. R. Tennant. "The Teaching of Ecclesiasticus and Wisdom on the Introduction of Sin and Death." *Journal of Theological Studies,* II (1901). Pages 207–223.

W. H. Wagner. "The Transfiguration and the Church." *Lutheran Quarterly,* 16 (1964). Pages 343–348.

R. E. Whitson. "The Concept of Origins." *Thought,* 37 (1962). Pages 245–268.

J. Wijngaards. "A two-fold approach to the Exodus." *Vetus Testamentum,* 15 (1964). Pages 91–102.

P. Winter. "Genesis 1: 27 and Jesus' saying on Divorce." *Zeitschrift A. T. Wissenschaft,* 70 (1959). Pages 260ff.

T. Worden. "The Meaning of Sin." *Scripture,* 9 (1957). Pages 44–53.

M. Zerwick. "The Hour of the Mother." *The Bible Today.* Pages 1187–1194.

NAME INDEX

Augustine, St., 20

Beare, F. W., 83n.
Bishop, E. T., 201 and n.
Botte, B., 8n.
Brown, R., 43

Chrysostom, St. John, 217

Daniélou, J., 217n.
Daube, D., 167n.
Davies, W. D., 59n., 173n.
Dawe, D., 126, 127n.
Dubarle, A., 28

Etheridge, J. W., 27, 30n., 67nn.

Ford, J. M., 216
Freedman, H., 52n.

Gaster, T. H., 128n., 129, 137n.,
    166n., 186, 223n.
Ginzberg, L., 68n.

Hamman, A., 12n.
Hayes, J. H., 236n.
Hippolytus, St., 4, 9, 12n., 16

Irenaeus, St., 96

Jacob, 214n.
Jeremias, J., 61n.
Josephus, 70n., 87, 88, 142

Kosmala, H., 134 and n.

Loewe, H., 89n.

Meeks, W., 196, 197n., 199n.
Monica, St., 19
Montefiore, C. G., 89n.

Philo, 27, 142

Ramsey, A. M., 61n., 62n.

Sanders, J. A., 87
Savignac, J. de, 214n.
Schlatter, A., 61
Simon, M., 52n.

Vainstein, Y., 55n.
Vèrmes, G., 236n.

Wigan, B., 21n.

BIBLICAL INDEX

245